Directed by Allen ̶U̶̶i̶̶l̶̶l̶̶i̶̶a̶̶m̶̶s̶

COMMERCE AND MASS CULTURE SERIES
EDITED BY JUSTIN WYATT

Directed by Allen Smithee

Jeremy Braddock and Stephen Hock, Editors

Foreword by Andrew Sarris

Commerce and Mass Culture

University of Minnesota Press
Minneapolis • London

Published by the University of Minnesota Press
111 Third Avenue South, Suite 290
Minneapolis, MN 55401-2520
http://www.upress.umn.edu

Printed in the United States of America on acid-free paper

The University of Minnesota is an equal-opportunity educator and employer.

Library of Congress Cataloging-in-Publication Data

Directed by Allen Smithee/Jeremy Braddock and Stephen Hock, editors.
    p. cm. — (Commerce and mass culture series)
    "This book represents the collective labors of the Allen Smithee Group
at the University of Pennsylvania"—Acknowledgments.
    Includes filmography.
    Includes bibliographical references and index.
    ISBN 0-8166-3533-1 (HC : alk. paper) — ISBN 0-8166-3534-X
(PB : alk. paper)
    1. Motion pictures—Production and direction. 2. Auteur theory
(Motion pictures) I. Braddock, Jeremy. II. Hock, Stephen. III. Series.
    PN1995.9.P7   D53   2001
    791.43'0233—dc21
                                                        00-012860

12 11 10 09 08 07 06 05 04 03 02 01   10 9 8 7 6 5 4 3 2 1

Contents

III Smithee Suggests

Foreword:
Allen Smithee Redux

Andrew Sarris

I wish to inform you that Allen Smithee is alive and well and living in a Hollywood trailer park where disappointed, disaffected, and discarded film directors drop off their unwanted movies and credits. He almost re-appeared very recently when Jocelyn Moorhouse, director of *A Thousand Acres*, repudiated the final studio cut with the threat of taking her name off the credits, and letting the ever available Smithee take all the credit or blame for the final result. Smithee had already put on his director's beret and Erich von Stroheim's Hapsburg Dynasty riding boots when Michelle Pfeiffer, one of the feisty stars of *A Thousand Acres*, reportedly stormed into the Disney office, and said that if Moorhouse took her name off the credits, Pfeiffer would take her name off as well, and she would see to it that Moorhouse never worked in the town again. Moorhouse backed down and shoved Smithee aside, but the damage was done to the movie's critical and commercial prospects, particularly with Moorhouse giving interviews badmouthing it at every opportunity. Siskel and Ebert picked up on the industry buzz and gave it two thumbs down, and most every other critic lambasted it. I've seen *A Thousand Acres* and it isn't that bad. In fact, it isn't bad at all. It could be described as the year's *Marvin's Room*, a joint vehicle for two brilliant actresses, Jessica Lange and Michelle Pfeiffer, just as *Marvin's Room* (1996) was a splendid opportunity for Diane Keaton and Meryl Streep.

Undiscouraged as always, Smithee saw another opportunity loom-
ing when Robert Altman thundered and roared that he would take his
name off the credits of *The Gingerbread Man* if Polygram persisted in
recutting the movie, but an item in the "ReelWorld" column of the 26
September 1997 *Entertainment Weekly* dashed Smithee's hopes: "Polygram will release Robert Altman's original 109-minute cut of *The Gingerbread Man* after all. The director threatened to remove his name from
the John Grisham–scripted thriller after the company re-edited the film
following lackluster test screenings. Opening date has been pushed from
Oct. 3 to early '98."[1]

So why are we honoring this leper of the cinema, this harbinger of
doom and disaster, this guarantor of mediocrity, incompetence, and in-
coherence? I suspect a certain degree of deviousness in those who would
take Smithee from his hovel of anomie and anonymity, give him a bath,
a haircut and a shave, spruce him up with a suit of academic tweeds, and
parade him in a carnival of deconstructionist whimsy to deny the importance of the *auteur* or author in the manufacture of sounds, speech, and
images on the screen. Smithee even comes equipped with a filmography
of about fifty titles, many of them on videotape, out of the thousands of
bad movies signed by directors other than Smithee.[2]

The question you may be asking at this point is, if I feel this way
about this enterprise why did I agree to write the foreword to this book?
I'm really not sure. At my age it's an honor to be invited even to the opening of a supermarket. It's not so much that I'm suffering from a midlife
crisis of identity. After all, I don't know many people who are 136 years
old. I suppose it's more an end-of-life crisis, a forlorn and foredoomed
attempt to explain who and what I am and have been, what I have thought
and felt over the years as I wrestled with the burdens of being attacked as
an alleged theorist, and an *auteurist* theorist besides, and not a terribly
original one at that. It's all so irresistibly déjà vu. After more than forty
years of polemics, I have reached the stage where I am regarded as too
much of an academic for the journalists, and too much of a journalist for
the academics. And so if I seem glib, blame the journalist in me, and if I
seem pompous, blame the academic in me. When James Agee wrote his

first movie column for *The Nation*, he described his relation to the movies as that of an amateur. That is what I am also, a lover of the magical medium that has enthralled me since early childhood, and will do so till the day I die. I know most of it is artistically worthless, but that doesn't matter, because the cinema, at least that part of it that relies on live action cinematography and narrative, is not entirely an art at all. Too much of living, breathing, aging and dying reality seeps into its pores for it to be studied as congealed creation. It will never die as long as there is human life on this planet, and with that one proviso it is infinitely renewable.

So spare me the examples of movies that seemed to need no director besides the deplorable Smithee. I have never been a defender of directors, per se. The Directors Guild of America has given me no special award, and why should they? I have panned most of their members at one time or another over the forty-two years I have been reviewing movies for one publication or another.

Actually, I began publishing my film criticism in 1955, the year in which both James Agee and Robert Warshow died. They have been two of our greatest film critics ever since. I noticed back in 1978 that John Simon made a kind reference to Otis Ferguson. Ferguson too was one of our greatest film critics. He too was dead. Manny Farber is still alive, and thus he is still regarded in too many quarters as hopelessly esoteric with his nebulous pronouncements on negative space. Farber and the rest of us living critics must reconcile ourselves to the fact that we will remain "controversial" into the foreseeable future.

I have no idea anymore where I belong on the critical scene, or where I want to belong. What was for me an outlet in the fifties and an obsession in the sixties has become a time-consuming profession in the nineties. I would like to think that I have evolved as both a critic and human being, and that I have kept an open mind on the cinema. Yet it somehow seems that the more I write the less I communicate, and that I shall forever be typecast as the stormy petrel who once took on the whole critical establishment single-handed. Have you added anyone to your Pantheon?, I am asked in a humoring tone of semiseriousness. Wait and see, I reply. The trouble is that I staked out my positions before I had an opportunity to explain them. The sixties were all stirring proclamations and calls to arms. The nineties have settled down into a tedious tidying up.

Part of my problem here may be that the cinema for me has always been at least a partial substitute for my unfulfilled sexuality, and that therefore my critical sensibility is inescapably neurotic. My original compact with the cinema was not conditional upon its changing the world in which I lived. All that I asked was that it provide me a second world, a parallel universe as it were, to which I could escape from time to time. I always knew that this second, surrogate world had some tenuous relationship with the real world, but I did not begin to explore this relationship until long after I had succumbed to the shadows on Plato's Cave in the movie palaces. To put it quite bluntly, I am a professional voyeur. My personal pattern was established in the voluptuous passivity of moviegoing. In my early childhood the medium was still invested with all the mystery and magic of popular filmmaking. The lights went out, the projector went on, the moonbeams bounced off the screen, and I was entranced. I had absolutely no control over what happened. It was a different kind of experience from that of television, over which one has the life-and-death power of channel-switching and channel-surfing. Hence, television generates an attitude in the viewer of ironic superiority if not downright arrogance. The cinema, by contrast, is a relatively religious experience, at least for the solitary moviegoer—but then I never participated in the blustering bravado of the boys in the balcony.

Of course, I now take a more active role in connection with my moviegoing. I write. I teach. I lecture in a variety of journalistic and academic capacities. I even participate in the political process from time to time. Still, I am a long way from being an activist with a radical program to alter the bourgeois capitalist system in which I have lived and worked all my life. But even if I were to be suddenly converted to some revolutionary philosophy, I doubt that I could integrate the cinema I have known into a plan of action. I would no longer be a movie-man. I would be something else—a street-man perhaps. There would be no place for me in Plato's Cave. As long as I remain a movie-man, however, my centrist politics and casual acquiescence in the status quo seem to be the logical consequences of my professional commitment.

If *auteurism* can be considered the delayed Romanticism of film scholarship, structuralism, semiotics, and deconstructionism can be considered the delayed New Criticism. The transition is also from Freud and Bazin to Lévi-Strauss, Eco, Lacan, and Foucault; from stylistic pluralism to a shared system of codes and signals; from film technique as a grammar to film technique as a language; from an emphasis on Promethean personalities to an emphasis on textual crossovers. Most structuralist, semiotic, and deconstructionist undertakings seem to have as their ulterior purpose a systematic critique of bourgeois values and vices as Marxism tiptoes in again through a back door.

The much maligned and much misunderstood term *auteur* still haunts the stately castles of film theory and criticism. Since I bear official responsibility for bringing the word into the English language I feel an obligation to explain at this late date why it still generates so much controversy. I first employed the term *auteur* in an article titled "Notes on the *Auteur* Theory in 1962."[3] It was published in *Film Culture*, an obscure journal of cinematic scholarship with fewer than ten thousand readers; in the eight years of its existence there had been no unusual repercussions from any of its articles. On this occasion, however, a stormy rebuttal from Pauline Kael, then an obscure film commentator from San Francisco, appeared in *Film Quarterly*, an equally obscure journal of film scholarship.[4] Somehow the Sarris-Kael debate caught on from coast to coast. Soon every film critic was taking sides. The great majority embraced Kael's debunking position, which was vaguely antitheory, antisystem, antifilm scholarship, and, above all, anti-taking-movies-too-seriously. Significantly, the word "trash" kept popping up in her article, and this was a reassuring code word for the cinephobic cultural establishment.

Overnight I had been transformed from a nonentity to a pariah. It seems I had been the bearer of bad news, to wit, that movies had to be studied seriously and studied intensely. Indeed, the *auteurist* controversy coincided with a widespread invasion of film studies into the academic curriculum. As the original *auteurist* critics—Rohmer, Chabrol, Godard, Truffaut, Rivette, et al.—became internationally renowned directors, the Romantic notion of *auteurism* as the key to personal creation in the cinema took hold around the world. The director, long an obscure artisan to the general public, became a glamorous celebrity. Kids of earlier generations had yearned to be movie stars; the new breed aspired to the rank of *auteur* director. I must say I view all the hoopla about *auteurism* with some misgivings. Far from giving a blank check to all aspiring *auteurs*, I have become skeptical about the excessive emphasis placed on personal expression in the cinema at the expense of communication with its audience.

Does it then follow that I have repudiated my earlier position? Not really. My own interpretation of the *auteur* theory was based originally on the weird notion that good movies did not just happen by accident; nor were they products of some mindless beehive of activity. I proposed instead a pattern theory in constant flux to explain certain stylistic signs of personal creativity in what had otherwise been dismissed as an industrial assembly line. My business was history, not prophecy. After looking at a score of films directed by Alfred Hitchcock, a score of films directed by John Ford, and a score of films directed by Howard Hawks, no one could tell me that Hitchcock, Ford, and Hawks were not authentic *auteurs*. This was not to denigrate the role of the actor, the writer, the cinematographer, the editor, the composer of the music, the sound technician, the set designer, and the myriad artistic and technical contributors to the finished motion picture. There were instances, in fact, in which the true *auteur* of the film was not the director at all, but a producer like Selznick, a cinematographer like Lee Garmes or Gregg Toland, a set designer like William Cameron Menzies, a special effects wizard like Frank Bashevi, a composer like Miklos Rozsa or Max Steiner, a writer like Ben Hecht, or actors like Garbo and Cagney, Sullavan and Stewart, Leigh and Olivier, Hepburn and Tracy, Dunne and Grant, Arthur and Boyer. My "theory" was intended as the first step rather than the last stop of film scholarship.

Actually, the word *theory* gave me almost as much trouble as the word *auteur*, which had been coined in its specifically cinematic connotation by François Truffaut back in the *Cahiers du cinéma* no. 31 of January 1954.[5] Truffaut wrote, however, not of a theory, but of a *politique des auteurs*, with *politique* meaning something closer to a "policy" than to a "theory." What Truffaut was describing was the editorial tendency he shared with his colleagues of championing the films of directors they liked at the expense of the films of directors they disliked. The bulk of Truffaut's article, however, was a savage attack on certain French directors such as Claude Autant-Lara and Jean Delannoy, and certain French screenwriters such as Jean Aurenche and Pierre Bost for foisting upon the public a "Tradition of Quality." I doubt that many admirers of Truffaut's celebrations of *L'Amour toujours* are familiar with his earlier vituperations against his many enemies in France. If I sound cool to Monsieur François, whom I have admired as an influence, a critic, and an artist, it is because he and his French colleagues ran for cover from the perils of Pauline when I was feeling the heat, and began modifying their earlier polemics to seem more cuddlesome. But that is now all water under the Pont Neuf.

There are times I feel like Mario Puzo, who said of his book *The Godfather*: "If I had known so many people were going to read it, I would have written it better." Still, if I had to do it all over again, I would reformulate the *auteur* theory with a greater emphasis on the tantalizing mystery of style than on the Romantic agony of the artist. Why, I wondered back in the mid-fifties, had so many Hollywood movies endured as classics despite the generalized contempt of the highbrows? The *auteur* theory turned out to be a very workable hypothesis for this task of historical revaluation. But I was never all that interested in the clinical "personalities" of directors, and I have never considered the interview as one of the indispensable weapons in my critical arsenal.

In any event, the *auteurists* of the fifties and sixties did not introduce the cult of the director. Dwight Macdonald and John Grierson were writing very knowledgeably about Hollywood directors back in the early thirties. The great majority of film histories around the world have been organized in terms of the collected works of individual directors. If, as the Allen Smithee adherents imply, all that *auteurism* represents is an emphasis on directors, this so-called theory should be banished for its banality.

Certain tendencies have clustered around *auteurism* to form a more solid base for inquiry. Among these tendencies have been the anti-montage writings of André Bazin, the many French meditations on *mise-en-scène*, Lawrence Alloway's celebration of pop art, David Thomson's socioaesthetic speculations, and Peter Wollen's valiant efforts to reconcile *auteurism* with semiotics.

Although in the long run the French critics could not have the last word on the American cinema, they gave many of us the first glimpse of this elusive entity. American film criticism has not been the same since. There was a time when movies were judged almost entirely in terms of an absolute fidelity to social reality. Good intentions alone were too often considered the paving stones to heaven. By establishing the notion of individual creation in even the Hollywood cinema, the French shifted the critical emphasis away from the nature of content to the director's attitude toward content.

This attitude was expressed through a somewhat mystical process called *mise-en-scène*, defined perhaps most eloquently by French critic-director Alexandre Astruc:

> But Mizoguchi knows very well that ultimately it matters little whether his films end well, just as he does not worry whether the strongest bonds between himself and his characters are those of tenderness or of contempt. He is like the voyeur who sees pleasure reflected in the face of the one he watches, even though he is well aware that it is more than this reflection that he seeks: perhaps it is quite simply the wearying confirmation of something that he has always known but cannot resist making sure of.
>
> So I see *mise en scène* as a means of making the spectacle one's own—but then what artist doesn't know that what is seen matters less, not than the way of seeing, but than a particular way of needing to see and to show.[6]

I once suggested a definition of *mise-en-scène* that includes all the means available to directors to express their attitude toward their subject. This takes in cutting, camera movement, pacing, the direction of players and their placement in the frame, the angle and distance of the camera, and even the content of the shot. *Mise-en-scène* as an attitude tends to accept the cinema as it is and enjoy it for what it is—a sensuous conglomeration of all the other arts, more an emotional recapitulation than an intellectual formulation.

At this late date I am prepared to concede that *auteurism* is and always has been more a tendency than a theory, more a mystique than a methodology, more an editorial policy than an aesthetic procedure. The cinema is a deep, dark mystery that we *auteurists* are attempting to solve, and, what is infinitely more difficult, to report our findings in readable prose. The cinema is a labyrinth with a treacherous relation to reality. I suppose that the difference between *auteurism* and Allen Smithee–worship is the difference between knowing all the questions before finding the answers, and knowing all the answers before formulating the questions.

I could go on and on and on, but I can see Allen Smithee out of the corner of my eye preparing to storm the podium to chastise me for raining on his parade. Sorry, Allen, I had to do it. As always, my back was to the wall, or at least, I thought so. For the rest of you, thank you.

Notes

This foreword is the text of Andrew Sarris's keynote speech at the Specters of Legitimacy conference held at the University of Pennsylvania, 27 September 1997.

1. Steve Daly and Gregg Kilday, "ReelWorld," *Entertainment Weekly* 26 Sept. 1997. All *Entertainment Weekly* articles are archived online at http://cgi.pathfinder.com/ew/.

2. See the appendix to this volume for a comprehensive Smithee filmography.

3. Andrew Sarris, "Notes on the *Auteur* Theory in 1962," *Film Culture* 27 (winter 1962–63): 1–8.

4. Pauline Kael, "Circles and Squares," *Film Quarterly* 16.3 (spring 1963): 12–26.

5. François Truffaut, "Une certaine tendance du cinéma français" ["A Certain Tendency of the French Cinema"], *Cahiers du cinéma* 31 (Jan. 1954): 15–29.

6. Alexandre Astruc, "What is *mise-en-scène*?" trans. Liz Heron, *Cahiers du Cinéma, the 1950s: Neo-Realism, Hollywood, New Wave*, ed. Jim Hillier (Cambridge: Harvard University Press, 1985) 267–68.

Acknowledgments

This book represents the collective labors of the Allen Smithee Group at the University of Pennsylvania: Jeremy Braddock, Yoonmee Chang, Jonathan Eburne, Justin Ginnetti, Stephen Hock, David Quintiliani, Scott Shrake, and Laura Spagnoli. The group formed out of a graduate seminar taught by Craig Saper at Penn in 1997, "*Auteurism* and Artificiality in Film Studies." Invaluable research as well as ideas that have directly informed this project have come from Tom Paulus, editor of *Andere Sinema* magazine; Sam Adams of the *Philadelphia City Paper*; Laura B. Johnson; Tyler Smith; and Jim English. The Smithee Group took inspiration from our predecessors Jon Keith Brunelle and Ian Toll, founders of the Smithee Roundtable in New York City in 1996. Their project is archived online at http://www.echonyc.com/~jhhl/Smithee/index.html.

We are grateful to those at the University of Pennsylvania who have supported this project, including Wendy Steiner, chair of the English Department; Eugene Narmour and Robert Rescorla, deans of the School of Arts and Sciences; Jean-Michel Rabaté, professor of English; Liliane Weissberg, chair of Comparative Literature; Lance Donaldson-Evans, chair of Romance Languages; Jerome Singerman of the University of Pennsylvania Press; and the Graduate Student Associations Council. We also thank Timothy Eburne of Watermill Ventures, who is Allen Smithee.

Rayna Kalas and Mark Miller generously read portions of this book, and offered us valuable comments. Thanks are also due to R. L. Rutsky, whose review was both challenging and encouraging. In helping us prepare the final manuscript, Justin Ginnetti provided an assiduous reading from which the book also benefits enormously.

We thank our editor at the University of Minnesota Press, Jennifer Moore, and also series editor Justin Wyatt, both of whom were generous and supportive. We would also like to thank the energetic and helpful staff at the University of Minnesota Press—and Robin A. Moir in particular.

PART I
THE FORGING OF SMITHEE STUDIES

CHAPTER 1

The Specter of Illegitimacy in an Age of Disillusion and Crisis

Jeremy Braddock and Stephen Hock

> Welcome, O life! I go to encounter for the millionth time the
> reality of experience and to forge in the smithy of my soul
> the uncreated conscience of my race.
> *27 April*: Old father, old artificer, stand me now and ever
> in good stead.
>
> —James Joyce, *A Portrait of the Artist as a Young Man*

Writing in his 1972 foreword to André Bazin's *Orson Welles: A Critical View*, François Truffaut remarked, "When the use of video cassettes becomes widespread and people watch the films they love at home, anyone who owns a copy of *Mr. Arkadin* will be lucky indeed."[1] Truffaut was referring to a relatively obscure film that featured Welles as writer, director, and actor: a film originally distributed in England in 1955 under the title *Confidential Report*, and released to American audiences a full seven years later, this time retitled *Mr. Arkadin*. In drawing attention to the film, Truffaut anticipated the degree to which technological innovation would create new cinematic marketplaces and enable a coming generation of nonspecialists nevertheless to become *auteurist* critics. The *auteurist* critic, after all, needed access to the director's entire corpus, not just the most influential works that could have been seen by the urbanite at the arthouse cinema, the student on the college campus, the suburbanite on network television. For Truffaut, the videocassette promised to usher in a golden age of film studies, which would be highlighted by the apotheoses of neglected works like *Mr. Arkadin*. This, at least, is one way to understand that comment. It is not impossible that Truffaut recommended the film for entirely different purposes.

In a key scene in *Mr. Arkadin*, Welles, playing the title role of the film's American version, confronts Guy van Stratten (played by Robert Arden) with the "confidential report" that is the title object of the British version of the film. The report is an assiduously compiled conspectus of van Stratten's life which includes the revelation that the man who goes by the aristocratic-sounding name "Guy van Stratten" was in fact born under the ethnically tinged "George Straitheimer." When van Stratten insists, "My father's name was Streeter," Arkadin responds by noting tersely, "Your father's identity does not seem to have been established." We soon learn that the "confidential report," with its unearthing of abandoned names and dubious paternities, is Arkadin's way of securing submission from rivals and competitors (van Stratten had been pursuing a relationship with Arkadin's daughter Raina). In a later scene, however, it is Arkadin who confesses to Guy that he does not know his own age, and, moreover, that he has no memory that predates the year 1927. Van Stratten presses Arkadin on this point:

> GUY: You don't have any memory of what happened to you before '27, right? So what makes you so sure your name is Arkadin?
>
> ARKADIN: Hmm?
>
> GUY: Well, maybe it's Arkadine, or Arkadini, or Arkapopoulos—or *Smithee!*
>
> ARKADIN: Don't be a fool. I know my own name.

In this manner, on the associative level of the name itself, *Mr. Arkadin* proleptically reveals both its own fundamental connection, as well as that of its title character, to Allen Smithee. But it will be fourteen more years until Smithee receives his first directorial credit with 1969's *Death of a Gunfighter*.[2]

Truffaut must surely have been aware of the troubled circumstances of *Mr. Arkadin*'s production, circumstances that in a later day would doubtless have nominated the film to be attributed to Smithee, the pseudonym that stands in for the names of directors who wish to take their names off of films over which they have lost control.[3] As Joseph McBride

Figure 1.1. *Mr. Arkadin.*

writes, "Welles felt *Mr. Arkadin* was 'destroyed' after the editing was taken out of his hands," a loss of control evidenced by the fact that the picture was released first in a Spanish version with "different actors playing some of the characters," as well as by the existence of two differing versions of the film which appeared under the two different names mentioned above. McBride further notes that Welles claimed that fourteen minutes of the film had been cut from his original version, though "much about the making of *Mr. Arkadin* remains obscure."[4] Of additional importance for those interested in Smithee as the pseudonym of directorial disavowal is the fact that the novelization of *Mr. Arkadin*, though credited to Welles, was in fact ghostwritten by Maurice Bessy, only to be disowned by Welles in the end. In fact, the novel contains a telling inconsistency. Its version of the above-quoted scene reads as follows:

> "Amnesia.... You're sure it was quite total?... You remember nothing?... Really nothing at all?..."

> Suddenly I realised that there was something not quite right. I said:
> "In which case, how do you know your name is Arkadin?"
> Now it was his turn to be taken by surprise.
> "Don't be a fool. I wouldn't forget my own name."
> But he was being the fool. He fell silent.
> "You say you don't know who you are, but you're quite certain your name is Gregory Arkadin. How? Perhaps that's the name of a cough mixture you'd been taking that winter before you lost your memory?"[5]

As if to affirm that film is the only medium that can register his presence, this literary accounting has removed Smithee from the story. It is a removal that suppresses in advance any indication of the film's troubled production history that could have been discerned through Smithee's signature presence in the text.

As Truffaut predicted, we are "lucky indeed" to have access to the film version of *Mr. Arkadin* (unsurprisingly, it is now far easier to obtain than the book), as it has allowed us to uncover Smithee's heretofore occluded association with the 1955 film. This association imparts to the film an unforeseen dimension of meaning that extends not only outside the film toward its production history, but is also reflected in the narrative of the film itself. In *Mr. Arkadin*, Welles's character commissions Guy van Stratten to construct a "confidential report" on Arkadin himself, a report that, we later learn, Arkadin will use in order to rub out everyone who holds information about him and his past, and thereby ensure the specter of power, mystique, and legitimacy that his name possesses. In the first of van Stratten's interviews, Arkadin's old acquaintance "Sir Joseph" provides important background—"with the understanding it is not to be quoted"—on the subject of Guy's inquiry:

> Gregory Arkadin is one of the shrewdest of all adventurers in high finance, and certainly the most unscrupulous. During the last war I had occasion to make inquiries into his past. In another epoch such a man might have sacked Rome or been hung as a pirate. Today we must accept him for what he is: a phenomenon of an age of disillusion and crisis.

The information Guy receives from Sir Joseph helps to explain his earlier unconscious association of Arkadin with Allen Smithee. As the pseudonym employed by Hollywood directors who do not wish to be associated with a compromised project, Allen Smithee is indeed the shrewd adventurer who enables the highly financed world of American cinema to turn a profit on even the most haphazardly constructed films. As we will see, Allen Smithee also represents "an age of disillusion and crisis" within the field of film studies.

The fact that it is the *director's* name that serves as the site of the place-holding pseudonym Smithee is evidence of the worldwide success of the *auteur* theory of film scholarship, whereby the director has been made both the focal point of all cinematic achievement, and the origin of filmic meaning. The *auteur* theory is also a rare instance of a critical mode that has totally reorganized the public imagination. As a result of the success of *auteurism*, the apparatus that surrounds a film's reception apparently cannot support the total omission of a directorial credit, and so the creation of the fictive director Allen Smithee has become a necessity. For example, in the 1989 film *Backtrack*, actor Joe Pesci simply declined to take a credit for his prominent screen role in the movie, while Smithee was required to assume the directorial credit that Dennis Hopper refused.[6] François Truffaut, Eric Rohmer, Jacques Rivette, and the other *Cahiers du cinéma* critics who pioneered the concept of the *auteur* could not have foreseen the ease with which *auteurism* was to be appropriated as a marketing strategy by the vast machinery of corporate Hollywood.[7] They may also have been surprised to note that this machinery has often been supported by an unwittingly compliant film studies that neglects the ironic context of Truffaut's initial use of the term and employs narrow conceptions of authorship. It does not therefore follow that Smithee's arrival in film studies necessarily announces a dismantling of the *auteur* theory. Rather, Smithee shows film to be an exemplary case of authorship, and his works to be those of an exemplary author. We present his oeuvre here with the aim of recovering a progressive strategy in the cause of *auteurism*. In order to understand how this could be the case, it may be necessary to construct a confidential report of our own on the history of the director known as Allen Smithee.

From his birth, Allen Smithee has been the bastard son of Hollywood: like Guy van Stratten, a child of dubious paternity; like Gregory Arkadin, a phenomenon of crisis. Perhaps the clearest description of Smithee's misbegetting appears in Don Siegel's autobiography, *A Siegel Film*. In describing his work on 1969's *Death of a Gunfighter*, Siegel tells a tale of the film's star, Richard Widmark, demanding that the film's original director, Robert Totten, be replaced with Siegel. In the end, Siegel recalls, "I worked nine or ten days on the film. Totten was on it twenty-five days. In re-editing the picture, picking up a few shots, I *guess* we broke about even on footage in the film."[8] Through the entire process of shooting the film, however, Siegel's account makes obvious the fact that it was actually Widmark who called the shots. When it came time for the film to be released, Siegel and Totten each refused to take credit for the picture. A solution had to be found to the problem of whose name would appear on the finished product, a name that could both assume responsibility for the film's market success and organize its cinematic meaning. Siegel describes the process as follows:

> When I refused to take directing credit for the film, as did Bob Totten, the Directors' Guild made up a pseudonym for Totten and myself: "Allen Smithee." As the picture was well received, I told all my young friends who wanted to become directors to change their name to Smithee and take credit for the direction of the picture. I don't know if anyone did this. I still think under certain circumstances, they might have cracked the "magic barrier" and become a director.
>
> I'm sorry I got involved in the making of the picture. I thought Totten made a mistake in taking his name off the credits when I did, as he was truly the director of *Death of a Gunfighter*.[9]

With this brief description of an after-the-fact solution to a problem that would not have existed had Hollywood not already been so invested in a certain notion of authorship (a notion in part misappropriated from the literary model of authorship), Siegel astutely identifies both the problems and possibilities that would attend the name Allen Smithee.

Many directors did follow Siegel's advice to change their names to Smithee, though not in the subversive way he intended. Instead, "Allen Smithee" (often "misspelled" "Alan Smithee"[10]) became the pseudonym set aside by the Directors Guild of America for those directors who feel—and, more importantly, can prove to the Guild's satisfaction—that their films have been taken out of their control. The removal of a director's name from a film, however, represents a fundamental problem for the Guild and for the model of the director that it wants to promote. In the Guild's view, the director should be recognized as the author of a film; this is why, for instance, the Guild requires that the director's name be the final name seen in a film's opening credits.[11] The Directors Guild hopes to promote an environment in which each director has complete creative control over his or her films, and is thereby able to assume credit as the author of all that appears on the screen. With this taking of credit for a film's successes, of course, the director must also assume responsibility for a film's failures. Accordingly, the Guild will not allow its member directors to take their names off their films for just any reason, or replace their names with just any pseudonym. The Smithee pseudonym is the only pseudonym sanctioned by the Guild, and the Guild exercises absolute authority over its use. In order to take his or her name off a film and replace it with Smithee's, the Guild's *Creative Rights Handbook* implies that a director must be able to give negative responses to a number of questions concerning the director's control over the finished film. These range from the particular ("Were you advised about editing of versions for ancillary markets and given the opportunity to participate in the editing?") to the all-inclusive ("Were you consulted about every creative decision?").[12] Once the Guild has approved the use of the Smithee pseudonym, its rules forbid the director from discussing his or her experience, to the point that the director must agree not even to acknowledge that he or she was in fact the original director of the film.[13] Smithee has thus become Hollywood's secret shame, the all-purpose sign that adopts those films that can claim an embarrassingly plural parentage, a mixed parentage that would put the lie to the Guild's official position that the director is a film's sole author, or, since paternity is the central metaphor employed in the *Creative Rights Handbook,* a film's sole and rightful father.

That the DGA's archetypal director should be a father is no mere linguistic idiosyncrasy. Rather, this fact foregrounds the real and imaginary gendered division of labor that has always underwritten the process of making films in Hollywood. The idiom cannot fail to remind us of the 1975 essay "Visual Pleasure and Narrative Cinema," in which Laura Mulvey foregrounds the absolute gender difference that underwrites the process of making filmic *meaning.*[14] Constance Penley has perceptively recognized that this process, too, is a "division of labor," one that "controls the narrative structure because it is the man who makes the story happen at every textual level."[15] As the DGA seems willing to acknowledge, men make the story happen at every extratextual level as well, by controlling the modes of production throughout the film industry. A purely historicist understanding of Smithee, then, could mistake the creation of the male pseudonym as being merely complicit with this gendered division of labor, a perception reinforced by the fact that, to date, no women directors have adopted the Smithee pseudonym.[16] The aspect, however, of Mulvey's formulation that was to become the central point of contention within feminist film studies may also indicate that Smithee need not be always already employed purely in the service of corporate patriarchy. As Mulvey explains, even as the origin of "visual pleasure" is the spectacle of the female body, this same representation of the female serves as a locus for anxieties on the part of the audience (figured as male) about castration. In this way, it serves the function of a fetish, both hiding and drawing attention to those castration anxieties. Smithee shares a structural similarity with Mulvey's female figure insofar as he, too, is a fetish serving the double role of concealing as well as announcing anxieties about directorial authorship, which is also traditionally figured as masculine. To accept Smithee simply as a complicitous symptom is still to obey the rules of interpretation that have been prescribed by the industry he ostensibly serves; namely, that Smithee is nothing more than a placeholder, a curiosity only to those who may wish to reunite a "real" director with his disavowed progeny. If, on the other hand, we take the figure of Smithee seriously, then these abandoned films have already found an author, and one who disrupts and destabilizes established models of authorship figured along masculinist lines.

To date, Smithee's progeny includes over fifty films and television productions, and a quick glance at Smithee's filmography conveys a sense of the films' status as the castaway orphans of Hollywood. Following *Death of a Gunfighter*, the Smithee name next appeared on the 1970 made-for-TV movie *The Challenge*. Smithee's credits have since included the 1980 ABC production *City in Fear* (introducing Mickey Rourke); a producer's credit on the 1981 satire of teen-slasher flicks *Student Bodies*; 1982's *Shock Treatment* (a not unremarkable sequel that failed to achieve the notoriety of its predecessor *The Rocky Horror Picture Show*); the aptly named *The Horrible Terror* in 1982; 1987's *Let's Get Harry*; the re-cut 1988 television version of David Lynch's 1984 *Dune*; 1989's *House III*; the 1991 video release *Bloodsucking Pharaohs in Pittsburgh*; the "Accidents Happen" segment of 1992's *The Red Shoe Diaries: Auto Erotica*; in the same year, the music video for Whitney Houston's "I Will Always Love You" (theme song to the film *The Bodyguard*); various made-for-TV movies such as 1994's *The Birds II: Land's End* or 1995's *The O. J. Simpson Story*; and, in 1998, the feature film *Sub Down*. The Smithee oeuvre culminates in *Burn Hollywood Burn: An Alan Smithee Film*, a satire of the Smithee phenomenon that became a victim of its subject when director Arthur Hiller took his name off of screenwriter Joe Eszterhas's recut version of the film. Eszterhas's version scored only marginally better with test audiences, however, and the film's release was delayed several times before eventually opening to a "select number of cities" in March of 1998.[17]

Smithee was born the year after the Motion Picture Production Code, the agreement that for nearly forty years had legitimated the censorship of all films produced in America, gave way to the Code and Rating Administration. The Code was originally conceived as a way of "holding in check" the tendency of the Big Eight Hollywood studios to produce salacious or sensational films, a strategy the studios turned to each time they felt threatened by dwindling box office figures. The death of the Code is symptomatic, then, of the dismantling of the structures that had grown up around the Hollywood studio system. These structures, even those that ostensibly regulated the studios, had hitherto enabled the Big Eight to function collectively as a monopoly. Individually, each studio operated as a factory that controlled the entire process of creating a film, from its inception to its distribution in studio-owned theaters nationwide. The dismantling of this system had accelerated in the years following the 1948 antitrust suit *United States v. Paramount*, and the fall of the Code was one of the key elements of this dismantling.[18]

It was from among the directors who worked under the studio system and within the strictures of the Code that François Truffaut and the *Cahiers* critics chose those directors they identified as *auteurs*. The *auteur*, for Truffaut, was originally a director defined by his ability to embed within his films his own stylistic signature despite the pressures of the studio system.[19] The death of the Code in the late 1960s would appear to have signaled a new era of freedom for the director working for the first time in decades without the threats of either MPPC censorship or significant studio interference. It also suggested the possibility that for the first time, the director, rather than the studio, could take primary responsibility (or *be held responsible*) for the films he directed. On the one hand, this freeing up of directors may be seen as one of the steps that led to the new generation of film school *auteurs* of the 1970s, a generation that included Martin Scorsese, Francis Ford Coppola, and Brian De Palma, aspiring directors influenced by Hollywood, the French art film, and, above all, by the *politique des auteurs*. At the same time, however, the shift away from studios and toward directors would also seem to be one explanation for the appearance of Smithee in 1969, since the very name of the director was now capable of bearing by itself both cinematic and economic value. With the death of the Code, one of those limiting structures of the studio system through which the *Cahiers du cinéma* critics defined the original *auteurs*, we come to the point in the history of Hollywood at which Allen Smithee, the apparent anti-*auteur*, becomes a necessary possibility.

This same year marks still another remarkable coincidence. At very nearly the same time that the Smithee challenge to the notion of the director as the author of a film was born in Hollywood, another attack on traditional literary notions of authorship was being launched in the form of French poststructuralism. Paris, of course, had earlier been the birthplace of the *Cahiers du cinéma*'s *politique des auteurs*, which Andrew Sarris had introduced to America as the *auteur* theory, and also of the *droit des auteurs*, the principles of which the Directors Guild of America had been trying to enshrine in Hollywood. Even as these traditional models of authorship began to be applied to film studies, however, French writers such as Roland Barthes and Michel Foucault launched innovative critiques of the same received literary notions. In 1968 Barthes proclaimed "The Death of the Author." The next year, Foucault responded to Barthes's essay, answering the question, "What Is an Author?" by demystifying the traditional model of literary authorship and replacing it with a model of what came to be known as the "author function," a function stripped bare of the glamour that film critics like Truffaut, Rohmer, and Sarris, as well as the Directors Guild, had been attempting to establish for film directors as *auteurs*. Today, of course, writers like Foucault, Barthes, and Jacques Derrida have become canonical authors in their own right within the body of work often grouped together as literary theory, many of the insights of which have been applied to film studies. These writers may themselves be taken to be the *auteurs* of the academy. Until now, however, no one has recognized that it is Smithee who provides the best opportunity to apply the insights of poststructuralism to the trope of the *auteur*. This should be done, we argue, not only by performing textual readings of a director's films, but also by studying the role of the post-Code film industry in constructing both filmic meaning and the cultural phenomenon of the director.

As early as April 1957, however, when André Bazin's well-known riposte to the younger *auteurists* appeared in *Cahiers du cinéma*, it had been argued that just such a nuanced consideration was necessary. Because "the cinema is an art which is both popular and industrial," Bazin stressed, the subject of analysis should be "not only the talent of this or that film-maker, but [also] the genius of the system."[20] This analysis could best be effected by "a sociological approach to [the] production" of "the American cinematic genius," a genius which, he noted, was not primarily individual but systemic.[21] Bazin was wary of the tendency of the *auteurists* to commit a kind of overdetermined intentional fallacy in their critical work, and the film that he used as a cautionary example was none other than *Mr. Arkadin* (Bazin calls the film by its English title):

> I think that not only would the supporters of the *politique des auteurs* refuse to agree that *Confidential Report* is an inferior film to *Citizen Kane*; they would be more eager to claim the contrary, and I can well see how they would go about it. As *Confidential Report* is Welles's sixth film, one can assume that a certain amount of progress has already been made. Not only did the Welles of 1953 have more experience of himself and of his art than in 1941, but however great was the freedom he was able to obtain in Hollywood *Citizen Kane* cannot help remaining to a certain extent an RKO product. The film would never have seen the light of day without the co-operation of some superb technicians and their just as admirable technical apparatus. Gregg Toland, to mention only one, was more than a little responsible for the final result. On the other hand, *Confidential Report* is completely the work of Welles. Until it can be proved to the contrary, it will be considered *a priori* a superior film because it is more personal and because Welles's personality can only have matured as he grew older.[22]

Although Bazin is in some way interested in the relative quality of each film, his true concern is the degree to which *auteurist* criticism defers to the *auteur*'s personality as both the origin and referent of a film's meaning, thereby effacing the "genius of the system" in which Bazin locates a principal origin of filmic meaning.

It is fitting that Bazin should choose *Mr. Arkadin* as the film with which he critiques these tendencies of the *auteurists*, since it is a film pre-eminently concerned with biographies constructed in order to efface the peripheral systemic figures from whose testimony emerges the persona of Gregory Arkadin. Arkadin would prefer to appear to be, like Welles, an *auteur* of the type described by the younger *Cahiers* critics. However, what is demonstrated by *Mr. Arkadin*, by Bazin's critique of that film, and by the uncanny emergence within it of the Smithee name as one possible origin for Arkadin, is the degree to which Arkadin and Welles, like Smithee, cannot be transcendent geniuses unto themselves, but are rather, in Bazin's words, products of "the social determinism, the historical combination of circumstances, and the technical background which ... determine [genius]."[23] As such, the film exposes the fact that the genius Welles and the pseudonym Smithee are both products of the same "genius of the system," thereby revealing that *Mr. Arkadin* can no longer claim to belong unequivocally to Welles's oeuvre, but must be at least shared with the social, historical, and technical phenomenon that is embodied by Allen Smithee.

Mr. Arkadin is a film deeply involved in the questioning not merely of credentials, but also of the authority that invests those credentials with the mark of legitimacy and authenticity. The disillusion and crisis that presently threaten the field of film studies have arisen because of a failure to make an analogous distinction. In naming the excluded authorial component, the "genius of the system," Bazin was also pointing to the way in which the American film industry profits by disguising its systemic nature under the cover of an individuated persona. The temptation to conceive of film studies mainly through the industry-endorsed models of *auteurist* scholarship (and here we may recall the colossal four-day Alfred Hitchcock centenary conference held in 1999 at New York University's Tisch School of the Arts, the leading film studies program in the United States[24]) habitually fails to engage with the historical and economic reification of the *politique des auteurs* into the marketing strategy and critical device that it has become. This temptation has also precluded theoretical approaches to film that differ from established models of scholarship, approaches that may challenge not only the grip of the *auteur* on his or her film, but also that of established critics on the shape film studies might take.

The idea for this collection of essays originated in a discussion among our colleagues of Derrida's *The Truth in Painting*.[25] Noting that Derrida's work had first entered film studies as part of the demythologization of *auteurist* writing on cinema, Craig Saper suggested that the question had become one of how to translate Derrida anew into *auteurism*. *The Truth in Painting*, along with other Derrida works such as *Signsponge* and *Glas*, offers a model of investigating the signature not simply as a legitimating mark, but also as a series of metaphors reiterated within the text, generated from the author's name: Hegel's work, for example, could be made to refer as much to eagles (*aigle*) as it would to the phenomenal author.[26] A consensus soon developed that no one's signature was more exemplary of these practices than Smithee's, not simply because Derrida's theorization requires no human author in order to function, but because the Smithee name already performs the work of this Derridean signature, by insisting on the place of work rather than the worker, the smithy rather than the smith, the "genius of the system" rather than the individual genius. From these discussions came the idea of producing an *auteurist* study of the collected films of Allen Smithee. The editors of this book, along with Laura Spagnoli, Justin Ginnetti, David Qunitiliani, Yoonmee Chang, Scott Shrake, and Jonathan Eburne, formed the Allen Smithee Group in order to study Smithee's films and to test the effects of the modes of criticism that were inspired by our viewings and readings of these illegitimate films.

In the process of creating this body of work, the members of the Allen Smithee Group experienced firsthand the difficulties of the process of forging and legitimating a new area of study. Initial responses often wondered about the purpose of studying films produced under the aegis of a "fake name," or suspected that the project was a "joke." In Italy, Laura Parigi won prizes for her work on Smithee (begun without knowledge of our group in Philadelphia), but at the same time had to fend off accusations that she had fabricated her subject matter. When the idea of studying Smithee films was described in organs of the popular press like *Entertainment Weekly* and the *Los Angeles Times*, it was either implied to be evidence of academia's frivolity or was incorporated into the discourse of the entertainment industry (*Entertainment Weekly* cited the project as "[f]urther proof that celebrity awards are out of control").[27] Whether or not any name could claim the status of "phony," as one reporter put it,

Smithee remained in the eyes of those working on the project the most "real" author possible, as we pursued the implications of Foucault and Derrida. Scott Shrake, one of the members of the Smithee Group, suggested further, "The goal [of studying Smithee] is to get to the bottom of some vital questions of authorship by interrogating a real, historical phenomenon, which is the existence of a group pseudonym at the Directors Guild. [This] is a lot less hallucinatory than most [academic topics] I've seen." It is our hope that readers will find the essays collected in this volume similarly nonhallucinatory.

Concluding the "Forging Smithee Studies" section, each of the two essays that follow this introduction theorizes an approach to film studies that offers alternatives to the prevailing paradigms of the discipline. In "Artificial *Auteurism* and the Political Economy of the Allen Smithee Case," Craig Saper traces two stages in the history of *auteurism* and argues for the necessity of the creation of a third. Moving from Andrew Sarris's translation of the *Cahiers* critics' *politique des auteurs* to an American audience, through what he calls the neo-*auteurism* that allowed for a politicized structural analysis not only of films and their *auteurs* but also of the experience of viewing, Saper arrives at his third term, artificial *auteurism*. Under this name, Saper designates critical methods that seek to reinvent film criticism as a metaphorical and performative practice, one that bears formal and political sympathies to the Neoist and Fluxus avant-garde groups.

Similarly, Robert Ray's "The Automatic *Auteur*; or, A Certain Tendency in Film Criticism," reconceptualizes film studies in the form of a surrealist game, while playing one such "critical game about *Allen Smithee*." In so doing, Ray rejects a film studies based on the formalist precepts of Sergei Eisenstein and David Bordwell, and champions the ideas of André Bazin and Roland Barthes, both of them theorists who, like the surrealists, privilege the *automatic* in order to de-emphasize that control that suppresses the generative power of the accident. Using François Truffaut's foundational essay "A Certain Tendency of the French Cinema" as a template, Ray theorizes an alternative approach to scholarship that is also an example of that approach in practice. Ray thereby works against what he calls a "path dependence" in contemporary film studies, a self-limiting devotion to prescribed and legitimated models of scholarship.

The next section of the anthology, "Smithee Studies," includes those pieces that engage directly with specific Smithee films. Donald Pease's "Allen Smithee's *Death of a Gunfighter*: 'A Casualty of Hollywood's Excluded Middle'" presents a close reading of Smithee's first film against the backdrops both of Sarris's *auteurism* and of suture theory. Between these two modes of analysis, Pease introduces the concept of the "smitheereen" to negotiate a middle ground between the theoretical fields staked out by *auteur* theory and those modes of film criticism influenced by Lacanian psychoanalysis. In the smitheereen, Pease locates an effect by which Smithee films unstitch both the sutures that attach *Death of a Gunfighter*'s characters to their social roles, as well as those that prescribe the spectator's position.

In "Smithee in *The Twilight Zone*," Jessie Labov considers the implications of the trial *The People v. John Landis et al.* for Hollywood's commercialized *auteurism* as well as for the Smithee name. The trial was an attempt to hold director John Landis legally responsible for the helicopter crash that killed actor Vic Morrow and two young children during the filming of Landis's segment of *Twilight Zone: The Movie*. This tragedy, in turn, caused a dismayed Anderson House to apply to remove his own name as second assistant director and replace it with Smithee's. As Labov shows, the trial marks one of the first major challenges to directorial autonomy that occurred after that autonomy was made possible by the death of the Code and the rise of the marketable *auteur*. As such, it has occasioned a rethinking of what directorial responsibility can mean, a question Labov asks in the context of the history of the pseudonym within Hollywood, particularly in the era of the blacklist.

Christian Keathley's "*Signateurism* and the Case of Allen Smithee" offers an extensive theorization of a *signateurist* approach to film studies, elaborated out of Derrida's *Signsponge*. Keathley's analysis shows Derrida's theorization of the signature to bear surprising and enlightening analogies to *auteur* theory as explicated by Sarris. Whereas *auteurism* offers interpretations of films that locate unified meanings centered on the director, Keathley's *signateurist* approach is more concerned with the productive effects of scattering meaning across the various names that appear in a film rather than confining meaning to the singular figure of the director. Keathley's case study of the Smithee-produced *Student Bodies* provides an example of the diffusive effects of such a *signateurist* reading.

Jeremy Braddock's essay, "Smithee's Incorporation," understands Smithee to be a directorial personality marked by his desire to dramatize the play between the singular and the general, between individuated and "corporate" identities. The received notion of *auteurism* seeks, on the other hand, to preserve a boundary between these categories, but, as evidenced by the Directors Guild of America's official publications, it requires an act of legislation to effect such a notion of individual cinematic genius. Following Derrida's eponymous meditation on Kafka's "Before the Law," Braddock reads Smithee's "three films of the law" (*Death of a Gunfighter*, *Backtrack*, and *Solar Crisis*) as films in which the law summons both Smithee's individuated and incorporated personae into being. Rather than strictly obeying the law, Smithee appropriates these films and reauthorizes them as representations of his own position within the film industry.

Stephen Hock's "This Is Too Big for One Old Name: Hitchcock and Smithee in the Signature Centrifuge" takes up the method of the signature experiment, as theorized by Derrida, Keathley, and Robert Ray, in elaborating a reading of Smithee's sequel to *The Birds*. Rather than conceding that the original film's production history of Hitchcock's sadistic treatment of Tippi Hedren is merely allegorically present in the original film, Hock's employment of the signature experiment reveals that both the film and its sequel bear witness to this history in a way that needs no recourse to Hitchcock's biography. The signature experiment generates these meanings from the names not only of the films' directors but also of their various casts, crews, and characters. In both his method and in the content that the method reveals, Hock works to disrupt the value that *auteurist* critics traditionally locate in the Hitchcock name, a value that Hitchcock, his heirs, the commercial apparatus surrounding his films, and sympathetic critics have constructed to function as if it were a corporate brand name.

The third section of the collection, "Smithee Suggests," speaks to the implications of the foregoing essays in contexts not immediately connected with Smithee. In the course of her work on Allen Smithee, Laura Parigi has compiled an exhaustive database of Americanized pseudonyms that were used by Italian directors for the three decades following the Second World War. These pseudonyms were not employed simply as frauds, however, whereby the pseudonym would merely have disguised an Italian film as American at the expense of an unwitting audience. Rather, in "The Fake Americans of the Italian Cinema," Parigi argues that this remarkable phenomenon manifested a collective agreement among filmgoers and filmmakers to participate in an "extrafilmic fiction" not unlike that fiction centered on Smithee himself. As Parigi shows, rather than being a footnote in the history of Italian cinema, this fiction proved crucial to the functioning of a national film industry at a transitional stage in its economic history, just as the fiction of Smithee both facilitated and marked a transition from the studio-driven movies of classical Hollywood to the director-identified film industry of the post-Code era. Parigi's article demonstrates the surprising affinities that Smithee studies may hold for a film studies that looks beyond the major American studios.

Jonathan Eburne's "The Cheerless Art of Industry: Marcel Duchamp and the Smithee Readymade" investigates the analogies between Smithee and Duchamp, insofar as the work of each artist reflects "a strategy for producing works of 'art' which understood this production as a proliferation of aliases." Like Duchamp's punning aliases, Smithee, according to Eburne, serves to distance the process of creating films from the director's persona. Eburne analogizes this function to Smithee's surprising appearance (dressed as a businessman on holiday) at the Penn conference held in his honor. His specific presence represented a "kind of 'cross-dressing' in the sense that it depicts a corporation dressed up to look like a man," and the mistake the audience could have made would have been to think that it was looking at anything but the pastiche of an actual man. Instead, Smithee came to stand for all the stages in the cycle of the industrial production of film, ranging from creation to reception to critical judgment. As such, Smithee does not only designate the productive processes of the film industry; he also becomes a productive industry unto himself.

In "A for *Auteur* and F for Fake," Tom Conley sees an allegiance with the work of Smithee in that of Raoul Walsh, the "Hollywood *auteur* par excellence." Because of both the quantity of Walsh's output and the speed with which it was produced, Walsh's *auteurist* signature was always difficult to identify, and the *Cahiers* critics concluded that what marked Walsh's work was an attention to "the surface-effects of the film and not the abstraction of its psychology." But since the "work of the author is anything but original or originary," each of Walsh's authorial signatures is genuine insofar as it possesses the power to expose itself as duplicated, serial, or falsified, in the manner suggested by Derrida's essay "Signature Event Context." This infinitely performative quality of the signature affirms all *auteurist* practices to be proliferations of simulacra, thereby demystifying the received notion of the *auteur* as a marketing strategy, while repoliticizing it in what Conley identifies as a "neo-Brechtian" manner.

Finally, in his afterword to the collected pieces, James English presents Smithee and the preeminence of the academic anthology as twin symptoms that show both Hollywood and academia to be dependent on the production and distribution of names. Rather than simply attacking the academic star system, English examines the ways in which our own work in the humanities, including even that work committed to a collective political agenda, depends on that proliferation of individual names. This is no less true of a discourse that interrogates the cultural function of names. In order for the work of this project to be complete, English argues that Smithee studies needs to include a dimension of "sociological self-scrutiny" that implicates its own practices and practitioners in the field it seeks to disrupt.

In the name of Allen Smithee, the essays collected here aim to use the evanescent director's oeuvre in order to try to conceptualize a film studies that can operate metaphorically while also providing critiques of film and film studies at the level of the industry's infrastructure. These essays therefore also operate in the spirit of Dennis Hopper's "Into the Issue of the Good Old Time Movie Versus the Good Old Time," a 1965 essay originally dismissed as an "apologia for bad American movies." Four years before he made *Easy Rider*, and twenty-four years before he himself would take a Smithee for *Backtrack*, Hopper praised the director Bruce Conner's assembling of movies from "the stockpile of films that lie decaying in the vaults of all the major studios," and implied that the possibility of an "American Art Film" must differentiate itself from its European predecessors by engaging directly with the Hollywood models it aimed at the same time to destroy.[28] Similarly, a meaningful American film studies must differentiate itself from its academic predecessors by engaging with films that, in Bruce Conner's time, would have lain "decaying in the vaults of all the major studios." In our present day of technological advance and profit maximizing, we are "lucky indeed" that these films instead sit innocuously and illegitimately on the shelves of video stores everywhere. We offer this book as an invitation to create illegitimate scholarship, scholarship that resists the conformist pressures of the academy and in that way is more fully able to realize the promise the Allen Smithee Project holds as an example of loosening the "principle of thrift in the proliferation of meaning."[29] Like Guy van Stratten, who declares, "Maybe I'll wind up an Arkadin myself someday!" this collection recognizes the transformative power of the name, in this case Smithee, not only for film history, but for a renewed film studies.

Postscript

In January 2000, MGM released the film *Supernova*, a science-fiction film whose production history was sufficiently vexed as to oblige original director Walter Hill to remove his name from the credits. Instead of being released as a Smithee film, *Supernova* was credited to the direction of Thomas Lee. As various observers noted, the decision to use the new

Thomas Lee pseudonym rather than the familiar Smithee name appeared to reflect a "feeling … that Mr. Smithee was getting too well known for his own good."[30] The irony of the decision to retire the Smithee name is that it affirms Smithee's status as a pivotal Hollywood director, one with a career that spanned three decades of significant change in the film industry. We may speculate that future pseudonymous production (whether done in Lee's name or not) will have to claim Allen Smithee as a forbear. As of this writing, no new Thomas Lee films have appeared, which leaves open the question of his further employment. The question *Supernova* poses to film studies now is whether Thomas Lee is a pseudonym for Walter Hill or for Allen Smithee.

Notes

1. François Truffaut, foreword, *Orson Welles: A Critical View*, by André Bazin (Los Angeles: Acrobat Books, 1991) 19.

2. The editors wish to thank Tyler Smith for discovering in *Mr. Arkadin* this important early reference to Smithee.

3. Indeed, it could be argued that Welles's later career was more prescient of the necessity for Smithee's arrival than was that of anyone else who worked in Hollywood before Smithee's appearance. The well-known battle which he lost with Universal Pictures over *Touch of Evil* (1958) is another such example of this same prescience.

4. Joseph McBride, *Orson Welles*, rev. ed. (New York: Da Capo, 1996) 130.

5. Orson Welles [Maurice Bessy], *Mr. Arkadin* (London: W. H. Allen, 1956) 89.

6. Smithee's version of the film was retitled *Catch Fire*. Hopper's 116-minute restored "Director's Cut" is easily found in video stores today. Pesci remains uncredited in both versions.

7. For some *Cahiers* critics, the category of *auteur* was a way of marking what they perceived as the radical attacks that directors made against consumer America from within Hollywood. Jean Domarchi's 1956 essay "Knife in the Wound," for example, identifies the "great American directors" as those who have either made "passionate or ironic critique[s] of the extremely commercialized American consciousness," or, more directly, have "violently denounced the fetishization of money." Translated by Diana Matias in *Cahiers du Cinéma, the*

1950s: Neo-Realism, Hollywood, New Wave, ed. Jim Hillier (Cambridge: Harvard University Press, 1985) 235–47. For an illuminating discussion of the more recent marketing of the *auteur*, see "The Commerce of Auteurism: Coppola, Kluge, Ruiz" in Timothy Corrigan's *A Cinema without Walls: Movies and Culture after Vietnam* (New Brunswick: Rutgers University Press, 1991) 101–36.

America's most prominent *auteurist*, Andrew Sarris, was himself the victim of another apparently mechanical appropriation of his *auteurist* principles, as the Oxford University Press typesetter of his recent book *"You Ain't Heard Nothin' Yet"* rendered the journal title *Cahiers du cinéma* as *Cashiers du Cinema*, thereby underscoring Corrigan's point about the contemporary "commerce of *auteurism*." Andrew Sarris, *"You Ain't Heard Nothin' Yet": The American Talking Film, History and Memory 1927–1949*, 1st ed. (New York: Oxford University Press, 1998) 264.

8. Don Siegel, *A Siegel Film* (London: Faber and Faber, 1993) 320.

9. Siegel 320–21.

10. The 1980s saw a boom in Smithee's output, during which period his first name came much more often to be spelled "Alan." In fact, the original spelling had been chosen in order to minimize the likelihood that it would coincide with a real person's name (the first name proposed, Alan Smith, was dismissed for this reason). The popular fable that "Alan Smithee" is a clever anagram of "the alias men" is therefore an anachronism. As the essays in this volume often depend on one specific spelling of the name, the editors have chosen to incorporate both spellings, deferring when possible to the director's "given" name, Allen Smithee.

11. There are several ways for directors to get around this particular requirement. George Lucas, for instance, chose to include no opening credits in *Star Wars*. He similarly kept opening credits off the *Star Wars* sequel *The Empire Strikes Back*, a sequel he did *not* direct. The sequel's director, Irvin Kershner, had no problem with this decision, but the DGA did, and fined Lucas $250,000. Lucas then sued the DGA, settled with it for $25,000, and promptly quit the Guild. See Dale Pollack, *Skywalking: The Life and Films of George Lucas* (New York: Harmony, 1983) 248–49.

Or, a director might choose never to join the Guild, as Quentin Tarantino has done, a decision that has allowed him the liberty to keep his name out of certain of his films' opening credits, but which has also kept him from directing television productions that have exclusive agreements with the Directors Guild.

12. *DGA 1996 Creative Rights Handbook*, Directors Guild of America, 5 Sept. 1997, http://www.dga.org/dga-info/dga_creative_rights_handbook.htm.

13. Justin Ginnetti, a member of the Allen Smithee Group, wrote to invite director Arthur Hiller to the Smithee conference from which this volume originates. It was hoped that Hiller would come discuss his experiences "taking a Smithee" on the recent Joe Eszterhas–scripted film *Burn Hollywood Burn: An Alan Smithee Film*. Brenda White, Hiller's executive assistant, wrote in return, "Mr. Hiller has asked that I thank you for your letter regarding your Alan Smithee Conference on September 27. Unfortunately, he is prohibited by Directors Guild Agreement to discuss publicly his own Alan Smithee experience and so will be unable to join your conference. We wish you well with it." Brenda White, letter to Justin Ginnetti, 23 July 1997.

In the case of the 1998 film *American History X*, director Tony Kaye applied to have his name replaced with Smithee's in order to dissociate himself from the longer cut of the film that had been authorized by Ed Norton, the film's star. The DGA refused his offer, however, because Kaye had already taken out advertisements in *Variety* and *The Hollywood Reporter* excoriating New Line Cinema for having taken control of the film's final cut. See Benjamin Svetkey, "X Marks the Spat," *Entertainment Weekly* 455 (23 Oct. 1998): 28–36.

14. Laura Mulvey, "Visual Pleasure and Narrative Cinema," *Screen* 16.3 (autumn 1975): 6–18.

15. Constance Penley, "'A Certain Refusal of Difference': Feminism and Film Theory," *Art after Modernism: Rethinking Representation*, ed. Brian Wallis (New York: Museum of Contemporary Art, 1984) 376.

16. In the foreword to this volume, Andrew Sarris describes the controversy that marked the release of *A Thousand Acres*, and nearly established Jocelyn Moorhouse as the first woman director to "take a Smithee." Moorhouse ended up assuming credit for the film, however, and the pseudonym has remained the privilege of male directors. Likewise, no nonwhite directors appear to have used the pseudonym, indicating that being able to take a Smithee is a luxury for those already rewarded by the divisions of labor in Hollywood.

17. Eszterhas became the subject of an interesting anecdote in the field of Smithee scholarship. A month before the staging of the conference for which many of these essays were originally written, Eszterhas phoned the Allen Smithee Group, and offered to send an early print of the film to Philadelphia, in order that it might be screened in conjunction with the conference. The screening was not

to be billed as a "premiere," however, and when the organizers asked if a small admission fee could be charged, in order to cover the rental of a 35mm projector, the offer was curtly rescinded by the film's producer, Ben Myron. The film eventually opened in a small number of American cities (Philadelphia not among them) in May 1998, receiving reviews that ranged from "it pretty much succeeds" (*San Francisco Chronicle*) to "spectacularly bad" (Roger Ebert) and "this huge, steaming pile" (*USA Today*). The film went on to win more Golden Raspberry Awards than any film before it, including the award for Worst Picture of 1998, an accomplishment that above all else argues for the status of Smithee as *auteur*, since the specter of his directorial reputation now precedes him to the extent that his latest film, despite having been released to a limited market and seeing a very short run, nevertheless commanded a reception that understood it to be formally consistent with his previous work.

18. For a consideration of the weakening financial position of the studios in the years following the 1948 *United States v. Paramount* ruling see Leonard J. Jeff and Jerold L. Simmons, *The Dame in the Kimono: Hollywood, Censorship, and the Production Code from the 1920s to the 1960s* (New York: Grove Weidenfeld, 1990). See also Frank Walsh, *Sin and Censorship: The Catholic Church and the Motion Picture Industry* (New Haven: Yale University Press, 1996).

19. Indeed, the less a director was indulged by a studio, the greater the chances that he could distinguish himself as an *auteur*, as Truffaut indicates in his review of *Giant* (1956): "I have come to a conclusion: *Giant* is everything that is contemptible in the Hollywood system, especially when the said system works for the benefit of a prestige movie, deliberately conceived to win a few Academy Awards.... This dead film won't take away from us the idea that American cinema is the most alive in the world when it offers us, for example, *Written on the Wind* [1956; Dir. Douglas Sirk], a small, successfully done *Giant*." Quoted in Wheeler Winston Dixon, *The Early Film Criticism of François Truffaut*, trans. Brigitte Formentin-Humbert (Bloomington: Indiana University Press, 1993) 87.

20. André Bazin, "On the *politique des auteurs*," trans. Peter Graham, *Cahiers du Cinéma, the 1950s: Neo-Realism, Hollywood, New Wave*, ed. Jim Hillier (Cambridge: Harvard University Press, 1985) 251, 258.

21. Bazin 251.

22. Bazin 254.

23. Bazin 251.

24. The conference did include "The Death of the *Auteur*" as a possible

panel title in its promotional material, but only as the last in a long series of celebratory panel subjects that served to deify the subject *auteur*. "Topics to Ponder," *Hitchcock: A Centennial Celebration, October 13–17, 1999*, 10 July 1999, http://www.nyu.edu/tisch/cinema/hitchcock/topics.html.

25. Jacques Derrida, *The Truth in Painting*, trans. Geoff Bennington and Ian McLeod (Chicago: University of Chicago Press, 1987).

26. "His name is so strange. From the eagle it draws imperial or historic power. Those who still pronounce his name like the French (there are some) are ludicrous only up to a certain point: the restitution (semantically infallible for those who have read him a little—but only a little) of magisterial coldness and imperturbable seriousness, the eagle caught in ice and frost, glass and gel.

"Let the emblanched [*emblémi*] philosopher be so congealed."
Jacques Derrida, *Glas*, trans. John P. Leavey Jr. and Richard Rand (Lincoln: University of Nebraska Press, 1986) 1.

For an extended discussion of *signateurism*, see Christian Keathley's article in the present volume.

27. Irv Slifkin, "Alan Anon," *Entertainment Weekly* (10 Oct. 1997): 13.

28. Refused publication by the magazine that originally commissioned it, the essay was published as a preface to the *Easy Rider* screenplay. Peter Fonda, Dennis Hopper, and Terry Southern, *Easy Rider*, ed. Nancy Hardin and Marilyn Schlossberg (New York: Signet, 1969) 7–11.

29. Michel Foucault, "What Is an Author?" trans. Josué V. Harari, *The Foucault Reader*, ed. Paul Rabinow (New York: Pantheon, 1984) 118.

30. Andrew Gumbel, "Hollywood Decides to Kill the Man Who Never Was," *The Independent* (16 Jan. 2000): 19.

CHAPTER 2

Artificial *Auteurism* and the Political Economy of the Allen Smithee Case

Craig Saper

In a *New York Times Magazine* article on the increasing importance of script doctors for Hollywood movies, the editors include a parodic movie poster to capture the odd jumble of talents lumped together in contemporary productions.[1] The poster advertises a movie called *Baseball Commandos* starring an absurd array of actors from Bruce Willis to Roseanne. The stars, rendered by cartoon-like drawings, are shown parachuting into a baseball park. In the style of a movie poster, the bottom of the illustration presents a long list of writers as well as actors, producers, and, last, the director. In the description of the corresponding fictional movie, the *New York Times* reporter, Jaime Wolf, describes how a hypothetical producer would hire nearly ten different writers to bring the script to fruition with "punched-up jokes," heightened action sequences, and other specialized aspects of a script. Each script doctor contributes her or his specific expertise. The target of the parody is Hollywood's current conveyor-belt approach to filmmaking. The poster reinforces the joke by including these *script doctors'* names as the writers, as if the script had been put together by a committee with no single author or singular authorial voice.

Oddly, the poster includes as director a name not found elsewhere in Wolf's article. To make sure that the reader does not miss the point, the director's name is placed at the end of the list of the film's participants and is further set off from the absurdly long list of scriptwriters by being rendered in a different colored typeface. The director, not mentioned in the reporter's hypothetical situation, is "Alan Smithee."[2] That name is a reference to something similar to the army of script doctors who have replaced a single writer in today's Hollywood. Smithee's name here is added by the illustrator to make a joke about Hollywood's relatively anonymous system of production. It also refers to the problem that Wolf's article points out is created by script doctors: formulaic schlock. No one would actually want to include her or his name on some of these films. Allen Smithee is the name often used by directors, who remain somewhat hidden behind the pseudonym, in order to mock a particularly kitschy production. The poster shows that this inside joke has now entered the popular parlance, as well as the importance of that name for understanding the socioeconomic structure of Hollywood.

Turning to the academic reception of Smithee, the Allen Smithee Group has described Smithee as "a director so reclusive and mercurial as to seem non-existent, and yet, his corpus includes more than fifty films."[3] Not only does this anthology seek to recover that corpus, but it also seeks to share some of Smithee's fame as a marker for a dissenting voice within a production system. The Allen Smithee Group has already received publicity unusual for academic publications. Articles and blurbs in the *Village Voice*, *Entertainment Weekly*, the *Los Angeles Times*, and *Le Monde* (as well as the more predictable mention in the *Chronicle of Higher Education*) suggest that writing about Smithee might mark an important shift in film and cultural studies. In fact, this anthology, and this article in particular, offers a model for these new directions in film and cultural studies. The shift that Smithee marks depends on understanding the importance of a director's name in contemporary culture and in the academic discipline of film studies.

We all know the director in Figure 2.1. And our immediate recognition is proof of the success of *auteurist* theories. A useful simplified definition of that approach to film studies is that the director is the key factor in the achievement of a film and that great directors mark films as significant rather than run of the mill. To suggest how much our common-sense perception of film has changed as a result of this approach, let me

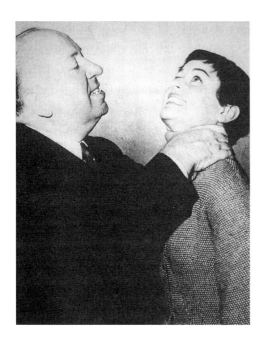

Figure 2.1. Recognizing this director is proof of the success of *auteurist* theories.

quote the 5 August 1954 review of *Rear Window* in the paper of record, the *New York Times*. The reviewer, Bosley Crowther, explains that "Mr. Hitchcock's film is not 'significant.' What it has to say about people and human nature is superficial and glib. But it does expose many facets of the loneliness of city life and it tacitly demonstrates the impulse of morbid curiosity."[4] Not many contemporary critics would argue with this description of the film's portrayal of human nature as "superficial" or "glib," but we would be hard pressed to find a critic or film student today who would take these apparent shortcomings as marks against the film's "significance." *Rear Window* is significant in no small part because Hitchcock directed the film in his unique style, and that style is marked by its playful superficiality, not by its subtleties or depth. *Auteurism* has so completely won the day that it has captured the common sense of movie fans everywhere.

During the 1950s the editors of *Cahiers du cinéma* introduced the notion of a film's director as the author of a movie; they called this idea *auteurism*. Using the French word for "author" was meant as an ironic attack on those critics who wanted to privilege the screenwriter's literary skills over the superficial stylistic panache of a film's director. François Truffaut attacked the "Tradition of Quality" with his famous remark that "a film is no longer made in France that the authors do not believe they are re-making *Madame Bovary*."[5] But the subtleties of their argument these days often have less influence either on attacks on authorship or on lists of "greatest directors" in popular magazines. The writers who introduced the idea of *auteurism* tended to focus on popular filmmakers like Alfred Hitchcock, Douglas Sirk, or Sam Fuller rather than on either so-called quality films and filmmakers or on big productions like *Ben Hur*. Because these critics' work has indirectly had a profound influence on popular opinion in the United States, film buffs might forget that many of the directors now considered *auteurist* geniuses received little, if any, scholarly attention before the *Cahiers* editorials appeared. Those editorials examined the aesthetic achievement of often quirky and unusual filmmakers working within the Hollywood industry. Truffaut championed an odd and interesting shot construction over the coherence of a story or the significance of a theme. Truffaut even championed a film because of the odd performance or tantalizing costume of the starlet. Now as then, Hollywood markets precisely this sort of superficial, but fascinating, type of filmmaking. What sometimes is referred to as *auteurism* is often its opposite—part of a high-brow marketing pitch—films with lasting thematic significance and beauty. Routinely, the industry markets those films that do not fit into the blockbuster "event film" category in terms of the director's reputation for producing a quality film. These directors might find themselves interviewed on a National Public Radio talk-show rather than appear on *Entertainment Tonight*, and their films might premiere at prestigious film festivals rather than opening on thousands of screens simultaneously. In this sense, not only does the Smithee name reference the history of *auteurism*, but it also highlights (and mocks) the way that the lionizing of directorial control now functions as public relations for a new "tradition of quality."

Among film scholars *auteurism* is so naturalized now that it simply makes the director into a great artist equal to an author. It puts film in the same lineage as other art forms such as painting and literature by effacing the inherently collective and industrial process involved in film-making. In common parlance, the term *auteur* has lost its ironic mean-ing, and its attack on the supposedly literary values of significant themes about human nature and society is muted. Now the term is usually used pejoratively to describe the snob appeal of "literary" filmmaking. *Auteur-ism* has become a minor mythology: it seems to stand for precisely the values it sought to disrupt.

In 1962 Andrew Sarris introduced *auteurism* as an approach to film criticism in the United States. He is always quick to point out that he is not a film theorist and simply used this approach as part of his journal-istic style. He wanted mainly to suggest that the film director is the key factor in the film's aesthetic result. That notion is difficult to deny. Sarris outlines three criteria for examining films: the director's techni-cal competence, the director's personality, and the interior meaning of the film.[6] The interior meaning is the director's personality mixing with the particular materials available in the film. This interior meaning is the "*élan* of the soul" or what Sarris goes on to describe as "that intangible difference between one personality and another."[7] I am not going to challenge this description, for—to be fair to Sarris—it was not intended as an elaborated theory but rather as a few rules of thumb; he writes that it is "the first step rather than the last stop in solving the mysteries of the medium."[8]

In a larger social context, Sarris became the whipping boy of acad-emics intent on attacking creative genius in favor of analyzing the polit-ical machinations and power of the studio system's visual style. The attacks on Sarris were contemporaneous with the attacks on authorship that began in literary studies later in the sixties. Roland Barthes's "The Death of the Author" stressed the reader's importance in creating mean-ing. Soon film theorists were focusing on spectators, audiences, and the interactions among films and spectators. In the academy, *auteurism* was considered passé at best. It simply found few supporters—either scholars adopted sophisticated theoretical models of spectatorial pleasures or they examined the general forms and structures of all films. *Auteurism* was, apparently, too simple and vulgar for any sustained analysis of film-making. More importantly, *auteurism* was taken as symptomatic of a "great man" theory of culture—for the *auteurists* were white men, as were the vast majority of Hollywood film directors—and so the sadistic power of Hitchcock's complete control now took on a sociopolitical tenor that was not particularly funny. The dark side of genius, to borrow the title of a trashy exposé about Hitchcock, now sullied *auteurism*.[9]

The second stage of *auteurism*, what I call neo-*auteurism*, grows out of these attacks on authorship and the sophisticated theories of spec-tatorship. Film scholars soon realized that there were other voices in the cinema that were marginalized. These voices needed to find an audience, and the role of film studies was understood to be introducing audiences to and preparing them for these alternatives to Hollywood movies. Kaja Silverman, for example, looked at female *auteurs* and combined her analy-sis with psychoanalytic theory to suggest new spectator positions offered by these identifications with the director's desires. In neo-*auteurism*, French and British feminist critics used psychoanalytic critical methods to interpret the structure of meaning by which classical Hollywood func-tioned, on the levels both of the *auteur* and of the audience. Their own films, like Laura Mulvey and Peter Wollen's *Riddles of the Sphinx* (1977) and Sally Potter's *Thriller* (1979), often bore a closer resemblance to their neo-*auteurist* theories than did the films made by the original *auteurist* critics (Godard, Truffaut, et al.) to their *auteurist* theories. Even if many theorists later rejected the initial *interpretive* paradigm introduced by Mulvey and others, these same theories encouraged an explosion of cre-ative activity that exceeded the intention of any particular reading or analytic practice. Because the analytic methodology became so influen-tial in cinema studies, Mulvey's achievement in encouraging and helping initiate the emergence of an *écriture feminine* in filmmaking receives rel-atively less attention. Although the phrase *écriture feminine* appears first in discussions of the work of Luce Irigaray, Hélène Cixous, and Julia Kristeva to describe an alternative literary writing practice, film theo-rists later used similar phrases to describe filmic writing practices as well. A feminine discourse could articulate the "unrepresentability" of the body in patriarchy by attempting to apply a different writing practice as an opposition to the patriarchal "social code." Annette Kuhn's description of "deconstructive" cinema, for example, examines this type of alternative practice. Such films break down and possibly analyze the modes of signification characteristic of dominant cinema.[10] Not only is the content feminist, the form is feminist as well. The practice of a filmic *écriture féminine* renders impossible the kinds of spectator identification typically set up by "realist" cinema. Through this breaking of identification, these films hope to engender a critical attitude the way a Brechtian play attempts to encourage critical thinking by distancing the audience. Kuhn hedges her bets by explaining that the final determining force for these films depends on the context of reception; the films need a setup. Instead of a modernist practice, this feminist filmwriting challenges the spectators to change their own conditions of consumption: to talk about these films differently and in different contexts than as entertainment. The crucial element of these discussions was the neo-*auteur*, in this case the woman director, who was an important indicator of new-found social and political power, and, more importantly, the peculiar presentational style of films by, and for, women. Only film scholars will recognize the woman in Figure 2.2 as the director of *Harlan County USA*, a documentary film about a coal-mining strike. In claiming her as an *auteur* we recover a usually marginalized political position, rescue her uniquely female perspective, and still recognize her name, Barbara Kopple, as a marker for other sociopolitical structures rather than her unique inner vision or her soul.

Peter Wollen converted *auteurism* into a structuralist project that explained how a director's name can organize a corpus of films and demonstrate a coherence across a series of films. Picking up from Wollen, Robert Self used Foucault's author-function to argue, for example, that "Robert Altman is a name that represents a certain cinematic heterogeneity and plurality.... Unlike classical narrative, which aims at homogeneity, the signature Robert Altman constantly restates the heterogeneous, the contradictory, the plurality."[11] Tim Corrigan explains that a director's name is "a kind of brand-name vision that precedes and

Figure 2.2. A marker for sociopolitical issues rather than a unique inner vision. Reprinted with permission.

succeeds the film."[12] James Naremore's work, especially his book on Vincente Minnelli, represents a sustained engagement with *auteurism*. He focuses particularly on the way the conjunction of designers, actors, producers, and social situations interacts with Minnelli to produce specific stylistic effects. In doing so, he examines in detail how Minnelli's window-dresser sensibility produces intensely artificial productions. I mention this approach to note that it once again advocates the play and aesthetic beauty of an artificial visual surface as opposed to an approach that searches for any great literary themes about human nature. It would be impossible to connect Minnelli's work in, for example, *Meet Me in Saint Louis*, to surrealism and to American mythologies without referring to a particular visual style and a peculiar flamboyance.[13]

Of course, as I mentioned above, *auteurism* is also now a marketing tool of Hollywood cinema. This marketing strategy usually targets a particularly literary-minded demographic, although the films themselves still use a superficial style of presentation. That is, visual style and poetic constructions are what make these films interesting, not their redeeming social values or thematic content. The Coen brothers (Figure 2.3), Spike Lee, Quentin Tarantino, David Lynch, and others are among these self-conscious film-school *auteurists*. They *began* their careers as *auteurists*. The marketing and controversies about their films circulate around thematic and moral issues, and in spite of the importance of the stylistic play, such style is usually ignored in the popular press. This film-festival and film-school *auteurism* is part of the neo-*auteurist* shift away from the great director toward efforts to make audiences or to use *auteurism* as a way to understand recurring structures in particular groups of films. The director is now a brand name.

And Hollywood is also marketing *stars* as self-made *auteurs* (Figure 2.4), self-invented creative geniuses behind a film's production (and in these scenarios the director is once again invisible). Self-invention of a unique personal style is now generalized throughout contemporary culture—*auteurism* is everywhere. Now someone who sells a tell-all autobiography invents herself as a celebrity.

Figure 2.3. The Coen brothers and Steve Buscemi at Cannes: they began their careers as *auteurists*.

Figure 2.4. Howard Stern, *auteur* of his peculiar lifestyle.

This anthology points to another stage in *auteurism* and in film scholarship in general. It overlaps with the classical moment in film criticism and builds on the neo-*auteurist* works. The anthology appears to present an homage to Allen Smithee, as a kind of hero of the cinema. Although the advance publicity for the conference that preceded this volume implied that the scholars were taking something frivolous seriously, as academics always seem to do, in fact the name Allen Smithee complicates the homage to a director just as the "hommage" of De Gaulle in Figure 2.5 becomes ironic as soon as it appears in quotation marks—especially in this context. Smithee is a citation of the *auteurist* director, and this homage to his accomplishments defamiliarizes all those other celebrations for war heroes, political leaders, and film directors. The Directors Guild of America claims that it provided the name for directors who declined to sign their films as long as these directors show "reasonable grounds" for not including their names. The credit often

Figure 2.5. "Hommage" becomes ironic as soon as it appears in quotation marks.

appears in films directed by more than one person, something that is perhaps the real threat to the Hollywood system. In that sense, this anthology functions much like an outing of a gay movie star. By bringing Smithee's identity into the public view, this book hopes to comment on the Hollywood structure of controlling the popular conception of a director (or a star). Smithee's name brings with it the politics of outing each time it appears and the audience notices the name; it functions like a double entendre, a secret sign, an ornament that has great significance, like an earring, a scarf, a key chain, a gesture, a phrase.

Related to that *politics of outing*, Smithee also suggests the "fronts" used by blacklisted directors during the McCarthy Red Scare (Figure 2.6). Directors at that time chose pseudonyms to enable their work to avoid the censors' prohibitions. The government's fears about communism and, more generally, fear of ambiguous and unsettling messages in films led to blacklisting and graylisting.[14] What fear of the censors does the name Smithee protect against? As soon as we ask the question, Why use the name Allen Smithee?, the connections to the politics of fronts appear. The answer to that question is perhaps not as obvious because we are still so close to the situation. One answer is to compare Allen Smithee to ghostwriters and script doctors, understanding that ghostwriting now functions as a metaphor for a profession that is fading fast: the individual author. Important ghostwriters are now given million-dollar contracts, while many news reports describe how literary publishers are cutting back on the publication of literary novels, how they are unwilling to take a risk on unknown authors and works that might not make a bestseller list. Script doctors assure Hollywood producers that the final product will contain the specific elements needed to market a movie successfully. The products become less differentiated and the risks involved in producing a movie are minimized when all scripts contain the necessary elements—for example, "punched-up jokes." Smithee is a metaphor for taking risks as well as a metaphor for the threat to the profession of *auteurist* directors who do not fit the predefined mold.

If we were to ask what Allen Smithee looks like, the question itself would suggest issues about the need to find an author. A work by the

Figure 2.6. The Hollywood Ten. From left, front: Herbert Biberman, attorney Martin Popper, attorney Robert W. Kenny, Albert Maltz, and Lester Cole. Second row, from left: Dalton Trumbo, John Howard Lawson, Alvah Bessie, and Samuel Ornitz. Top row, from left: Ring Lardner Jr., Edward Dmytryk, and Adrian Scott. Copyright AP/Wide World Photos; reprinted with permission.

photographer Nancy Burson, Figure 2.7, graphically illustrates the challenges in finding one image for a name that represents a compilation of personalities. Burson combined images of many people of different races according to their proportion in the world population. Although she sought to make an aesthetic comment about the look of the "average person," the image can function as a figurative image of Allen Smithee: a figure of sociopolitical situation and struggle.

Artificial *auteurism* allows a scholar to understand these more figurative dimensions of the Smithee name. It allows for the study of the role of the director as a socioeconomic structure, the function of names and naming in Hollywood films. This figurative dimension of *auteurism* allows one to study it as a language system, or what Wittgenstein calls a "language game."[15] How do we speak this language and defamiliarize it enough so that we can see it as a language—to see its figurative potential? How do we invoke its ability to be neither just another myth to demythologize, nor another natural fact to be accepted unproblematically, nor even an alternative to Hollywood, but to function as a way of

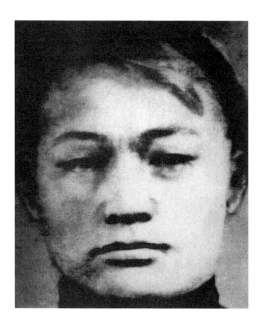

Figure 2.7. Is this the real Allen Smithee? Nancy Burson, *Mankind,* 1983–84. Copyright 1983–85 with Richard Carling and David Kramlich; reprinted with permission.

writing that uses this structure as a generative procedure? Even if we can do these things, the question becomes, What will the name produce?

As soon as we appreciate Smithee figuratively as a way to perform the conflicts and issues surrounding creative control and collective authorship, the signature functions as a performance. Using the Smithee name in a performance, directors create a type of artwork in the titles. This signature as artwork suggests the many conceptual connections already discussed in this essay. Using pseudonyms as a type of experimental art has a tradition that includes works produced under collective names like Fluxus and works produced anonymously by pseudonyms shared by many participants. Artists' networks and publications contain apt examples of how the author's name can function in a sociopolitical artwork. One of these figurative and performative uses of a pseudonym arose out of calls for what participants termed an art strike. Gustav Metzger, who had previously worked with Fluxus, called for an art strike to last from 1977 through 1980. Although this strike had limited impact, it did inspire Stewart Home to make a similar call in 1985; he intended the strike to last from 1990 through 1993. Home's explicit awareness that his hoped-for artists' strike would fail suggests both his effort to caricature the pompous calls for social change through avant-garde artwork as well as "the effect such a strike will have upon my own—and any other's artist's—identity." Home goes on to explain that "such a 'refusal of creativity' ties in with my interest in plagiarism and multiple names, since all three concepts stand in opposition to contemporary Western notions of identity."[16] He wanted to use the strike as "a means of encouraging critical debate around the concept of art."[17] The art strike also helped disseminate Home's Neoism (i.e., the movement set against the individual identity of an artist). This movement depended on the use of an invented name, Monty Cantsin, that any artist could use as a pseudonym. When that name became too closely identified with a few individuals, another name, Karen Eliot, appeared.[18] The Cantsin name served as an "open pop star" to democratize the star system. Not only did Neoists promote these anonymous names, they also insisted that anyone could issue the periodical *SMILE*, initiated by Home in 1984.[19]

That assembling wanted to continue the debate about artistic merit begun in three other periodicals, *FILE*, *VILE*, and *BILE*, to challenge authorship itself; the quality of the issue could no longer depend on an artist's individual skill because the artists and editors involved remained anonymous. No one will ever know how many unidentified editors and contributors were able to participate anonymously. Supposedly over fifty different versions of *SMILE* appeared. Later *Slime* and *Limes* also continued the rhyming and anagrammatic title lineage. Neoism was the largest effort to challenge the framing of artworks with a lineage of authenticity and, therefore, market value. Everything produced was inherently a fake.

In a similar move, Malcolm McLaren produced ideas, not products, and in doing so he helped invent punk fashion and the Sex Pistols as purposefully failed products: failed products but provocative ideas. This was his intended challenge to the mercantile system that packaged music and fashion as commodities. His project was a "great rock-n-roll swindle," a trick on the market. His fashion designs were purposefully failures, the music he produced was bad (at least in terms of the contemporary norms of rock), the band he managed produced only one album and had a disastrous tour in America. Yet it was clear to everyone that this was precisely the point of these works: ideas not products. So it is with Allen Smithee, famous for producing bad movies, or movies too controversial for the market; his very name loosens the marketing machine a bit and inserts an idea in the space where fans usually find a product. Now the director is an idea, an art strike, a Karen Eliot attack, and a McLaren-esque fashion-statement, not a product.

Allen Smithee, not just a pseudonym, but a kind of conceptual art project, uses the Hollywood marketing and spin machine as part of its canvas. It has more recently spread into the legal system and into academia. In fact, the case filed against the Directors Guild of America by the director Tony Kaye on 23 November 1998 not only highlighted some of the central issues of the Allen Smithee phenomenon but also directly involved the author of this essay in the Smithee celebrity machine. The lead lawyer on the case, Mark Lane, who is most famous for representing Lee

Harvey Oswald, filed suit against the Guild in what looked like a publicity stunt or, more accurately, the blurring of Hollywood spin and legal truth. The well-known case is worth relating here to tease out the nuances relevant to understanding artificial *auteurism* more completely.

Tony Kaye had been hired by New Line Cinema to direct *American History X*. Although Kaye had never directed a full-length motion picture, he had garnered enormous praise for his commercials, which usually featured young children and cinematic effects. In the advertising world, his prima donna arrogance became part of his reputation as an *auteurist* of the short commercial form. So, in hindsight, it seems unsurprising that a dispute arose between Kaye and the film's lead, Edward Norton. Norton wanted to cut a number of scenes and reinsert some scenes that Kaye had cut. The producers sided with Norton, allowing him to change the final quarter of the film. After complaining publicly about how Norton and the producers compromised and ruined the film, Kaye filed a "grievance" with the Directors Guild of America. He requested permission to use the name Allen Smithee, but because the Guild reserved that name for directors who agreed not to publicize their differences with a producer, and because Kaye had already spoken publicly about the problems with the film, the Guild rejected his request. Kaye then asked to use the name Humpty Dumpty. This name was to comment on how the producers and Norton had ruined the film in the editing room, on Kaye's ruined kingly reputation, and, most importantly, it suggested that the use of these types of pseudonyms is not about anonymity. The name Humpty Dumpty was not a challenge to the fetish of the author's name; it challenged the system of using names as merely literal monikers for individuals rather than markers of, or commentary on, disputes, collaborations, and experimentation. The name Allen Smithee often allowed directors to work outside their own reputations: to experiment, to take a risk, to challenge the "tradition of quality." It was not about working anonymously, it was about using the name as a commentary on an often contentious social situation or dispute.

As a consolation, the Directors Guild gave Kaye a choice of six *other* names from which he could choose the one pseudonymous name that would appear in the publicity for the film. But because the dispute was not about the anonymity of the director, but about the importance of the name as a figure for a reputation (*auteurism*), a peculiar style (neo-*auteurism*), and a commentary on a social situation (artificial *auteurism*), these alternative names were not adequate. Kaye rejected these choices. If the Allen Smithee phenomenon were simply about a challenge to critics' and marketers' almost fetishistic need for a director's name, then Kaye would have accepted any one of the six alternative names.

At this point in the dispute, Kaye was now claiming that New Line Cinema had "raped" the film and his reputation, that Edward Norton was "a narcissistic dilettante," and that producer John Morrissey was "Pompous Pilot." In light of this continuing bad press, the producers offered to allow Kaye to use the name Allen Smithee after all. When the DGA again rejected the request, Kaye filed suit. He thought of the DGA as the "Dinosaur Guild of America" precisely because they sided with the efforts to secure a market for even the worst Hollywood films (the Allen Smithee name is available only if the director does not interfere with the marketing of the film) rather than the defense of an *auteurist*'s vision. Significantly, Kaye thought of himself as "the greatest English filmmaker since Alfred Hitchcock," connecting his work not just to a pantheon of great directors, but to the epitome of *auteurism*. John Morrissey explained that the name Allen Smithee was not merely a pseudonym, but allowed Kaye "to treat the movie like Hype Art.... And like all of Tony's work, he was its subject. The ads in the trades and all the controversy he created—it was all a giant conceptual art piece about him."[20] This sounds like a description of the Sex Pistols' Situationist-inspired strategies or the work of the Neoists described above. Artificial *auteurism* initiates a field of study that allows for all of these works to be understood not as opposites (mass culture versus avant-garde or film versus music), but as related by the use of the name as a figure or as something resembling a conceptual artwork.

Soon after Kaye filed suit against the DGA, one of his lawyers contacted me, described the case in detail, and hired me as an expert witness. To refer to James English's afterword to this volume about the compensation and fame of academic "stars": as an expert witness I participated in an alternative "star" system and (judging by the fees I was initially offered for my potential testimony on the use of the Smithee name) one which offers a more lucrative compensation than academia. The Allen Smithee name circulates in a market system so large that it might in some future histories engulf much of the humanities as a footnote. English's essay suggests that an academic market based on use and citation does not need a corrective challenge with something like the use of the Allen Smithee name. He notes that much of the resistance to theory and cultural studies from within academia arises from an almost puritanical resentment of the relatively small salaries of academic "stars," including cultural theorists. He argues persuasively that academia might actually benefit from more recognition of the big names. From that conclusion, he insinuates that the problem might be the widespread local power of professors in less interdisciplinary, less theoretical, and less experimental areas. These professors use their status as defenders of the "tradition of quality" (that is, the traditional approaches, medium-specific disciplines, and historical periods) to castigate the influential academic stars as trendy, too creative, and undeserving.

English interprets the use of the Smithee name as a challenge to directors as stars; in academia this attack on a fledgling star system would stifle creativity. But if Smithee were merely a challenge to the fetishistic need for academics' names, then there would be little need for it in Hollywood, either. In Hollywood, Smithee offers protection. The name always functions as a figure rather than as a literal origin, and artificial *auteurism* might help to highlight how stages of *auteurism* have functioned, or might potentially function, in a wider sphere of intellectual production. Academics have already used the school name, like the Yale School, to allow for protection against the ever-vigilant attacks from those powerful defenders of the "tradition of quality." One such collective name might be the Allen Smithee Group. In Robert Ray's chapter in this volume, the names Allen Smithee and the Allen Smithee Group mark precisely the type of experimentation in film studies that will both defend itself against the inertia of academic traditions and suggest models of working that depend on shared strategies of construction and openness to the play of contingencies.

Both those film directors who take the name of Allen Smithee and those outside the film industry who choose to use the Allen Smithee dynamic in their own work and publicity comment on systems in which the names of directors, authors, or scholars circulate as legitimation. The performance of the Allen Smithee name (or other similar strategies) allows one to understand the political economy of this circulation. It plays with this artificial *auteurism*: an art that works on the level of infrastructure, an art that means little to those not prepared to think beyond the literal naturalized level of a director's name.

Film and cultural scholarship faces a crisis; it is the crisis that we may be losing the ability to think about our culture with a metaphoric or figurative approach to these well-known natural facts. The social-scientific analyses, economic explanations, cognitive studies, legal approaches, and histories of directors may yet all play important roles in this version of film and cultural studies. The key factor that Allen Smithee and this anthology highlight is the possibility that surface structures may hold a usually overlooked figurative and even allegorical dimension that will speak volumes about a culture's past, present, and future, and about the cinema's possibilities beyond the simple framing of a worldview. Some will see Allen Smithee as only a façade, an artificial construction. And, although the term "celluloid" has had since its invention in the late nineteenth century a connotation of "cheap imitation," some will not see the figurative potential and sociopolitical importance of stand-ins, doubles, camoufleurs, fronts, stunt-doubles, body doubles, and *auteurist* doubles. Is Smithee a Jacob or an Esau, or is that the wrong question, a moot point? Perhaps one should rather wonder about Smithee's allegorical story?

To use this anthology as a blueprint, take special note as the essays here do not unmask, demythologize, or simply gawk, tabloid-style, at a scandal, but rather use Smithee as a marker for a new approach to film studies: artificial *auteurism*. The artificial *auteur* is not a product but an idea. In the form of Allen Smithee, the director is no longer a product for

Hollywood to market, it is now an idea, a provocation, a fashion statement waiting for someone to project. To those interested in becoming Smithee, to performing artificial *auteurism*, and to intervening in a political economy of the *auteurist's* name, good luck.

Notes

1. Jaime Wolf, "The Blockbuster Script Factory," *New York Times Magazine* 23 Aug. 1998: 32–35. The poster accompanying the article is by Roberto Parada.

2. As explained in the introduction to this volume, Smithee's first name was originally spelled Allen.

3. See the website created to publicize the Smithee conference, Specters of Legitimacy, 27 Sept. 1997, http://www.english.upenn.edu/Smithee97.

4. Bosley Crowther, review of *Rear Window*, *New York Times* 5 Aug. 1954: 18.

5. François Truffaut, "A Certain Tendency of the French Cinema," *Movies and Methods: An Anthology*, ed. Bill Nichols, vol. 1 (Berkeley: University of California Press, 1985) 232.

6. Christian Keathley's chapter in the present volume provides an explication of Sarris's three criteria in light of Jacques Derrida's theory of the signature.

7. Andrew Sarris, "Notes on the *Auteur* Theory in 1962," *Film Theory and Criticism*, ed. Gerald Mast and Marshall Cohen, 2d ed. (New York: Oxford University Press, 1979) 663.

8. Andrew Sarris, "Auteurism is Alive and Well and Living in Argentina," *Film Comment* 26 (July/Aug. 1990): 21.

9. Donald Spoto, *The Dark Side of Genius: The Life of Alfred Hitchcock* (Boston: Little, Brown, 1983). Stephen Hock's chapter in this volume examines in detail the construction of the Hitchcock "brand name," and how the early critical reviews of Hitchcock's *The Birds* closely resemble the negative reviews of a film by Allen Smithee, *The Birds II*.

10. Annette Kuhn, *Women's Pictures: Feminism and Cinema* (New York: Routledge, 1986) 160–67.

11. Robert Self, "Robert Altman and the Theory of Authorship," *Cinema Journal* 25.1 (fall 1985): 4.

12. Timothy Corrigan, *A Cinema without Walls: Movies and Culture after Vietnam* (New Brunswick, NJ: Rutgers University Press, 1991) 128.

13. James Naremore, *The Films of Vincente Minnelli* (Cambridge: Cambridge University Press, 1993) 10. Jeremy Braddock provides a longer discussion of Minnelli in chapter 7 of the present volume.

14. For a more thorough consideration of Smithee in the context of blacklisting, see Jessie Labov's chapter in the present volume.

15. See Ludwig Wittgenstein, *Philosophical Investigations*, trans. G. E. M. Anscombe, 3rd ed. (Oxford: Blackwell, 1967).

16. Stewart Home, *Neoist Manifestos* (Stirling: A. K. Press, 1991) 4. See Clive Phillpot, "Artists' Magazines: News of the Art Strike, Monty Cantsin, and Karen Eliot," *Art Documentation* (fall 1992): 137–38.

17. Home 137.

18. Because many people used the name, the name sometimes appears as Karen Elliot, and like the Allen Smithee name, it eventually had multiple spellings.

19. *SMILE* is available online. *SMILE: A Magazine of Multiple Origins*, http://www.thing.de/projekte/7:9%23/smile_index.html.

20. John Morrissey as quoted in Benjamin Svetkey, "X Marks the Spat," *Entertainment Weekly* 455 (23 Oct. 1998): 28–36.

CHAPTER 3

The Automatic *Auteur*; or,
A Certain Tendency in Film Criticism

Robert B. Ray

This essay appears in fifteen sections. Since it concerns a theoretical *tendency* involving photographic automatism, I decided, in the spirit of the surrealists' games, to use François Truffaut's famous essay "A Certain Tendency of the French Cinema" as the source for the sections' titles, which generated what follows: a critical game about *Allen Smithee*.

1. Ten or Fifteen Minutes.

The name "Allen Smithee" is a mark of failure resulting from discord. It is shorthand for "a bad movie." Except for daily reviewing, however, we have little serious writing about "bad cinema." Nevertheless, we do have one provocative remark. During his ten-year stay in Hollywood, Man Ray was often given to a particular observation:

> The worst films I've ever seen, the ones that send me to sleep, contain ten or fifteen marvelous minutes. The best films I've ever seen only contain ten or fifteen valid minutes.[1]

Figures 3.1 through 3.6 show stills from some of those minutes.

If we want to use the Allen Smithee phenomenon to think about film and about film criticism, this remark provides us with our first clue. Where do these ten or fifteen marvelous minutes come from? Why can they appear in both good and bad films?

Figure 3.1. *Grand Hotel.*

Figure 3.2. *Red Barry.*

Figure 3.3. *Murder in a Private Car.*

Figure 3.4. *Fly Away, Baby.*

Figure 3.5. *Sunrise.*

Figure 3.6. *Eureka.*

Man Ray, of course, was an official adherent of surrealism, the movement defined by its founder, André Breton, as

> Psychic *automatism* in its pure state.... Dictated by thought, *in the absence of any control exercised by reason*, exempt from any aesthetic or moral concern.[2]

As a name, "Allen Smithee" indicates certain problems with control. Does it therefore also suggest something to do with *automatism*?

2. Directors' Films.

The theory, history, and practice of Hollywood cinema have turned on a single issue: control. The studio heads modeled their operations on Henry Ford's factory, with its geographical concentration, division of labor, standardized parts, and hierarchical management. For Marcus Lowe, Nicholas Schenck, L. B. Mayer, and Irving Thalberg at MGM, this arrangement had the advantage of reining in, or eliminating, film-making's unpredictable elements (an extravagant director like von Stroheim, a capricious environment like the Italian location for *Ben Hur*). With production largely confined to MGM's own sets, with scriptwriters and directors reporting to line producers, and with Thalberg overseeing the entire operation, making movies would become, or so it appeared, *rationalized*. At MGM, even Allen Smithee, or especially Allen Smithee, would have been welcome. In some ways, in fact, the MGM system converted all of its directors into Allen Smithee.

In the 1950s and 1960s, launched in 1954 by Truffaut's manifesto, the *auteur* theory would offer an alternative view of this situation, suggesting that the greatest directors had managed to slip those restraints in order to impose their own recognizable signatures on the films they made. In fact, of course, *auteurism* merely relocated the site of control from producer to director: the theory still presumed a predictable, rationalized process.

But just how rationalized was the process of filmmaking, even in a Hollywood studio like MGM? In *The Avant-Garde Finds Andy Hardy*,[3]

I argued that under Thalberg, MGM's filmmaking (and by implication, that of the other studios) had less in common with Ford's assembly lines than with surrealism's Exquisite Corpse, a game, now known as MadLibs, that asks four players, working independently of each other, to fill in the slots of a paradigm:

> What is a [noun]?
> A [noun], [adjective] and [adjective].

With its reliance on fragmentation (the isolated detail), automatism (players producing elements only on the basis of their grammatical value), and recombination (the unexpected juxtapositions), the Exquisite Corpse mimics photography. Significantly, Breton once described automatic writing, a similar game, as "a true photography of thought,"[4] and we should note this linking of automatism to photography as our second clue.

And studio filmmaking? With its system organized around stars and genres, with its commitment to hire and retain the best technicians (cameramen, set designers, light and sound experts), MGM could define its production process as a syntax, like the Exquisite Corpse's question-and-answer, in which could occur an infinite number of variables. In fact, Breton's game amounts to a diagram of MGM's procedure:

> What is [name of a star]?
> A [character], [adjective] and [adjective].
> > Hence, *Grand Hotel*:
> What is Garbo?
> A ballerina, fading and desperate.
> > Or *Flesh and the Devil?*
> What is Garbo?
> A temptress, faithless and destructive.

The process is even more subtle. Who, for example, is in control of the shot from *Grand Hotel* shown in Figure 3.7? Edmund Goulding, the movie's director, never a candidate for *auteurist* canonization? Garbo? Barrymore? William Daniels, the cameraman? Cedric Gibbons, the art director? Adrian, the costumer? As Thalberg knew, changing any one of these elements would result in a dramatically different shot. A *Grand Hotel* with Warner's Joan Blondell or Dick Powell? Garbo directed by Howard Hawks?

As a game, the Exquisite Corpse rewards players with rich vocabularies: "interesting" nouns and adjectives produce the most appealing metaphors, even if they seem accomplished by utter accident. Compiling a literate team stacks the deck, increasing the chances of turning out striking phrases. In Hollywood, Mayer and Thalberg quickly intuited something similar: having Garbo, Barrymore, Gable, and Harlow amounted to having the best "nouns," the ones capable of entering into the most lively combinations when inflected by the studio's "adjectives," the most reliable directors and scriptwriters, the most innovative

Figure 3.7. Greta Garbo in *Grand Hotel*.

cameramen, set designers, and costumers. Thus, the shot from *Grand Hotel* amounts, at the least, to this Exquisite Corpse:

> What is Garbo?
> A *ballerina* (the role created by the writers), *photographed*
> by William Daniels, and *paired* with John Barrymore,
> *dressed* by Adrian, on a *set designed* by Cedric Gibbons.

Having established this syntax, and collected MGM's stars and technicians, Thalberg could relinquish control of the movies' details, certain that the results would fall within a range of acceptable possibilities. Studio filmmaking, therefore, resulted from a delicate balance of accident and design, of automatism and control.

3. Today No One Is Ignorant Any Longer.

Since its first appearance in English in 1970, Walter Benjamin's essay "The Work of Art in the Age of Mechanical Reproduction" has become one of film studies' most often-cited pieces. Today no one is ignorant any longer of Benjamin's association of fascism with the nostalgia for the "aura" of unique objects. But how many people know that in its first draft, Benjamin's essay began with this sentence: "The most important social function of films is to create a balance between the human being and technology." And how many people remember that the published essay contains this warning: in the age of mechanical reproduction, art acquires "entirely new functions, among which the one we are conscious of, the artistic function, later may be recognized as incidental."[5]

4. That Famous Mechanical Reproduction.

The most interesting thing that I have read about Benjamin's "Work of Art" essay is Lindsay Waters's forthcoming article, "Walter Benjamin's Dangerous Idea." Drawing his inspiration, and indeed his title, from Daniel Dennett's *Darwin's Dangerous Idea: Evolution and the Meanings of Life,*[6] Waters suggests that both Darwin and Benjamin "put forward a powerful mechanistic explanation of a process that seemed before to work only because of divine intervention." What is frightening about

Darwin's idea "is that it explains how evolution takes place in an orderly way without God: there is design to the process, but it operates without the intervention of mind." So, too with Benjamin, whose dangerous idea is that the mechanical aspect, not authors, best accounts for the work of art. In Waters's words, "Those people who seek some divine source for art are the equivalent of creationists."[7] Film criticism brought the divine source back, and labeled it the *auteur*, but that move is regressive, resisting Benjamin's observation that the machines have taken over, and we are merging with them. Let us think about retitling Benjamin's essay. One possibility: "The Work of Art in the Age of Allen Smithee"?

5. What Annoys Me.

Méliès.
The Cabinet of Doctor Caligari.
Ivan the Terrible.
2001: A Space Odyssey.
Tim Burton.
Tom Petty's videos.
Oliver Stone.

What do these names signify? A suppression of accident, regarded less as opportunity than as noise. An allegorical propensity, in which the idea dominates the image. A refusal of automatism's possibilities. The elimination of life crowding in at the edges of the frame. In Truffaut's terms, a disguised return of the scriptwriter-dominated film, with directors conceiving of images as syntactical blocks, capable of communicating relatively unambiguous meaning.

6. Unmask.

The surrealists used games to simulate the automatism intrinsic to photography and required by psychoanalysis. Indeed, the psychoanalytic session, utterly dependent on the strange but strict rules proposed by its inventor, has all the earmarks of a game designed to encourage automatism. Here are Freud's instructions to a patient "beginning the treatment":

What you tell me must differ in one respect from an ordinary conversation. Ordinarily you rightly try to keep a connecting thread running through your remarks and you exclude any intrusive ideas that may occur to you and any side-issues, so as not to wander too far from the point. But in this case you must proceed differently. You will notice that as you relate things, various thoughts will occur to you which you would like to put aside on the ground of certain criticisms and objections. You will be tempted to say to yourself that this or that is irrelevant here, or is quite unimportant, or nonsensical, so that there is no need to say it. You must never give in to these criticisms, but must say it in spite of them—indeed you must say it precisely because you feel an aversion to doing so. Later on you will find out and learn to understand the reason for this injunction, which is really the only one you have to follow. So say whatever goes through your mind. Act as though, for instance, you were a traveler sitting next to the window of a railway carriage and describing to someone inside the carriage the changing views which you see outside. Finally, never forget that you have promised to be absolutely honest, and never leave anything out because, for some reason or other, it is unpleasant to tell it.[8]

Although these instructions seem simple enough, Freud soon discovered that they were extraordinarily difficult to follow. In fact, Freud invented a term to describe this difficulty, one that threatened the whole psychoanalytic project. That term was *resistance*.

Having intuited this problem, the surrealists invented games that would encourage the freedom of response necessary to psychoanalysis, the automatism that Breton saw so closely resembling photography. The games were practice sessions in automatism. I am playing one now, a modified version of "Directions for Use" whose instructions go like this:

Using the style and format of the *Directions* to be found on the labels of household products, D.I.Y. kits and other ordinary items, apply them to items that do not require such instructions.

An example:

> THE HEART
>
> To retain its perfect freshness, keep THE HEART dry. UNLIKE similar products, THE HEART WILL EXPAND WHILE DRYING OUT. All actions performed with THE HEART are therefore derivative.
>
> . . . .
>
> IMPORTANT: THE HEART acts like a cement, so delirium must never be added to previously prepared sentiment, nor should it be "dwelt on" too long. THE HEART hardens in two hours. Increase the dosage of HEART in the first few seconds if you desire a sentiment with firmer consistency.[9]

For my "Directions for Use," I have chosen the fifteen section titles from Truffaut's "A Certain Tendency of the French Cinema." Can the manifesto of *la politique des auteurs* become the manifesto for Allen Smithee, the automatic *auteur*?

7. So Be It, They Will Tell Me.

The oldest trick used to refute any interest in or use of the avant-garde is to say that "the avant-garde" is itself old-hat. A recent reviewer plays this well-worn card:

> Perhaps any professedly avant-garde criticism ought to consider the possibility that "progressive" art and its associated commentary have, over a century, built up their own clichés. Anybody trying to make the academy more avant-garde might reflect upon the academicism of the avant-garde itself.[10]

These two sentences, ironically themselves clichés, amount to the equivalent of the very young child's discovery that the statement "Everything is a lie" is itself a lie. If the Allen Smithee Group is condemned for trafficking in The Avant-Garde, we will refer our critics to Brecht's *Messingkauf*, the buyer-of-brass:

> I can only compare myself [Brecht wrote] with a man, say, who deals in scrap metal; and goes up to a brass band to buy, not a trumpet, let's say, but simply brass. The trumpeter's trumpet is made of brass, but he'll hardly want to sell it as such, by its value as brass, as so many ounces of brass. All the same, that's how I ransack your theater for events between people, such as you do more or less imitate even if your imitations are for a very different purpose than my satisfaction. To put it in a nutshell: I'm looking for a way of getting incidents between people imitated for certain purposes; I've heard that you supply such imitations; and now I hope to find out if they are actually the kind of imitations I can use.[11]

The *Messingkauf*'s unembarrassed invention-by-appropriation thrives on infidelity to the theoretical source, and it encourages experimentation. It frees a film scholar, for example, to use surrealism without having to become a surrealist. The Hollywood studios, after all, modeled *their* system on Henry Ford's, but they didn't make cars.

And if they tell us that this, too, is only another construction, let's remind them that after having demonstrated the utterly social basis of morality, Nietzsche paused to advise: "Supposing that this also is only interpretation—and you will be eager to make this objection?—well, so much the better."[12]

8. One of These Days,

we will begin to realize how radical André Bazin's ideas were. He was among the first to notice that with photography, for the first time in human history, an exact representation of reality *could be made by accident.*

9. The Influence of Impressionism and Existentialism Is Immense.

At the origins of the French New Wave lies a previously undetected contradiction: a celebration of the image combined with an insistence on authorship. If Barthes's "Third Meaning" correctly locates the filmic's definition in precisely those details that *escape* authorial control,[13] then why would an avant-garde filmmaking group, avowedly on the side of the autonomous image ("the *mise-en-scène*," in *Cahiers*-speak), resort to *la politique des auteurs*? The answer lies in the process of invention: the French New Wave, like every avant-garde, worked by extrapolation. Its sources' contradictory elements survived in their new combination.

In his book *Heuretics: The Logic of Invention*, Gregory Ulmer demonstrates that creativity works more systematically than popular mythology assumes, proceeding as much by emulation as inspiration. In fact, Ulmer argues, avant-garde manifestoes "belong to the tradition of the discourse on method" and "tend to include a common set of elements." Those elements, he suggests, can be mnemonically summarized by the acronym CATTt, representing the following operations:

C = Contrast

A = Analogy

T = Theory

T = Target

t = tale (or form in which the avant-garde will work)[14]

If we take as the New Wave's manifesto three essays, Alexandre Astruc's "*La Caméra Stylo*,"[15] Truffaut's "A Certain Tendency of the French Cinema," and Godard's 1962 interview with the *Cahiers du cinéma*, we can observe the same pattern of invention. Contrast?—"the tradition of quality," those formally conservative, big-budget French films controlled by scriptwriters rather than directors, movies explicitly compared to the academic *grands machines* of Salon painting against which the impressionists had rebelled. Analogy?—Astruc, Truffaut, and Godard all rely on the literary notion of authorship and writing: the camera will become a *stylo* when filmmakers become like writers. Theory?—the traditionally Romantic notions of heroic, self-expressive (and proprietary) authorship, descended from the French impressionist painters, but even more immediately, from Sartre's existentialist insistence on individual responsibility. After all, the issue of who was to be responsible for what appeared on the screen remained the question that defined New Wave practice. The Target, of course, was the French film industry, and the tale or form was that hybrid of documentary and fiction that Godard labeled "research in the form of a spectacle."[16]

Just as this method of invention-by-appropriation thrives on infidelity to the theoretical source (Breton did not want to be a doctor), it can also work with something less than a profound knowledge of it (Breton had not read all of Freud). The avant-gardist is always in the position of the photographer who can extract a beautiful image from something he knows little about. We will probably never learn exactly how much of Sartre Astruc, Truffaut, and Godard had read. We do know that by the time the *Cahiers* proclaimed *la politique des auteurs*, Sartre and his vocabulary had entered what Sherry Turkle calls "a sociology of superficial knowledge."[17] His 1945 lecture "Existentialism Is a Humanism," printed in a cheap, paperback version in 1946, had become the breviary of that movement, and the echoes of his phrasing are unmistakable in Godard:

> Man is nothing else but that which he makes of himself.... man is responsible for what he is. Thus, the first effect of existentialism is that it puts every man in possession of himself as he is, and places the entire responsibility for his existence squarely upon his own shoulders.[18]

> The cinema is not a craft. It is an art. It does not mean teamwork. One is always alone; on the set as before the blank page.[19]

> the moral choice is comparable to the construction of a work of art.[20]

> A dolly shot is a moral statement.[21]

> Who can give an answer to that [a moral dilemma] *à priori*? No one.... You are free, therefore choose—that is to say, invent. No rule of general morality can show you what you ought to do: no signs are vouchsafed in this world.[22]

> The problem which has long preoccupied me ... is: why do one shot rather than another?...

What is it ultimately that makes one run a shot on or change to another? A director like Delbert Mann probably doesn't think this way. He follows a pattern. Shot—the character speaks; reverse angle, someone answers.[23]

This is what I thought: for the most banal event to become an adventure, you must (and this is enough) begin to recount it.[24]

People pigeon-hole adventure. "We're off on holiday," they say, "the adventure will begin as soon as we are at the seaside." They don't think of themselves as living the adventure when they buy their train tickets, whereas in the film everything is on the same level: buying train tickets is as exciting as swimming in the sea.[25]

While these parallels suggest why the French New Wave directors insisted on the notion of authorship (in fact a code term for the more metaphysical, and *au courant*, idea of *responsibility*), they do not tell us why these men also championed the image. That secret lies in the movement's buried connections to another theory, surrealism. Almost certainly, the *Cahiers* critics knew that earlier avant-garde less from its works than from the extraordinary, surrealist-inspired screening practices of Henri Langlois's *Cinémathèque Française*. In a theater where foreign-language films ran without subtitles, where programs changed without notice, where movies collided unpredictably, without regard for genre, period, or assumed value, the New Wave directors, "the children of the Cinémathèque," experienced "the heightened, autonomous image" that Breton and his colleagues had sought through their own eccentric moviegoing:

When I was "at the cinema age" ... I never began by consulting the amusement pages to find out what film might chance to be the best, nor did I find out what time the film was to begin. I agreed wholeheartedly with Jacques Vaché in appreciating nothing so much as dropping into a cinema when whatever was playing was playing, at any point in the show, and leaving at the first hint of boredom—of surfeit—to rush off to another cinema where we behaved in the same way, and so on.... I have never known anything more *magnetising*: it goes without saying that more often than not we left our seats without even knowing the title of the film which was of no importance to us anyway. On a Sunday several hours sufficed to exhaust all that Nantes could offer us: the important thing is that one came out "charged" for a few days.[26]

The New Wave, in other words, invented itself by combining impressionism, existentialism, and surrealism, movements whose lessons and strategies it translated into another domain—filmmaking. There, "responsibility" reappeared as "authorship," and the decontextualized image as "*mise-en-scène*," forced to live side-by-side as incompatible intellectual heirs. When we remember that another figure who acknowledged similar intellectual debts, Roland Barthes, listed "fidelity" as one of his "Dislikes,"[27] and when we consider that Truffaut, who had sympathized with translation, ended up, in Godard's eyes, making the kind of films he had earlier denounced, we might consider this maxim: the more unfaithful the translator, the more original the work of art.

10. Eisenstein Is To Be Regretted.

Film history's conceptual neatness depends on its dual provenance in those great opposites, Lumière and Méliès, documentary and fiction. Inevitably, film theory took longer to appear, but after World War I, it quickly developed into two analogous positions, only one of which was attached so neatly to a single name.

That name, of course, was Eisenstein. With his insistence that Filmmaking-as-an-Art depended on repudiating the camera's automatic recording capacity, Eisenstein aligned himself not only with Méliès, but also with pictorialism, the movement that sought to legitimate photography by disguising its images as paintings. Eisenstein avoided that retrograde move while nevertheless sharing its fundamental premise: that a medium's aesthetic value is a direct function of its ability to *transform* the reality serving as its raw material. For Eisenstein, the means of such transformation was montage, the ideal tool for deriving significance (chiefly political) from the real details swarming in the footage.

As his theoretical essays appeared in the 1920s, Eisenstein assumed the role simultaneously perfected by T. S. Eliot—the artist-critic whose writings create the taste by which his own aesthetic practice is judged. Eisenstein's sensational films enhanced the prestige of his theoretical positions, which quickly triumphed over the alternative proposed by the French impressionists and surrealists. If Eisenstein saw the cinema as a means of argument, the French regarded it as the vehicle of revelation, and the knowledge revealed was not always expressible in words. "Explanations here are out of place," Louis Delluc wrote about the "phenomenon" of Sessue Hayakawa's screen presence, an example of what the impressionists called *photogénie*. "I wish there to be no words," Jean Epstein declared, refusing to translate the concept that he posited as "the purest expression of cinema."[28]

The concept of *photogénie*, especially in the surrealists' hands, emphasized precisely what Eisenstein wished to escape: the cinema's automatism. "For the first time," André Bazin would later elaborate, "an image of the world is formed automatically, without the creative invention of man."[29] Moreover, for reasons that the French could not define, the camera rendered some otherwise ordinary objects, landscapes, and even people luminous and spellbinding. Lumière's simple, mesmerizing films had proved that fact. And just turning on the camera would do the trick: in René Clair's words, "There is no detail of reality which is not immediately extended here [in cinema] into the domain of the wondrous."[30]

In his first published essay, Louis Aragon suggested that this effect did not result from "art" films alone:

All our emotion exists for those dear old American adventure films that speak of daily life and manage to raise to a dramatic level a banknote on which our attention is riveted, a table with a revolver on it, a bottle that on occasion becomes a weapon, a handkerchief that reveals a crime, a typewriter that's the horizon of a desk, the terrible unfolding telegraphic tape with magic ciphers that enrich or ruin bankers.[31]

This response seems, in retrospect, an acute description of the way movies are often experienced—as intermittent intensities (a face, a landscape, the fall of light across a room) that break free from the sometimes indifferent narratives that contain them. Why, then, was the impressionist/ surrealist approach so rapidly eclipsed by Eisenstein's?

First, its emphasis on fragmentation poorly suited the rapidly consolidating commercial cinema whose hard-earned basis lay precisely in its continuity system. Both the impressionists and the surrealists, in fact, often regarded narrative as an obstacle to be overcome. "The telephone rings," Epstein complained, pointing to the event that so often initiates a plot. "All is lost."[32]

Second, by insisting that film's essence lay beyond words, the *photogénie* movement left even its would-be followers with nowhere to go. By contrast, Eisenstein had a thoroughly linguistic view of filmmaking, with shots amounting to ideograms, which, when artfully combined, could communicate the equivalent of sentences. As the hedonistic twenties yielded to the intensely politicized thirties, Eisenstein's propositions seemed a far more useful way of thinking about the cinema.

11. Bazin's Realism, Both Real and Psychological.

One of the most decisive moments in the history of film theory occurred during a span of twelve months from late 1952 to early 1953. During that period, Bazin published essays in which, for the first time, someone suggested that the two most prestigious schools of filmmaking (Soviet montage and German expressionism) were wrong. The movies' possibilities, Bazin insisted, were more radical than those ways of working had indicated. The Soviets and Germans, according to Bazin, had betrayed cinema's sacred purpose (a recreation of the world in its own image) by "putting their faith in the image" instead of in reality, convulsing the camera's objectivity with abstracting montages and grotesque *mise-en-scènes*.

Since about 1970, this position has been represented as fantastically naive, another version of Western culture's longing for what Derrida calls "presence." In a passage often singled out for critique,

Bazin had even praised *The Bicycle Thief* as "one of the first examples of pure cinema": "No more actors, no more story, no more sets, which is to say that in the perfect aesthetic illusion of reality, there is no more cinema."[33]

In fact, however, behind Bazin's realist aesthetic lay an intuition about the cinema's most profoundly radical aspect: its automatism. If an absolutely accurate representation of the world could be made by accident, this miraculous revelatory power made the Soviet or expressionist imposition of subjective meanings seem a kind of misguided vanity.

This argument amounted to a revival of the impressionists' *photogénie* and the surrealists' automatism. For the impressionists, *photogénie* was untranslatable but intentional. For the surrealists, on the other hand, it was often accidental, and thus capable of appearing anywhere—even in a film by Allen Smithee.

12. Mise-En-Scène, Metteur-En-Scène, Texts.

Like the surrealists, Bazin could occasionally find what he valued in forgettable movies. He devoted, for example, a page-long footnote in one essay to what he called "an otherwise mediocre English film," *Where No Vultures Fly*, praising a single moment that abandoned "trickery" and "banal montage" to show parents, child, and a stalking lioness "all in the same full shot."[34] In general, however, Bazin preferred to associate his cinematic ideal with a particular set of strategies deliberately employed by an elect group of filmmakers. Renoir, De Sica, Murnau, Flaherty, Wyler, and Welles were great because in relying on long takes and deep focus, they had modestly permitted reality to speak for itself.

With this argument, Bazin was retreating from his thought's most radical implication, his sense of the fundamental difference between previous representational technologies and the new "random generators" like the camera. In the hands of his followers, the *Cahiers* critics, Bazin's attitude toward intentionality became even more ambivalent. *La politique des auteurs* seemed to renounce altogether the surrealist faith in chance, celebrating even Bazin's beloved "reality" less than the filmmaking geniuses who could consciously summon its charms. But at the heart of the *Cahiers* position lay a privileged term that evoked both *photogénie*'s ineffability and the surrealist's automatism.

That term was *mise-en-scène*. As the *Cahiers* critics used it, *mise-en-scène* quickly left behind its conventional meaning ("setting") to become a sacred word, shared by friends who could invoke it knowing the others would understand. At first, it appeared to be simply another version of *photogénie*, a way of talking again about the untranslatable "essence of the cinema." Hence, Jacques Rivette on Preminger's *Angel Face*:

> What tempts Preminger if not the rendering audible of particular chords unheard and rare, in which the inexplicable beauty of the modulation suddenly justifies the ensemble of the phrase? This is probably the definition of something precious, its enigma—the door to something beyond intellect, opening out onto the unknown.
>
> Such are the contingencies of *mise en scène*.[35]

Auteurism's basic problem, however, involved just this kind of attribution. More than even most theoretical groups, the *Cahiers* critics had a sense of themselves as a visionary, well-educated, sensitive elect. As long as they were associating the delights of *mise-en-scène* with filmmakers like Jean Renoir, they could continue to insist on the conscious aspect of a director's decisions. Renoir, after all, was aesthetically well-bred, politically liberal, and personally sympathetic. But the *auteurist* position increasingly prompted them to celebrate directors who had often made bad films, and who sometimes seemed neither particularly smart nor especially nice. Directors, for example, like Otto Preminger. Faced with this situation, the *Cahiers* writers revised their praise, directing it less at individual filmmakers than at the medium itself. Thus, the *Cahiers*'s American operative, Andrew Sarris, could explicitly modulate *la politique des auteurs* into a revival of surrealism's praise of automatism:

> For me, *mise-en-scène* is not merely the gap between what we see and feel on the screen and what we can express in words, but it is also the gap between the intention of the director and his effect upon the spectator.

… To read all sorts of poignant profundities in Preminger's inscrutable urbanity would seem to be the last word in idiocy, and yet there are moments in his films when the evidence on the screen is inconsistent with one's deepest instincts about the director as a man. It is during those moments that one feels the magical powers of *mise-en-scène* to get more out of a picture than is put in by a director.[36]

13. They Will Still Say To Me

that all of these games, this play, is ludicrous, and we will respond by citing André Breton, who observed that "'all things that have come to be recognized in poetry as conscious qualities—beauty, a sense of the sacred, magical power—are implied from the outset in the primary quality of the game.' It is clear that to shut oneself off from game-playing … is to undermine the best of one's own humanity."[37]

14. All Bourgeois.

The roots of the *mise-en-scène* move lay in Bazin's tacit renewal of the impressionist/surrealist branch of film theory. Bazin's ability to re-route film theory, at least temporarily, amounted to a rare instance of a discipline escaping from what economic historians call *path dependence*.

"Path dependence" developed as a way of explaining why the free market's invisible hand does not always choose the best products. Beta and Macintosh lose to inferior alternatives, while a clumsy arrangement of keyboard symbols (known as QWERTY, for the first six letters on a typewriter's upper left) becomes the international standard. Although an initial choice often occurs for reasons whose triviality eventually becomes evident (momentary production convenience, fleeting cost advantages), that decision establishes a path dependence almost impossible to break. Superior keyboard layouts have repeatedly been designed, but with every typist in the world using QWERTY, they have no chance.[38]

Bazin recognized that film theory was especially prone to path dependence. The vagaries of film preservation, the industry's encouragement of amnesia (before television, only a handful of films were regularly and widely revived), the small size of the intellectual community—these factors all encouraged theoretical consensus. While the impressionist and surrealist films, with a few exceptions, had disappeared from sight, Eisenstein's had remained in wide circulation, serving as advertisements for his position. As a result, Eisenstein's rationalist, critical branch of film theory had triumphed, establishing a path dependence that Bazin challenged with all his energy.

Bazin attacked on two fronts. First, he challenged the Eisenstein tradition's basic equation of art with antirealism. Second, he encouraged, without practicing himself, a different kind of film criticism: the lyrical, discontinuous, epigrammatic flashes of subjectivity cum analysis that appeared in the *Cahiers*, and that prefigured the New Wave's hybrid filmmaking.

Bazin's moment lasted only fifteen years. It was swept away by the events of May 1968, which stimulated different questions about the cinema's relationship to ideology and power, ones more suited to the semiotic approach that descended from Eisenstein. Since the mid-1970s, film theory has issued from an academic world whose vast oversupply of Ph.D.s has fostered a concomitant oversupply of publications desperately produced, in the best bourgeois spirit, to satisfy a buyer's market. Time is critical. To have any chance of landing a job, a graduate student must have already published. Earning tenure in an American research university typically requires a book, which must be written and accepted within the first five to six years of employment. This situation inevitably furthers film studies' tendency toward path dependence. Meaghan Morris has described the result:

> Sometimes, reading magazines like *New Socialist* or *Marxism Today*, or flipping through *Cultural Studies*, I get the feeling that somewhere in some English publisher's vault there is a master-disc from which thousands of versions of the same article about pleasure, resistance, and the politics of consumption are being run off under different names with minor variations.[39]

The problem, as Roland Barthes once put it in his autobiography, is "Where to go next?"

15. Like Giving Oneself a Good Address.

"It is always good to conclude," Truffaut said in the final section to "A Certain Tendency of the French Cinema." "That gives everyone pleasure."[40] For Truffaut, the "giving oneself a good address" that he condemned was the tendency of French directors to align themselves with the received tradition of quality that he opposed: the polished, old-fashioned, script-writer-dominated, politically correct, literary adaptations that ignored the mysteries of *mise-en-scène* and automatism. We've seen these movies, Truffaut said, and "it isn't necessary to repeat a grade indefinitely." We've seen contemporary film studies, and we have no need to repeat it. Let us say that Allen Smithee stands not for failure but for the unexamined, for those aspects of the movies gestured to, if not defined, by surrealist automatism, impressionist *photogénie*, and New Wave *mise-en-scène*. And to paraphrase Truffaut's final words, included in a footnote to his article, "It really will be necessary to use Allen Smithee to start an ultimate quarrel with film studies' tradition of quality, before it has dropped definitively into oblivion."

Notes

1. Man Ray, "Cinemage," *The Shadow and Its Shadow: Surrealist Writings on the Cinema*, ed. Paul Hammond (London: BFI, 1978) 84.

2. André Breton, *Manifestoes of Surrealism*, trans. Richard Seaver and Helen R. Lane (Ann Arbor: University of Michigan Press, 1972) 26.

3. Robert B. Ray, *The Avant-Garde Finds Andy Hardy* (Cambridge: Harvard University Press, 1995).

4. Quoted in Rosalind E. Krauss, *The Originality of the Avant-Garde and Other Modernist Myths* (Cambridge: MIT Press, 1985) 103.

5. Walter Benjamin, *Illuminations*, trans. Harry Zohn (New York: Schocken, 1969) 225.

6. Daniel Dennett, *Darwin's Dangerous Idea: Evolution and the Meanings of Life* (New York: Simon and Schuster, 1995).

7. Lindsay Waters, "Walter Benjamin's Dangerous Idea" (unpublished essay).

8. Sigmund Freud, "On Beginning the Treatment," trans. James Strachey, *The Freud Reader*, ed. Peter Gay (New York: Norton, 1989) 372.

9. Alastair Brotchie, ed., *Surrealist Games* (London: Redstone Press, 1991) 42–43.

10. David Bordwell, "The Avant-Garde Finds Andy Hardy," review of *The Avant-Garde Finds Andy Hardy*, by Robert B. Ray, *Film Quarterly* 50.4 (1997): 44.

11. Bertolt Brecht, *The Messingkauf Dialogues*, trans. John Willett (London: Methuen, 1965) 15–16.

12. Friedrich Nietzsche, *Beyond Good and Evil*, trans. Walter Kaufmann (New York: Vintage, 1966) 30–31.

13. Roland Barthes, "The Third Meaning," trans. Richard Howard, *The Responsibility of Forms* (New York: Hill and Wang, 1985) 41–62.

14. Gregory L. Ulmer, *Heuretics: The Logic of Invention* (Baltimore: The Johns Hopkins University Press, 1994) 8–11.

15. Alexandre Astruc, "The Birth of a New Avante-Garde: *La Caméra Stylo*," *The New Wave*, ed. Peter Graham (Garden City: Doubleday, 1968) 17–23.

16. Jean-Luc Godard, "Interview with Jean-Luc Godard," *Godard on Godard*, trans. Tom Milne, ed. Jean Narboni and Tom Milne (New York: Viking, 1972) 181.

17. Sherry Turkle, "Dynasty," *London Review of Books* 6 Dec. 1990: 3, 5–9.

18. Jean-Paul Sartre, "Existentialism Is a Humanism," trans. Philip Mairet, *Existentialism from Dostoevsky to Sartre*, ed. Walter Kaufmann (New York: Meridian, 1956) 291.

19. Godard, "Bergorama," *Godard on Godard* 76.

20. Sartre, "Existentialism Is a Humanism" 305.

21. Godard 60.

22. Sartre, "Existentialism Is a Humanism" 296, 297-98.

23. Godard, "Let's Talk about *Pierrot*," *Godard on Godard* 223.

24. Jean-Paul Sartre, *Nausea*, trans. Lloyd Alexander (New York: New Directions, 1964) 39.

25. Godard, "Let's Talk about *Pierrot*," *Godard on Godard* 221.

26. André Breton, "As in a Wood," *The Shadow and Its Shadow* 42–43.

27. Roland Barthes, *Roland Barthes*, trans. Richard Howard (New York: Hill and Wang, 1977) 117.

28. Richard Abel, ed., *French Film Theory and Criticism*, vol. 1 (Princeton: Princeton University Press, 1988). The three essays quoted are Louis Delluc, "Beauty in the Cinema," trans. Richard Abel, 138–39; Jean Epstein, "The Senses

I (b)," trans. Richard Abel, 243; and Jean Epstein, "On Certain Characteristics of *Photogénie*," trans. Richard Abel, 315.

29. André Bazin, "The Ontology of the Photographic Image," *What Is Cinema?* vol. 1, trans. Hugh Gray (Berkeley: University of California Press, 1967) 13.

30. Quoted in Paul Willemen, *Looks and Frictions: Essays in Cultural Studies and Film Theory* (Bloomington: Indiana University Press, 1994) 125.

31. Louis Aragon, "On Décor," *The Shadow and Its Shadow* 29.

32. Epstein, "The Senses I (b)," *French Film Theory and Criticism*, vol. 1, 242.

33. André Bazin, "Bicycle Thief," *What Is Cinema?* vol. 2, trans. Hugh Gray (Berkeley: University of California Press, 1971) 60.

34. Bazin, "The Virtues and Limitations of Montage," *What Is Cinema?* vol. 1, 49.

35. Jacques Rivette, "The Essential," trans. Liz Heron, *Cahiers du Cinéma, the 1950s: Neo-Realism, Hollywood, New Wave*, ed. Jim Hillier (Cambridge: Harvard University Press, 1985) 134.

36. Andrew Sarris, "Preminger's Two Periods: Studio and Solo," *Film Comment* 3.3 (1965): 13.

37. Quoted in Brotchie 138. Breton, in the first sentence of the passage I quote, is citing Johan Huizinga's *Homo Ludens*.

38. See Paul A. David, "CLIO and the Economics of QWERTY," *American Economic Review* 75.2 (1985): 332–37. See also Peter Passell, "Why the Best Doesn't Always Win," *New York Times Magazine* 5 May 1996: 60–61.

39. Meaghan Morris, "Banality in Cultural Studies," *Discourse* 10.2 (1988): 15.

40. François Truffaut, "A Certain Tendency of the French Cinema," *Movies and Methods*, vol. 1, ed. Bill Nichols (Berkeley: University of California Press, 1985) 235.

PART II
SMITHEE STUDIES

Allen Smithee's *Death of a Gunfighter*: "A Casualty of Hollywood's Excluded Middle"

Donald E. Pease

The Allen Smithee Story:
"A Casualty of Hollywood's Excluded Middle"

In 1967 Universal Studios began production of a Joseph Calvelli script that had adapted Lewis B. Patten's novel *Death of a Gunfighter* to the screen as a "noir" Western. The shooting script retold the familiar story of a Western town whose citizens wanted to dissociate themselves from the gunfighter turned lawman whose code of frontier justice had facilitated the town's development. Richard E. Lyons, the film's producer, cast Richard Widmark in the lead role as Marshal Frank Patch, a gunfighter who had outlived his usefulness to the town that hired him to keep the peace. The supporting cast included Lena Horne as Claire Quintana, the Madame of the *Goliad*; Carroll O'Connor played Lester Locke, the owner of the *Alamo*, Cottonwood Springs's rival saloon. John Saxon appeared as Sheriff Lou Trinidad, a Mexican immigrant commissioned by the town council to arrest Frank Patch.

Universal executives provided the film with the "studio treatment" conventional to a middle-budget action Western. They commissioned Robert Totten as director with instructions to shoot a Technicolor film with a soundtrack featuring Oliver Nelson's musical score and an original lyric, "Sweet Apple Wine," sung by Lena Horne. But twenty-five days into the shooting, tension between Totten and Widmark prompted anxious studio authorities to replace Totten with director Don Siegel, in the interests of bringing the film in within budget. When Universal Pictures released the final cut two years later in 1969, however, Siegel requested that his name be removed from the film's list of credits. In place of either "Don Siegel" or "Robert Totten," the name "Allen Smithee" appeared as the director of record of *Death of a Gunfighter*.

Andrew Sarris's elevation of Don Siegel to the rank of *auteur* a year earlier provided the studio with an artistic warrant for its economic decision to replace Totten with Siegel. But Sarris's promotion of "*auteur* theory" might also be invoked to establish a cultural context for Siegel's decision to substitute "Allen Smithee" as the name of the film's director. Sarris, who was arguably the leading American film critic of the 1960s, described Siegel's direction of Richard Widmark in *Madigan* as "among the most stunning displays of action montage in the history of the American cinema."[1]

In executing this judgment, Sarris had ascribed to Siegel's directorial talents qualities that French theorists had described as the mark of the *auteur*. François Truffaut, and many of the other critics writing in the journal *Cahiers du cinéma*, had defended American cinema against the charge that Hollywood mass-produced commercial spectacles that pandered to vulgar tastes.[2] They did this by substituting the *auteur* as a synonym for a film's director, thereby distinguishing the creative efforts of artists like Orson Welles from the hackwork of "*metteurs en scène*." The "*metteur*" routinely combined the formulaic plots, stereotypical situations, and stock characters through which the studios shaped the market appeal of their products, but the *auteur* reshaped these materials into a cinematic worldview that assumed the contours of "his" creative personality. In his application of literary terminology to aesthetic problems specific to post–World War II Hollywood films, Truffaut overturned a European cultural prejudice that had written off Hollywood as little more than a factory for the production of disposable entertainments. The *Cahiers* school's interpretations would eventually transfer literature's cultural legitimacy onto the cinema.

Whereas Truffaut and his coterie had initiated the debate a decade earlier, throughout the 1960s Andrew Sarris was embroiled in a homegrown variation of the controversy over whether American films should be construed as high art or as an industrial enterprise. When he introduced the *auteur* into this debate, Sarris intended to reacquire for Hollywood films the aesthetic values that French theorists had already discerned in them. In adapting French *auteur* theory to his needs, Sarris distilled the concept of the *auteur* into the opposed factors of technical know-how and creative virtuosity. Sarris thereafter claimed the power to recognize the work of a genuine *auteur* through the discernment of an "interior meaning" operating within the film's technological apparatus as its regulative principle. An *auteur*, according to Sarris, was the effect of a director's ongoing substitution of artistic for commercial concerns. A director's capacity to render economic criteria extraneous to his film's organizing principles produced the interior meanings through which Sarris recognized his merits. "Interior meaning," Sarris observed, was the outcome of a tension between the force of an *auteur*'s creative personality and the technical and economic materials through which he gave it expression. Discriminating its aesthetic significance from Hollywood's commercial values, Sarris turned the *auteur* into an American film critic's substitution for the Oscar. But the directors Sarris granted the title *auteur* differed from those Hollywood awarded Oscars in that the latter often received the award as a consequence of a studio's publicity campaigns rather than artistic achievement.

The *auteur* permitted Sarris to criticize the judgments of a film industry governed by an interest in profits rather than inner meaning. But his redefinition of the term also significantly lowered the French standard. The French theorists who elevated Hollywood films' aesthetic standing were interested in demonstrating the cultural power of the criteria they invoked to accomplish this feat. When they restricted the figures to whom they awarded the title *auteur* to directors whose cinematic visions exemplified features of their theory, they transposed these Americans into precursors for François Truffaut and Jean-Luc Godard, whose films were based on the *auteur* theory. It is no small irony that at the same historical moment in which Sarris would invoke *auteur* theory to legitimize the Hollywood film industry, Truffaut and other French filmmakers experienced the deleterious economic effects of that industry's monopolizing power.[3]

In proposing that the aspiration to transcend economic and ideological constraints be construed as the precondition for membership within his club, Sarris was enhancing the cultural status of the American director. Many directors were still recovering from the public (and private) humiliation that they had suffered at the hands of the House Un-American Activities Committee and greedy studio executives.[4] In the film reviews and essays he wrote between 1962 and the release of *Death of a Gunfighter* in 1969, Sarris invoked *auteur* theory to produce a complex taxonomy of Hollywood directors. Multiplying the categories through which he could distribute the title *auteur*, Sarris rehabilitated the reputations of numerous directors. Whereas the directors whose names appeared on Sarris's lists could reclaim an integrity that was predicated on their works' autonomy from economic as well as ideological pressures, Sarris did not choose to legitimize the entire Hollywood film industry. Sarris organized his hierarchically ranked classification of Hollywood directors by genre and theme as well as by the budgets the studios allotted individual directors.

Sarris's energetic application of the *auteur* concept in his influential study *The American Cinema: Directors and Directions 1929–1968*[5] significantly elevated Don Siegel's cultural status, along with that of the other Hollywood directors considered in the book. Siegel's 1956 film *Invasion of the Body Snatchers* had been read as an allegory of the hyperconformity that had followed in the wake of HUAC and the Cold War. Sarris discussed Siegel's work as an example of "Expressive Esoterica," a category that also included Stanley Donen and Arthur Penn. Characterizing *Invasion of the Body Snatchers* as "one of the few authentic science fiction classics," Sarris observed that his most successful films express the "doomed peculiarity of the antisocial outcast."[6]

Overall, Sarris ranked Siegel in the third tier of American directors—beneath Cecil B. DeMille and Orson Welles, but above Billy Wilder and John Huston and Richard Brooks. Having recognized Siegel as an *auteur*, however, Sarris concluded his account of the director's achievement with a somewhat ominous observation: "For the present, Siegel seems most assured with the middle budget action film, and it is to be hoped that he does not become a casualty of Hollywood's excluded middle."[7]

It is likely that Sarris intended that concluding turn of phrase to be playfully ironic, a gentle barb directed against the film industry's penchant for investing the majority of its resources in "major motion pictures" rather than the "middle budget action" genre in which Siegel excelled. When juxtaposed with the assessment of Siegel's accomplishment, the phrase also discloses how Sarris validates his principles of selection. Here and elsewhere, Sarris's judgment derives from his power to discriminate between an *auteur*'s occult meaning and a studio's budget. By giving expression to his vision despite economic constraints, Siegel had refused to compromise his craft. Sarris interpreted that refusal as the tell-tale sign of the *auteur*.

When it is referred to the contractual conditions that surrounded Siegel's hiring, the phrase "a casualty of Hollywood's excluded middle" also invites alternative readings. When Universal Studios signed him to direct *Death of a Gunfighter* midway through the film's shooting, their decision was based in part on Siegel's standing. But the fiscal constraints on a middle-budget Western made it necessary for Siegel to assume the persona of *metteur* in place of practicing the craft that had established his reputation.

When they recruited him to complete Robert Totten's film, Universal executives had implicitly confined his directorial responsibilities to the application of his proven ability to complete the picture under budget. Because they wanted the film to make a profit, studio executives did not ask that Siegel exercise artistic control over every aspect of the film's production. They could not afford an *auteur*. Nor did they request that Siegel start the movie from the beginning. The studio wanted him to complete a middle-budget action Western according to formula.

In sacrificing the different storyline he might have developed, Siegel proffered what Sarris had described as the primary value of an *auteur*, namely, his "creative personality," as a possible referent for a "casualty of Hollywood's excluded middle." Having agreed to make the movie according to the studio's terms, Siegel was compelled to abandon rather than develop the themes and characters that constituted his film's "interior meaning." He had begun to explore the prototype for Marshal Frank Patch through the role Richard Widmark had played in *Madigan* in 1967. In *Dirty Harry*, released in 1971, Siegel returned to the theme of the lawman who violated the law that he also upheld. Nine years after the completion of work on *Death of a Gunfighter*, Siegel directed *The Shootist*, whose story concerned a theme—the relationship between a dying gunfighter and his surrogate son—left underdeveloped in the earlier film.[8]

The Western that Universal wanted Siegel to film was not the one Siegel wanted to make; it was the one Totten had already botched. *The Man Who Shot Liberty Valance* had established the prototype for the film Universal wanted five years earlier. It was composed of familiar plot sequence and stereotypical characters of the Hollywood Western, yet it would tell the tale of the passing of the old West (in which the gunslinger "took the law into his own hands") with the emergence of the modern Western town. But Calvelli's screenplay presented Siegel with the same insuperable difficulties it had posed for Totten. The story it told represented an internally divided social order. It included evidence of racial and ethnic tensions that the cowboy Western had previously ignored— and *The Man Who Shot Liberty Valance* had erased.[9]

In foregrounding the political short-sightedness of the formula Western, the script represented a moment in which the town of Cotton-wood Springs was about to undergo an irreversible transformation. But the demographic and political configurations of that change could not be subordinated to the stock conventions of the movie-house Western. Moreover, despite the film's title, the shift from the old to the new Cot-tonwood Springs was not wholly reducible to the change in fortunes of the town's gunfighter. The commercial modernization recommended by its town council posed a threat to the changes in the town's multiracial community that Marshal Patch had safeguarded during his twenty years in office. Traces of the changes in the town's demographic order are leg-ible in the buildings—the Catholic Church; the *Goliad*, Claire Quin-tana's multiracial saloon; and Rosenbloom's Merchandise Emporium—

that constituted significant deviations from the Hollywood setting of a typical Western town.

While none of the film's characters claim ownership of this knowledge, the changes the town council recommends would involve a reversal of the political gains of its ethnic and racial minorities. Following Patch's murder, the town council would be free to close down the *Goliad* that Claire Quintana had opened under the marshal's protection, as well as the Catholic Church and Rosenbloom's Emporium. Intimations of danger to these structures as well as the groups they represent are alluded to throughout the picture and specifically by way of Sheriff Lou Trinidad, whose character is composed out of these tensions. If they do not fully enter the film's visual field, those tensions are nevertheless expressed by way of a series of questions that the narrative leaves unanswered: Why did Marshal Patch decide to marry Claire Quintana on the day of his assassination? How did the *Goliad* become multiracial? Why hadn't the *Alamo*? What did Lester Locke, the saloonkeeper of the *Alamo*, expect to gain from Patch's death?

Siegel would appear to have communicated the restrictions that the studio imposed on his shooting time to the narrative when he eliminated crucial linkages between its represented actions and the film's plot.[10] Siegel provided a structural warrant for these lapses in the story line by emplotting the narrative in the form of a flashback. The action as narrated takes place in the interval in between Claire Quintana's watching as a group of men transport a coffin from a wagon onto a train at the film's beginning and her climbing aboard that same train at its conclusion. Representing the narrative's conclusion as the film's opening scene regulates the spectatorial desire that it also produces. The conclusion restricts the subsequent actions to a sequence of events that would provide the spectator with the narrative coordinates necessary to explain the corpse as well as Claire Quintana's decision to leave town. No matter what narrative sequences they might have otherwise developed, the significance of each of the film's subsequent frames is overdetermined by the opening's finality.

But when the film returns at its conclusion to the scene with which it had opened, Claire Quintana's presence on the train platform poses an enigma that the story of "the gunfighter who had (quite literally) out-lived his time" has not resolved. Her decision to get out of Cottonwoood Springs and to take Patch's corpse with her reopens the narrative that the flashback had short-circuited. It gestures toward un-narrated intermedi-ary stories that, in addition to reasking all of the questions mentioned earlier, posed several others.[11] Was the corpse that she watched the townspeople load onto the train Frank Patch's? Was his death the only casualty of the people of Cottonwood Springs? Or had they murdered other clientele of the *Goliad* as well? Neither Claire Quintana's decision nor the answers to those questions have been narrated within *Death of a Gunfighter*. The narratives in which they might have been included were, like Don Siegel's "interior meaning," "casualt[ies] of Hollywood's excluded middle."

Despite their absence from the final cut of *Death of a Gunfighter*, however, these alternative tales were not disclaimed altogether. When Don Siegel substituted the name Allen Smithee as director of *Death of a Gunfighter*, that name claimed the narratives he could not claim. An anomalous Western, *Death of a Gunfighter* neither fit the generic expec-tations of the formula Western nor told the complete story of Cotton-wood Springs. In refusing to integrate the film into the symbolic field organizing his other work, Siegel had not abandoned it. Naming it an Allen Smithee film called attention to the differences between the West-ern's conventions and narratives that did not fit into them. While the narrated movie disowned those stories, Allen Smithee renarrated them. As the name the director of *Death of a Gunfighter* substituted to disown the released film, Allen Smithee reclaimed the unnarrated film that had become "a casualty of Hollywood's excluded middle."

Between *Auteur* and *Metteur*

The concluding statement of this essay's opening section—that "Allen Smithee reclaimed [Don Siegel's] unnarrated film"—has provided a nar-rative account of Smithee's emergence. But the formulation also raises a number of questions that such an observation begs. The statement has proposed that Allen Smithee be understood as having originated from two separate operations: from Don Siegel's excision of *Death of a Gun-fighter* from the list of films accredited to his direction, and from his inscription of a name that would incorporate the film's excluded narrative(s). But hasn't this explanation of Don Siegel's decision to substitute Allen Smithee's name as director uncritically accepted Sarris's *auteur* concept as its grounding presupposition?

In addition to disclaiming Universal's film, Siegel's act of substitution restored the economic considerations—the historical conditions of mass production and the Cold War state—out of whose exclusion Sarris had constructed the American *auteur*. As the name that stands for the negotiation between a director's artistic concerns and these socioeconomic interests central to every cinematic production, Allen Smithee would have been written off of all of Sarris's lists. But as an index for the commercial constraints with which every director must contend, Allen Smithee names the studio system and the surveillance state as the two interlocking *mise-en-scènes* internal to every director's work.

In calling attention to the forces of production that Sarris's taxonomy had effaced, Siegel might be understood to have added Allen Smithee as an additional character to *Invasion of the Body Snatchers*. That film allegorized the historical moment when the film industry became part of the state's surveillance of U.S. citizens. Whereas Sarris's *auteur* system constitutes an effort to forget that episode when "naming names" could ruin Hollywood careers, Don Siegel has encrypted that disclaimed history within the name Allen Smithee.

The invention of Allen Smithee also complicated the distinction that Sarris adduced between the *auteur* and the *metteur*. Operating at the border between *auteur* and *metteur*, Allen Smithee reestablishes the *metteur* at the ideological limit of and as the economic precondition for the work of the *auteur*. The *auteur* and *metteur* do not exist in a relationship of diachronic opposition. *Metteur* and *auteur* work with the same materials—shooting script, location, budget, technology, editing equipment. Each constitutes and is constituted by the work of the other. The *metteur* supplies the materials for the *auteur*'s design; the *auteur* provides the means of shaping the materials assigned to the *metteur*.

Suture

Film theorists have proposed a term that might provide another means of relating the way Don Siegel unstitched *Death of a Gunfighter* from his credits, and the way other directors stitch the name "Allen Smithee" to their films, that might explain the pertinence of both activities to Sarris's *auteur*. These autonomous and asymmetrical operations—unstitching and stitching—both involve "suturing." Film theory borrowed this term from the Lacanian school of psychoanalysis, which describes suture as "the psychical mechanism whereby the subject takes up a place, is stitched into the signifying chain—just as a surgeon sews up a wound. . . . thereby constituting it as a subject."[12] In their application of this process to film, theorists have used it to refer to the complex process whereby the spectator is drawn into the film's multitude of shots in order to confer a kind of coherence upon them.

Suturing is manifestly in operation when a film's shot/reverse-shot sequence asks the spectator to hold the place in between two opposed looks. But suturing also effectively inscribes the position the viewer is presumed to occupy throughout the film. Elizabeth Cowie has discerned three distinct threads involved in interweaving the spectator into the film's preconstituted position: "As a process in which the viewer is positioned as a cinematic subject, as a process in which the viewer is stitched into, takes his or her place in the cinematic discourse, and as, therefore, a mechanism of ideology."[13]

If suture names the position effected whenever a subject projectively identifies with the unified position that secures coherence, it bears a resemblance to Andrew Sarris's account of the *auteur*. The *auteur*, according to Sarris, named the placeholder for the view that provided the spectator with a privileged knowledge of the film's "interior meaning." What Sarris called an *auteur*'s creative personality articulated the intentional force that guaranteed a film's meaning. As the source of its "interior meaning," the *auteur* held a supervisory position outside the cinematic field. But as the masterful coordinator of the film's other elements—cinematography, sound, camera movement, lighting, special effects—the *auteur* was also immanent to its design.

The position to which the film sutured the spectator resulted from an identification with the *auteur*. As its source, the *auteur* named the subject position that the spectator presupposed the film already to have provided. The imago of the *auteur* became the means through which the spectator recovered the pleasure of an imaginary fullness and presence.[14]

As the subject that the film solicits to hold the position central to the production of its meaning, however, the spectator should also be distinguished from the *auteur*. The latter figure, at least according to Andrew Sarris' definition, must be presumed not to suture. The *auteur*, that is to say, is presumed to know more than the spectator who is positioned in relation to a knowledge sufficiently different from the viewer's in order to produce a film out of those differences.

The *auteur* holds the position within the film that is central to the construction of its significance and that the spectator can only belatedly reconstruct. Considered from this perspective, then, the notion of the suture acknowledges the difference between *auteur* and spectator. The spectator in effect presupposes the work of the *auteur* as the precondition for the position he or she assumes within the chain of shots. By positioning the subject in between shot and reverse shot, the suture specifies the spectator's place in the film.

Paradoxically, in stitching that position into its itinerary as the agent responsible for its continuity, the sequence of shots might be understood to constitute the spectator. After having been stitched into the filmic chain of events as the point of view assumed responsible for its overall significance, however, the sutured subject also holds the supervisory position presupposed in the very notion of the *auteur*. If, as Andrew Sarris has argued, the *auteur* constitutes the organized singularity of the film's "look," that position can appear only retroactively as the effect of the sequence it organizes. As the "look" that a film solicits heterogeneously throughout the process of its showing, the suture effects an identification between spectator and *auteur*.

The suture, then, discloses a contradiction that is inherent to the position of the spectator. As the figures to whom the film appeals for significance, neither the *auteur* nor the spectator can be understood to exist prior to the suture. No spectator can inhabit this position crucial to the film's significance until the film asks for it. Yet the film's signification can only accomplish itself in and for this position. The position is constituted out of what might be called the film's desire for a spectator whose interpretation the film thereafter imagines itself to represent. The spectator's position materializes retroactively as what will have provided a film with the qualities of narrative consistency and thematic unity that a sequence of shots lacks.

In "The *Auteur* Theory Revisited," an essay that Sarris first published in 1977 and republished as an afterword to *The American Cinema: Directors and Directions 1929–1968*, Sarris has reflected on the paradoxical identity that the film viewer shares with the *auteur*.[15] In ruminating over the work that the *auteur* performed in improving American cinema's cultural standing, Sarris has posited a significant distinction between the *auteur* as a datum and *auteurism* as a spectatorial fantasy. "Auteurism," Sarris reflected, has "less to do with the way movies are made than with the way they are elucidated and evaluated."[16]

In "The Auteur Theory Revisited," Sarris acknowledges that he intended the *auteur* concept to be, in part, an idealization of the space that the spectator holds in the cinematic apparatus. *Auteurism* not only elevated cinema into a hieratic art; it also permitted Sarris to refashion himself as a high priest able to interpret "movies as sacred relics."[17] By way of this admission, Andrew Sarris might be described as having encountered Allen Smithee in the process of formulating his *auteur* fantasy. Sarris might be understood to have encountered Allen Smithee, that is to say, in between the spectatorial position that he invented the *auteur* to idealize and his knowledge of the economic and political conditions that impeded this idealization. Sarris encountered the knowledge he wanted to suppress at the very site in between the *auteur* and the *metteur* within which Don Siegel would subsequently inscribe the name Allen Smithee.

The distinction Sarris adduced between the *auteur* and *metteur* articulated a structural difference between the film as narration and the film's means of production. But as we have already seen, *auteur* and *metteur* describe interdependent practices rather than antithetical personalities. When Sarris defined an *auteur* as the effect of a creative personality's having suffused every aspect of a film's production, he produced that effect by actively suppressing knowledge of the heterogeneous factors—sound, cinematography, camera movement, color, lighting, editing—outside a director's complete control. But in revealing the matters out of whose erasure Andrew Sarris had constituted the "interior meaning" of the *auteur*, Allen Smithee also facilitated the return of this suppressed knowledge.

If a spectator must remain ignorant of the technologic-economic apparatus undergirding a film's production as a precondition for viewing the film, an Allen Smithee film exposes the spectator to an apparatus incommensurable with the film's narrative logic. Allen Smithee changed the ratio between knowledge and nonknowledge. An Allen Smithee film knowingly consolidates the interior meanings subtending an *auteur*'s work yet also supplements them with parallel "disclaimed" narratives. The name for a film that no *auteur* could sign, Allen Smithee splits the difference between the spectator as an effect of suture and the *auteur* as an ideal spectator.

The Smitheereen

The description of an Allen Smithee film as taking place in between *auteur* and suture indicates the range of effects that this signature encompasses. An Allen Smithee film emerges at the unbreachable divide between the film as narration and as the formalization of its technological apparatus. A film's technological apparatus provides the syntax across which a director communicates a narrative; but a director can communicate a coherent narrative only by suppressing a spectator's knowledge of this apparatus. If this syntax should coincide with the film's narrative grammar, it would threaten to replace the story with a revelation of its technological and economic means of production.

Because of the pervasive interference it effects in between knowledge of its narration and the means of its production, a Smithee film invariably releases the (non)knowledge that no *auteur* could ever (want to) master. As the difference between directorial mastery and a technological apparatus beyond the director's control, Allen Smithee takes place as the constitutive failure to take up the position of *auteur* intrinsic to every directorial practice. An Allen Smithee film communicates this mis-take to its spectators as an intense oscillation between fascination and aversion, between their drive to know more than the film can disclose and their need to refuse this knowledge. The alternation between these irreconcilable needs results in the characteristic effect of the spectator having experienced an unclaimable filmic event that might be described as a "smitheereen."

A smitheereen should not be confused with "smithereen." The latter word is derived from the Gaelic *smiodirin*, denoting a fragment. But a smitheereen refers to the unstitching procedure that splits the *auteur* and spectator in an Allen Smithee film into irreconcilable portions. Such unstitching is a potential effect intrinsic to every shot sequence. But the smitheereen refers typically to the spectacular disturbance of the suturing that would otherwise connect one shot with the next or link adjacent sequences into a meaningful sequence.

Jacqueline Rose's commentary about the estrangement of the look in Alfred Hitchcock's *The Birds* might be invoked as an illustration of the limits of the suturing operation that would also explain the smitheereen's retroactive effect that is discernibly at work in *The Birds II: Land's End*, Rick Rosenthal's 1994 remake of Alfred Hitchcock's classic, released as a Smithee film. The suture "mimes the dialectical" relationship between *auteur* and spectator, Rose observes, but renders it vulnerable to reversibility. Rose finds in the camera's shuttling from shot to reverse shot an estrangement of the spectator from the masterful position of *auteur*. Instead of confirming the belief that he or she is central to constituting the film's meaning, the shot/reverse-shot sequence exposes the spectator-*auteur* as a stand-in for the camera. In alternating between the shots, the camera holds the position of a "third look" that "cancels the observer's centrality and subjects the observer as well as the observed to a gaze whose signified is attack."[18]

In looking back at the subject from the perspective of its own ideal ego, the camera dispossesses the spectator of the power to confer significance that the film has solicited. Following this alienation of the subject from the look out of which it had been constituted, *The Birds*, according to Rose, then exposes this alienated look to a vulnerable position within the film's visual field. An aspect of filmviewers' pleasure in Hitchcock's original derives from their ability to achieve mastery over this anxiogenic look.

Rosenthal's sequel depends for its success upon filmgoers' scopophilia—their desire to re-see what they had not fully visualized in the original. That desire requires that a spectator actively forget what Rose analyzes as the scopophobic effect in Hitchcock's original. By visualizing the entirety of *The Birds II* from the viewpoint of the smitheereen, however, Rosenthal's unstitching produces a scopophobia that he manages to sustain throughout the film. Rosenthal, that is to say, successfully detaches the spectator from the desire to re-see the original and re-evaluates the relationship between re-seeing and not seeing in the latter's favor. Once repositioned within the smitheereen that operates its effects within the visual field Rose has called the third look, a spectator becomes detached from the scopic pleasure associated with *The Birds*. As effects of the visual trauma occasioned by Hitchcock's original but that Rosenthal was unable to work through, his film's smitheereens activate an ongoing desire for visual forgetting that only an Allen Smithee film could accomplish.[19]

The *Auteur* Who (Does Not) Know(s) Too Much

Thus far we have proposed that an Allen Smithee film emerges when interference from the film's technological and economic apparatus causes the film to lose track of the elements that would permit the transition from one shot or sequence of shots to the next. We have also described that event as the precipitating context for the release of the smitheereen, the signature effect of an Allen Smithee production. But these formulations do not explain the relationship between the disavowed or disclaimed elements of the film and the narrative line that we observed Don

Siegel had invented the signature Allen Smithee to reclaim. In addition to the acknowledgment of the economic concerns that the *auteur* suppressed, Allen Smithee also preserves the narrative traces of the movie Don Siegel could not afford to make. As he reclaims the narratives Siegel could not include in his film, this addendum-director implicitly hollows out a space in the narrated film for the projection of these disavowed narratives. Smithee reclaims the narrative that Siegel disowned.

In the scene just before the conclusion of *Death of a Gunfighter*, Siegel thematizes the difference between the desire to know more about the film's production than the film is at liberty to disclose and the director's need to foreclose this surplus knowledge as a character's desire to lay claim to an otherwise unclaimable event. The scene to which I refer involves a shoot-out between Marshal Frank Patch and Will Oxley, the son of the town's newspaper publisher, Andrew Oxley. Will attempts to kill Patch in the wake of his father's suicide, in which he correctly believes the marshal to have played a hand. Patch has already indicated the extent of his responsibility at the scene of Andrew's suicide, by belatedly promising Andrew's corpse, "I wouldn't have talked."

Patch's promise to the dead man indicates his understanding of the centrality of disavowal to his rule of law. In promising to have kept quiet about whatever it was that Andrew had done in the past, Frank Patch was able to maintain his power over him. Following his father's suicide, however, and just before his own death, Will Oxley asks, "Why did my father kill himself?" In asking this question, Will wants to know the source of the marshal's power over his father. His interrogative harbors an accusation in search of a criminal who might be punished for his father's death. In responding to Will's tacit accusation that he was indirectly responsible for his father's suicide, Patch adopts the eerily consoling voice of a parent about to tell a bedtime story to an upset child. Then Patch tells the story he had promised the corpse of Andrew Oxley he would not tell.

"A long time ago," Patch begins his account in a voice that remains as evasively nonresponsive as the story's elements, "a man was shot."

WILL: My father did it.

PATCH: No one knew for sure.

WILL: You knew. Why didn't you hang him?

PATCH: There was nothing to be gained from hanging.

Throughout this dialogue, Frank and Will enunciate nonconvergent formulations—what Patch gives as vague, indirect statements in the passive voice, the boy rephrases in the active voice as direct assertions of guilt. The dying son's demand to know why his father killed himself expresses his wish for a world in which crime gets punished. But the story Patch begins to tell has references to a murder for which no one was ever publicly accused or held criminally responsible. Their cross-purposes result in an exchange that might be described as a jointly constructed denegation—the affirmation of the truth of events through their negation.

Upon hearing Patch redescribe as a murderer the man he still believes to be his father, Will demands the operation of the juridical apparatus—witnesses, accusers, trial by jury, execution—that is missing from the social order. Its absence, as Will suggests, had made it necessary for his father to shoot himself when the law should have hanged him. With the phrase "There was nothing to be gained by hanging," however, the dialogue whose cross-purposes had previously been held together by the logic of denegation has now jumped the tracks of the narrative in which it had been positioned. At this precise instant, the signature Smithee effect takes hold. The smitheereen emerges after Patch enunciates this piece of knowledge that the symbolic order as narrated simply cannot accommodate. The actions that follow this phrase might as a consequence be imagined as taking place in the unsuturable space that lies in between Patch and Will as characters enclosed within the film's narrative and the *mise-en-scène* required to keep them anchored to those positions. In the remainder of the scene, Patch shifts his place of enunciation to the scene in which he established the contract that founded Cottonwood Springs's social order.

When articulated to the promise "I wouldn't have told anyone," the phrase "There was nothing to be gained from hanging" reenunciates the speech act that has constituted the social contract between Patch and the town of Cottonwood Springs. In *Death of a Gunfighter*, Marshal Frank Patch practices the law from a split-subject position: he represents the law as well as the violence required to enforce its rule. The violence with which Patch regulates Cottonwood Springs assumes the symbolic form of knowledge of their past transgressions that the people have collectively disavowed. The power that the town council transferred to Patch resulted from a reciprocal exchange between the people's submission to Patch's occasional use of deadly force and the memories of violence that force had screened. The murder Andrew Oxley committed represents synecdochically all of the other townspeoples' transgressions. It also established the limit the other townspeople's transgressions could not exceed.

In defense, Patch links the assertion that there "was nothing to be gained by hanging" with a fact that Will not only does not know, but that he cannot know and remain himself: "The dead man had a son." And the man who murdered him, Patch continues, "agreed to raise that boy as his son." In sharing this knowledge with Will in the instant before the boy's death, Marshal Patch has also transformed the position that the son of Andrew Oxley has occupied in the social order. Will entered the scene as a son who had accused the lawman of having had a hand in his father's suicide. Will comes to seek revenge. Just before his death, Will has discovered that his biological father had been murdered. The man who murdered him was the suicide he had come to revenge. But the publisher Andrew Oxley has already acted upon the son's revenge against a patricide by killing himself. Will is not only not Andrew Oxley's son; he is also the site wherein father and patricide coincide. With the disappearance of the man he believed was his father, the son he believed himself to be vanishes as well.

The story Patch tells recounts the series of substitutions upon which the ruling order of Cottonwood Springs was founded: Andrew Oxley agreed to place himself in the position of Will's father after Marshal Patch in his turn had promised not to hang Andrew for this capital offense. But Marshal Patch agreed not to prosecute Andrew only so long as Andrew agreed to perform the duties of the parent he had murdered. When Patch demanded that Andrew adopt the son of the man he had murdered in exchange for the foreclosure of the knowledge of that murder, he turned the disavowal of the father's murder into the basis for all of the town's social relations. This compact turned each townsperson into a placeholder for this knowledge that could not be acknowledged.

If the symbolic action in which the town participated entailed the collective disavowal of the knowledge of this murder, the sheriff's revelation of this knowledge to Will renders untenable every social position sutured by way of this disavowal. In killing Will, Patch repeats, this time within the social order, the scene of violence responsible for the founding of it. As the means whereby his father's murderer paid his debt to the social order, Will was not the son of Andrew Oxley but the means whereby Patch positioned the townspeople's disavowal of the knowledge of patricide. Without Will as his means of compelling the citizenry to remain anchored in legally sanctioned positions in exchange for his refusal to prosecute them for their violent past, Patch lacks the power to inhibit the repetition of their violence. Lacking this substitution, the townspeople feel compelled to reenact the collective violence that preceded the founding of their social order.

Communication of this fact does not merely dismantle the phrases of the social compact. As the revelation of the event in whose collective disavowal Cottonwood Springs was founded, this piece of information also unstitches the thread holding together the events as they had been previously narrated, reducing all of the actions and agents of *Death of a Gunfighter* to smitheereens.[20]

Notes

1. Andrew Sarris, *The American Cinema: Directors and Directions 1929–1968* (New York: Da Capo, 1996) 137.

2. *Cahiers du cinéma* was founded in 1951, as the successor to *La Revue du cinéma* (first issue in 1946). Its editors were André Bazin, Jacques Doniol-Valcroze, and Eric Rohmer. For an excellent edited volume on *auteur* theory, see

the anthology *Cahiers du Cinéma, the 1950's: Neo-Realism, Hollywood, New Wave*, ed. Jim Hillier (Cambridge: Harvard University Press, 1985) 148–59.

3. Thomas Elsaesser scrutinizes this historical irony along with several other unintended consequences of the *auteur* movement in "Two Decades in Another Country: Hollywood and the Cinéphiles," *Superculture: American Popular Culture and Europe*, ed. C. W. E. Bigsby (London: Elek Books, 1973) 199–216.

4. Elsaesser has remarked that French cineastes' "interest in Hollywood during the 1950s might be said to have coincided with that shown by McCarthy and the House of [sic] UnAmerican Activities Committee's special investigation" (214).

5. Sarris published the first edition of *The American Cinema* with Dutton in 1968. The 1996 edition includes the afterword "The Auteur Theory Revisited."

6. Sarris 137.

7. Sarris 138.

8. All of these films presuppose popular television series from the 1960s as intertextual narratives. *Gunsmoke* and *The Rifleman* had adapted the formula Western to the audience demands of their popular television soap operas. But while Claire Quintana's relationship with Marshal Frank Patch recalls Miss Kitty's with Marshal Dillon in episodes of *Gunsmoke*, the television censors would have prohibited the film's representation of their cross-racial sexual intimacy. Chuck Connors's role as Johnny Crawford's biological father in *The Rifleman* posed a model for Patch's acting as surrogate parent to the orphan Dan Joslin. But *The Rifleman* shored up the patriarchal authority that Dan Joslin discredited in *Death of a Gunfighter*. In visualizing scenes that no network could televise, Allen Smithee's film might be described as having produced missing episodes for both of these television series.

9. Virginia Wright Wexman has discussed *Liberty Valance*'s "repressed issues of land values and racial difference" in *Creating the Couple: Love, Marriage, and Hollywood Performance* (Princeton: Princeton University Press, 1993) 113–29.

10. The elimination of such linkages are central to the meaning of Smithee's later film *Solar Crisis*, as Jeremy Braddock shows in "Smithee's Incorporation," chapter 7 in the present volume.

11. Complete discussion of *Death of a Gunfighter*'s excluded narratives would require another essay. But it should be noted that these narratives coalesce around the return of Lou Trinidad. When Trinidad reenters Cottonwood

Springs as county sheriff, he activates the ethnic and racial tension that the organizing narrative disavows. These tensions emerge in two separate scenes— Lester Locke's bar and Marshal Patch's office. Council members take Sheriff Trinidad to the *Alamo*, the one saloon in town that has remained monoracial, to talk over his assignment. But its owner, Lester Locke, refuses to serve him the drink he requested. Offering Trinidad "American whiskey" in place of "wetback" brand, Lester then guides the group to a back room rather than the main bar.

Trinidad provides a history for Locke's segregation policy in Patch's back room office. He continues that history in his subsequent confrontation with Patch. After delivering the council's "complaint" against Patch, Trinidad recalls that most of the town council had threatened to leave town after Patch had appointed him deputy ten years ago, "You shoved me down their throats," Trinidad recalls, "Just like they're shoving me down your throat now."

As Trinidad's remarks suggest, Patch represented the racial threat the town feared as well as the double onto whom the townspeople projected everything they needed to disavow. Trinidad's encounter with Patch focalizes the town's racism, which the film associates with the 1960s civil rights movement and positions as its narrative's political unconscious. The film thereafter correlates Patch's violence with the symbolic violence of the multiracial social order that he "shoved down their throats." *Death of a Gunfighter* thereby communicates a collective racist fantasy of a small town's overthrow of the multiracial social order that the law had imposed. Claire Quintana's need to get out of town indicates that Cottonwood Springs has overturned that order following Patch's death.

12. Elizabeth Cowie, *Representing the Woman: Cinema and Psychoanalysis* (Minneapolis: University of Minnesota Press, 1997) 114. See also Jacques-Alain Miller, "Suture (Elements of the Logic of the Signifier)" *Screen* 18.4 (winter 1977–78): 34. Jean-Pierre Oudart's influential "Cinema and Suture" can be found in the same issue of *Screen* (35–47).

13. Cowie, *Representing the Woman*, 115.

14. In "The Art of Analysis: Mary Kelly's Interim and the Discourse of the Analyst," Parveen Adams's remarks about the fantasies spectators project onto artists are pertinent as well to the *auteur*-spectator relationship. Adams proposes that the *auteur* be construed the placeholder for a spectator's needs for a source of meaning: "Although she knows very well that the truth of the painting is already invested in the painting and not in the intention of the artist. . . . knowing this doesn't stop our fantasies about the artist, not so much as a person but as

a function, the vanishing point at which the picture and its truth would intersect as the source of the picture's correct interpretation. We may call this fantasy of the artist the ego ideal of the spectator, the place from which the spectator's interpretation may be felt to be validated. At this point, when it works, we do indeed think that we are looking at a masterpiece." *October* 58 (fall 1991): 90.

15. Sarris represents this paradoxical identity by way of the substitution of the word *auteurism* in the following *mise-en-scène*: "In the beginning, particularly, its preoccupation with visual structure and personal style was largely a reaction against the sloganized vocabulary of social significance and socialist realism. The open-minded and open-hearted French attitude toward myth and genre enabled a new generation of American critics to rediscover and reclaim the American cinema. Suddenly there was credit to parcel out for America's long despised output, whereas before the auteurists there was only blame" (271–72).

16. Sarris 278.

17. Sarris 277.

18. Jacqueline Rose, "Paranoia and the Film System," *Feminism and Film Theory*, ed. Constance Penley (New York: Routledge, 1988) 147.

19. Apropos of the smitheereen's renegotiation of the relationship between spectator and *auteur*, Timothy Corrigan has observed that "within the commerce of culture it [*auteurism*] has become, as both a production and interpretive position, more critically central yet massively different from what it once may have been. Since the early 1970s, the commercial conditioning of this figure has successfully evacuated it of most of its expressive power and textual coherence; simultaneously, this commercial conditioning has called renewed attention to the layered pressures of auteurism as an agency that establishes different modes of identification with its audiences." Timothy Corrigan, *A Cinema without Walls: Movies and Culture after Vietnam* (New Brunswick: Rutgers University Press, 1991) 135–36. In "Authorship and the Cultural Politics of Film Criticism," James Naremore takes Corrigan's remarks about the change in its status to another level and declares *auteurism* dead, adding that debates about it were likewise finished. See *Film Quarterly* 44.1 (fall 1990): 20. Dudley Andrew builds on both Naremore's and Corrigan's arguments in "The Unauthorized Auteur Today" in *Film Theory Goes to the Movies*, ed. Jim Collins, Hilary Radner, and Ava Preacher Collins (New York: Routledge, 1993) 77–85. For another consideration of *The Birds II*, see Stephen Hock's essay, chapter 8 in the present volume.

20. Although it emulates this effect, the independently produced film *Smithereens* (1984) was not directed by Allen Smithee.

CHAPTER 5

Smithee in *The Twilight Zone: The People v. John Landis et al.* and Other Trials of Authorship

Jessie Labov

> The spectacle manifests itself as an enormous positivity, out of
> reach and beyond dispute. All it says is: "Everything that appears
> is good; whatever is good will appear." The attitude that it demands
> in principle is the same passive acceptance that it has already secured
> by means of its seeming incontrovertibility, and indeed by its
> monopolization of the realm of appearances.
>
> —Guy Debord, *The Society of the Spectacle*

When the name "Alan Smithee" appears on the screen, it signals a masking, or a covering-over of a truth behind the film.[1] Smithee is unlike any other pseudonym in that it is not a singular identity created by an author to replace that author's true identity (a one-to-one relationship), but is a collective claim to anonymity (which can contain any number of authors in just one name). The only label that shares this capacity of Smithee is "Anonymous"; yet this signature marks an absence of name (*an-*), and lacks the insistence on falsehood, personification, and disguise (*pseud-*) that arises with the Christian name "Alan" in combination with the surname "Smithee." What personification *does* Smithee imply? The conditions under which a director may assume the Smithee identity have been made explicit by the Directors Guild of America: he or she must prove a loss of creative control over the film. The motivation seems clear. Removing one's professional name from a product that does not satisfy certain criteria can enable one's filmography to remain free of "bad" films, that is, films that could damage a reputation because of artistic or financial failure. It guards against the most stringent of Hollywood's ultimatums: *you are only as good as your last picture*. Smithee absorbs Hollywood's failures and protects the autonomy of the director.

Yet there is one Smithee credit that does more than shelter its author from financial or artistic devaluation. It is a tiny exception to the rule—a second assistant director credit on *Twilight Zone: The Movie* (1983)—that I claim as a challenge to our assumptions about the signification of Smithee. The Smithee credit on *Twilight Zone: The Movie* must be understood in a different register than the one in which the logic of supply and demand determines an author's (or even an *auteur's*) success. To insist on this shift is to invoke a moral and ethical dimension of the Smithee pseudonym, a dimension that includes the entire history of disguising one's identity and naming names, particularly in Hollywood. In the end, as in Guy Debord's vision of the spectacle, Smithee absorbs more than just a loss of creative control. As Smithee masks and personifies the pseudonym, it also covers over whatever else gets in the way of making a movie.

Twilight Zone: The Trial

In the credits as they appear today, Alan Smithee is listed instead of Anderson House as the second assistant director on John Landis's segment of the three-part film, *Twilight Zone: The Movie*. This case stands out as a rare example of an *assistant* director taking a Smithee credit (at least according to the Smithee filmographies assembled thus far). Why would someone who is only a notch higher than a production assistant in the hierarchy of filmmaking apply to the Directors Guild for a pseudonym?[2]

The answer lies in the anomalous motivation behind House's taking of the pseudonym, which dates back to 22 July 1982, when a fatal helicopter accident on the set of *Twilight Zone* caused the untimely death of Vic Morrow, the film's star, and two children, Myca Dinh Le and Renee Shinn Chen.[3] Several members of the crew, including director John Landis, were tried for involuntary manslaughter. They were eventually acquitted, although the process took almost five years (the final verdict was not reached until May 1987). The accident occurred around

2:30 A.M., while the crew filmed the second take of the last sequence to be shot in Landis's segment of *Twilight Zone*—a night scene that simulated the bombing of a Vietnamese village. It is still unclear precisely what caused the accident. Several things did go wrong: a series of explosives went off prematurely, a helicopter filming the scene flew too close to the explosives, became disabled, and crashed to the ground, killing the three actors below. The production team had broken several industry regulations in their effort to create a spectacle of this dimension, most prominently a prohibition on using child actors after 6:30 P.M.[4] Landis's defense team would later argue that it was an unforeseeable accident, which could just as easily have killed the director himself (Landis was only a few yards away from the site of the crash); Landis, the defense reasoned, was no more to blame than the fire safety officials or the special effects technician, none of whom were being prosecuted.

The trial represented the first time that a director was charged with a crime resulting from an accident on the set of a film, and the publicity and controversy surrounding the incident had far-reaching effects on the movie industry. Immediately after the accident, the Directors Guild of America instituted a safety committee and a "safety hot-line" to advise inexperienced directors and film crews about shooting potentially dangerous special effects sequences. Richard Brooks, who had directed the extended fire sequence in *Elmer Gantry* (1960), was put in charge of "fire safety." He commented on the prosecution of Landis:

> The industry—and in particular the Directors Guild—feels it's on trial.... When [the *Twilight Zone*] trial is over, it won't be over. There's going to be a civil suit, and the Legislature is going to say the director has too much autonomy. They'll want to put an overseer on the set, a policeman, but what will that person know about making movies?[5]

At first glance, Brooks is expressing a concern about the mechanics of filmmaking: who will be at the top of the chain of command on the set? This question is symptomatic, though, of the more general concern about a threat to the autonomy of the director. Since the dismantling of the Motion Picture Production Code, the Directors Guild had steadily been gaining greater autonomy for its members, approaching the point where a director could be in almost complete control of the film.[6] Before the trial, the DGA had even taken steps to forestall a proposal that would have given safety officials the final say over a director's decisions on the set.[7] The measures taken after the *Twilight Zone* tragedy represent a reversal in DGA policy, and were one of the first limits to a director's autonomy that the DGA would acknowledge.

"What we have here is the *auteur* theory of homicide," wrote Randall Sullivan in a controversial article in *Rolling Stone*.[8] Sullivan claimed that Landis had done everything he could to take full credit for the successes of his previous two films, *Animal House* (1978) and *The Blues Brothers* (1980), and had every intention of doing the same with *Twilight Zone: The Movie*[9] until the accident intervened: "The question is whether credit has another side, an obverse angle, a yin for its yang; that is, responsibility." The *Rolling Stone* piece accused Landis directly and sensationally; Sullivan's statements about the connection between *auteurism* and Landis's "denial of what's real" were provocative enough to draw a written response from Hollywood directors:

> Randall Sullivan asserts that because the *auteur* theory gives the director total artistic credit for a film, he also bears total moral and legal responsibility for everything that happens in the course of production.... Sullivan dismisses as "blatantly outrageous" the idea that John Landis on *Twilight Zone* was only "the artistic director." In fact, this is a basic truth of filmmaking.
>
> All directors must rely on their colleagues to carry out the actual making of the film. No director, for instance, can prevent a camera operator from shooting a scene out of focus or even know that it is happening.... Someone else is at the controls.[10]

This letter, which appeared in *Rolling Stone* a few months after Sullivan's article, was signed by sixteen directors, including Billy Wilder, Francis Ford Coppola, George Lucas, and John Huston. Steven Spielberg, who co–executive produced *Twilight Zone* with Landis, was noticeably absent.

The Los Angeles County grand jury indictments of Landis and his four codefendants were unsealed on the same day that the movie opened, 24 June 1983. In their account of the trial, Stephen Farber and Marc Green draw attention to the synchronicity of these events:

> As the list of credits rolled for the Landis segment, it looked like a duplicate of Gary Kesselman's witness list before the Los Angeles County Grand Jury. But one name was unfamiliar: the second assistant director, Alan Smithee.... Anderson House, whose involvement in the tragedy had sickened him, was determined to dissociate himself from the finished product. He asked that his name be removed, despite the fact that working on *Twilight Zone*, his first studio-financed feature, had represented a major career break when he took the assignment a year earlier.[11]

House was one of the few crew members other than the defendants who was in a position to know about the potential danger of the scene in question, as well as the illegal use of child actors in an overnight shoot. More than once during preproduction, he objected to the use of child actors in the scene, suggested using dolls, and even provided the names of midget stunt doubles who could be hired instead.[12] House's repeated attempts to dissuade his superiors from using children in the scene became the centerpieces of prosecutor Lea D'Agostino's case against Landis. She even brought it up in her opening arguments:

> The fatal scene, D'Agostino contended, "could have been done without sacrificing any artistic reality, so to speak, without sacrificing any human life whatsoever."
>
> For example, second assistant director Anderson House, she said, will testify that he suggested using midgets or dolls rather than the children. However, House was told by [unit production manager] Allington that Landis "did not think dolls or dummies would give him the real-life effect...."[13]

After John Landis rejected the suggestions, House became increasingly eager to conceal the fact that children were involved. On the night of the filming, for instance, House issued orders that the children be referred to as "the Vietnamese" on all headset communication, so that fire and safety officials would not become aware of their presence on the set.[14] Eventually, House was granted immunity from prosecution in return for his testimony.

House's parallel decisions, first to become a "friendly witness," and then to "dissociate" himself from the disaster by taking a Smithee credit, situate him in this essay. When he applied for the name "Smithee," thus refusing to include *Twilight Zone* in his filmography, the movie became a part of the Smithee oeuvre. But House's motivation differs from that of other Smithee directors because this was his first chance to work on such a high-profile, big-budget feature, and (if not for the accident) the film would have been a stepping stone to larger projects. By erasing the film from his resumé, House was trying to erase his involvement in, and perhaps responsibility for, the accident on the set.

It was not the artistic or financial performance of the film, therefore, that prompted the Smithee pseudonym, but the task of keeping the (assistant) director "good." As it happened, House's career in film never materialized, and whether this was due to the absence of the *Twilight Zone* screen credit, common knowledge about his role in the tragedy, or House's testimony against Landis and the rest of the crew, we will never know for sure. It is worth resting a little with this last possibility, however. No matter how real the moral outrage against Landis and his crew, House still sat in the witness chair and named the names of his former employers. After the grand jury indictment, crew members of *Twilight Zone* who cooperated with the prosecution reported being "blackballed" in the film community (camera operator Steve Lydecker and at least thirty others, according to the *Los Angeles Herald Examiner*), but their claims were impossible to support in a period of generally high unemployment in the movie industry.[15] Given the role that informers have played in Hollywood's history, could the Smithee credit also represent House's futile desire to remain anonymous in the midst of media attention concerning the trial? To dissociate his name from the equally career-damaging label of "informer"?

Blacklisting and Self-Censorship

> Only by a witness's naming names and giving details, it was said,
> could the [House Un-American Activities] Committee be certain
> that his break with the past was genuine. The demand for names
> was not a quest for evidence, it was a test of character. The
> naming of names had shifted from a means to an end.
>
> —Victor Navasky, *Naming Names*

There are many reasons why an artist would attach a name other than his or her own to a work of art as a matter of historical or (more simply) public record. Stage names can be used to cover an ethnic identity; a name can be too politically charged to publish either in a regime of state censorship or in an environment such as the one that prevailed during the McCarthy era. In each of these cases, the writer or artist might not want the work in question to taint his or her "record," if it involved a political or an aesthetic compromise.[16] More recently, pseudonyms have been adopted by screenwriters brought in as "script doctors" on films that they would rather not be associated with permanently.[17] Whenever a pseudonym is employed, these possibilities are invoked, whether or not the different conditions are present.

The strategies for working through and around censorship developed by those blacklisted in Hollywood during the McCarthy era (either for being named by a witness friendly to the HUAC, or by refusing to name names), have led us directly to the pseudonym as *person*, in the guise of "Alan Smithee." Within five years after the sentencing of the Hollywood Ten, for example, there were already several systems in place which allowed one to work under a false name.[18] One possibility was to find a "front," that is, a writer who was not blacklisted who would stand in from beginning to end for the blacklistee in negotiations with the studio. Another option was to work directly with the producer and director of a film while using a pseudonym. One could also more or less freelance using a pseudonym, because there was an active black market for scripts at that time. Some blacklisted writers had so much success writing under a pseudonym that they were able to sell their work to studios (on the black market) on the basis of their pseudonymous filmography.[19] There were even a few instances of pseudonyms themselves being officially blacklisted, after the real identities of the authors had become well known.

The twisted logic at work here has created entertaining moments as well as painful ones. In his recent memoir of the blacklist era, Frank Tarloff relates the following anecdote of how he and his director, Sheldon Leonard, came to find the right pseudonym:

> Well, go think up a name. Suddenly, the only name in the world was Frank Tarloff. I think it was my wife who solved my problem. Our son's name is Erik Sheppard Tarloff; why not become Erik Sheppard.
>
> I told Sheldon that's who I now was and he submitted Erik Sheppard to the William Morris Agency, who represented the show, as a new writer he'd discovered.... I didn't understand until some time later why the Morris Agency balked.
>
> "So pick a name that sounds like every other comedy writer's name," Sheldon told me.
>
> Every other comedy writer had a name like Hal Kanter, Larry Gelbart, Sid Dorfman, Artie Stander, Danny and Doc Simon, Milt Josefsberg, Aaron Rubin, Mel Tolkin, Sherwood Schwartz, Hal Goodman.... There were about a hundred-or-so of us writing all the comedy on TV in those days, and I'd say at least ninety percent of them had names in that ethnic persuasion.
>
> With that little hint, I eventually came up with David Adler. Sheldon submitted David Adler to the William Morris Agency as his new "find," received their blessing, and I understood why Erik Sheppard, while prettier, had never stood a chance.[20]

What Tarloff discovered was that a screenwriter's pseudonym needed to signify Jewishness—that same characteristic that actors have traditionally altered their names to avoid. According to Sheldon Leonard, the name "Erik Sheppard" was understood by the William Morris Agency to represent one of two unacceptable possibilities: either the writer was not of the stereotypical ethnic background, or the name was an easily detectable pseudonym. This was still relatively early in the blacklist era, however, and as the fifties progressed, and Hollywood continued to react to McCarthyism, pseudonyms acquired a distinctive life of their own.

In Tarloff's case, which was the most typical, the pseudonym had a monetary life: "He'd have to pay me, as a 'new' writer, a bit less for the first script written by the pseudonym, but by the second one, I'd be back to my normal fee." It is in the process by which a false name takes on an exchange-value of its own, or is treated as a real name by the censoring authorities, that we detect the first echoes of Smithee. A false name could be *notorious*; it could mean more than the absence of a proper name. Furthermore, because of the unusual circumstance that many pseudonyms were in use at the same time in the same industry, there arose an opportunity for a certain slippage of signification between them.

By this point in the late 1950s, writers like Dalton Trumbo (who technically ended the blacklist when he got screen credit for *Spartacus* in 1960) had achieved a distinct kind of notoriety. In 1957 Trumbo won an Oscar for Best Original Screenplay for *The Brave One*, using the name "Robert Rich." The inquisitive press realized that this was a pseudonym, and that Trumbo was the most likely blacklisted writer with that particular pseudonym. When he was interviewed about it by *The Nation* soon after the Academy Awards, Trumbo admitted to having written many scripts for the black market, and allowed that he had even won Oscars for "some of them." In an article detailing Trumbo's career as a blacklisted writer, Jeffrey Smith comments:

> The interview helped Trumbo enhance his exchange value by allowing him to dissociate himself from bad films that he had written while, at the same time, linking himself to excellent films with which he had actually no connection.[21]

Smith argues further that "a blacklisted writer's name had become a rather unusual form of product differentiation."[22] In other words, by the time the blacklist had ended, numerous unclaimed scripts had been publicly lauded, and any of their possible authors could become a valuable commodity. Thereafter, an obscure name acquired new power: all authorless successes lined up behind the pseudonym, all B-movies or flops were forgotten. Smithee shares with the blacklist-era pseudonym the capacity to absorb failure and reconstitute an author's good name.

Twilight Zone: **The Franchise**

Something apart from our knowledge of the accident sets Landis's segment of *Twilight Zone* apart from most of the other Smithee films. This film differs in content, and in tone, from Smithee's usual thrillers (*Appointment with Fear*, 1987), romantic comedies (*The Iron Cowboy*, 1969), and made-for-TV movies (*City in Fear*, 1980). Probably because of the legacy left by Rod Serling in his original television series, Landis's contribution to *Twilight Zone: The Movie* takes a political position—the fight against racism and bigotry—and creates a cautionary moral tale out of it.

The film is designed as an "anthology" divided into four segments, each roughly the length of an episode of the original *Twilight Zone* series. Landis directed the prologue and first episode; the other three episodes were directed by Steven Spielberg, Joe Dante, and George Miller. Landis's segment is much truer to the original series than are the other two new stories in the compilation (the last is a remake of an episode from the original show). A voice reminiscent of Serling's introduces the narrative segment, which takes place in the present and teaches a bigoted protagonist the lesson of "walking a mile in the shoes" of those he hates. In the parallel—and morally just—universe of the Twilight Zone, the protagonist Bill Connor (Vic Morrow) inexplicably finds himself in Nazi-occupied France, the Klan-dominated South, and wartime Vietnam, where he is hailed as Jewish, black, and a member of the Vietcong, respectively. Landis's segment, by far the most politically heavy-handed of the four, was criticized by reviewers for its clumsiness.[23] In the early 1980s, the segment's tone was unusual, a throwback to Serling's era, when one's political point of view was more visibly at stake in the entertainment industry. Rod Serling created the series in 1959, in fact, partly to provide a refuge for writers of leftist persuasion from the political pressures of the blacklist and McCarthyism. Television's relatively low profile in the late 1950s ensured that the genre of the "science fiction parable" was virtually ignored by the censors and could be employed as a vehicle for social critique.[24] The angry, moralizing voice of the *Twilight Zone* series was the embattled left's response not just to social problems (such as bigotry and class prejudice), but also to the censorship and self-censorship of the blacklist era that was still a recent and personal memory.

The shift in authorship from the writer to the director (a subject of much of the dialogue around Smithee) is a vital part of the scenarios of both *The Twilight Zone* and blacklisting. Serling's series, which ran until 1964, encompassed and enacted this historical moment of transition. During that time Serling transformed himself from a writer of radio and television plays, to the writer *and* director of *The Twilight Zone*, to a figure on camera, a television *auteur*, who would stand in for both the writer and director. Serling might even be regarded as the embodiment of the pseudonym—no matter who wrote the script or directed the episode, Serling, as host, subsumed their authorship. Eventually Landis would utilize Serling's ghostly authority in his own anachronistic morality tale. Meanwhile, the scriptwriters who had been targeted by McCarthyism found themselves in a studio- and, later, in an *auteur*-driven entertainment industry, where one might even say they were "relieved" of their official capacity as authors. This shifted the burden of interpretation, authorship, and responsibility to the role of the director.

What Is Behind Smithee?

> The Writers' Guild had allowed people to use pseudonyms for years.... But at the Directors' Guild we wanted to be careful about any use of a pseudonym. There had to be a good reason for a guy not to put his name on a show. We felt that if a fellow did the work, he should be held accountable.
>
> —John Rich, executive producer of *MacGyver*[25]

With the idea of the responsibility of the director in mind, we can return to the question of who wrote what. In 1991 Larry Ceplair posed this exact question—"Does it matter who wrote what?"—to several ex-blacklistees.

> Abraham Polonsky answered: "Yes it matters, no it does not matter." If it is a good movie, an award-winning movie, or a history-changing movie, then he thinks it matters. For the ordinary run of movies, however, it does not.[26]

If we ignore the first two conditions ("good" and "award-winning"), which by definition do not characterize the Smithee oeuvre, we are left with "history-changing." Is this, too, part of what *cannot* be behind Smithee? Can a history-changing film become a Smithee film?

In order to receive a Smithee credit, a director has to prove his or her case to the DGA: to prove that he or she has been unfairly burdened with the responsibility of a picture going sour.

> "It's like going to court," said one such [anonymous] director who recently went through the process. "They ask a lot of hostile questions. If they suspect you want to remove your credit because you're embarrassed by your own work or because the studio re-cut a scene, they tell you to piss off."[27]

What prevents these mock trials from absolving the Smithee director of responsibility? After all, some blacklisted artists used their anonymity to hide from their mistakes (or to make easy money writing B-movies), but these lapses of judgment have not made it into the archetype of the blacklisted writer. On the contrary, they have come to define Smithee.

Perhaps the Smithee oeuvre is judged more harshly by critics than films that are simply not commercially or artistically successful because of a perceived absence of ideological meaning in the pseudonym. What does it mean, in the context of other pseudonymous products, to call the Smithee decision "ego-driven," for example? It is more than a critique of the director's personality; it could be read as a moral judgment on the use of the pseudonym for personal or aesthetic reasons, and not socio-historical reasons. Should we, then, set the record straight? Should the study of Smitheeness recuperate each minitrial of authorship at the Directors Guild, assigning Smithee movies to others' filmographies and biographies? Judging from the responses to Ceplair's question, "Does it matter who wrote what?," the answer is no. Polonsky, the blacklisted writer who thinks that "for the ordinary movie it doesn't matter," will not reveal the titles of the movies he wrote—he will only acknowledge them if they are credited to him by another source.[28] Yet the last year has seen (in the "celebration" of the fiftieth anniversary of the blacklist) significant revision of 1950s screen credits, with several pseudonyms replaced by the true names of blacklisted writers. Is there an argument, then, that David Lynch should be "outed" as the deposed director of the television version of *Dune*?[29] Perhaps we should insist instead that the films have two authors: Smithee, and a parenthetical one.

Rather than fully engage with the dialectics of lustration, I would like to consider the origins of the impulse to out the Smithee directors. Each pseudonymous product discussed here has a blind spot necessary for its functioning. A collective lapse of memory must occur along with a personal one. Everybody knew, for example, that Dalton Trumbo wrote the screenplay for *The Brave One* and won an Oscar, but it could not be publicly acknowledged at that time. Not until 1985 did the Academy award Oscars to Michael Wilson and Carl Foreman for writing *The Bridge on the River Kwai* in 1957. And everybody knew that the director and crew of *Twilight Zone: The Movie* were in some way responsible for the accident on the set—even if it were only for an act of recklessness—and that they would not be held legally responsible in the public record. The only remaining evidence of something unsettled in the case is an obscure film credit to Alan Smithee.

To locate this blind spot behind Smithee is not to blame Landis and House for their roles in the *Twilight Zone* accident, but rather to point to the hubristic nature of the moviemaking itself. Landis's hubris was to make the scene as realistic as possible, to recreate the conditions of the Vietnam War with meticulous care. The three people who were "disguised" as Vietnamese during the shooting of the scene (Vic Morrow as Bill Connor as a Vietcong soldier, the two children referred to as "the Vietnamese" over the headsets) were actually killed. The connection between the filmmaker's quest for realism and the nature of the accident was by no means overlooked by those involved in the trial, either. In fact, Judge Brian Crahan's decision at the preliminary hearing to proceed with a trial was based entirely on the director's quest for "cinematic reality":

> All of the principals on the production had one object in mind: the creation of a final illusion which had dynamics, explosives and a feeling of the awesome import of simulated eventual death and hopelessness.... Unfortunately, the attempt to obtain visual truth led to death, without any articulated specific rhyme or reason.[30]

Chief prosecutor D'Agostino would refer to this motivation throughout the jury trial, as well, claiming that Landis's "desire to achieve absolute realism at any cost.... led to the deaths of the three actors."[31] Gradually, the assumption that the accident was caused by the film's realist aspirations became commonly accepted by the wider Hollywood community, where the tragedy was linked to advances in technology and special effects that "str[ove] for greater and greater realism." Yet this claim presents a paradox: was it the progressive presence of special effects and advanced technology (the explosions, the helicopter shot) or the reactionary absence of them (Landis's assertion that dolls or dummies "would not give a real-life effect") that was to blame? The appeals court judge who upheld Judge Crahan's decision invoked one of the most notorious cases of a "real-life effect," D. W. Griffith's climactic ice floe sequence in *Way Down East* (1920):

> "This isn't Nickelodeon time anymore," [Judge Gordon Ringer] said. "I should have thought that after 75 years somebody might have thought it inappropriate to put Lillian Gish on an ice floe and send her into the middle of Niagara Falls to make a movie."[32]

According to an appeals court judge with a good memory, the impulse that got Landis in trouble has been around since the early days of American film; Griffith filmed the famous sequence during a brief thaw in a blizzard, before special effects as we know them set new standards for cinematic realism.[33] Judge Ringer's pointed comment implies that Landis's quest for verisimilitude was not necessarily a result of special effects or their misapplication. Rather, the urge to obtain a "real-life effect" is inherent to filmmaking; all films contain the capacity for this kind of tragedy.[34] As established in one trial of authorship—the dimension of the pseudonym—House's Smithee credit could be read as the kernel of moral responsibility in the Smithee oeuvre, or, what happens when Smithee is invoked to keep the last picture "good" and not just successful. In the trial of authorship presided over by Judges Crahan and Ringer, however, the Smithee credit in the *Twilight Zone* tragedy reveals the burden that accompanies all films striving for cinematic realism. It is a goal that seems to bear no more moral responsibility now than it did before the accident.

One could go even further, and read Landis's hubris in terms of the film's content[35] (as opposed to the legal record or the act of simulating war). The film metonymically fuses the experiences of the Holocaust, of racial terror in the South, and of the Vietnam War into one moral lesson. Vic Morrow does not undergo any physical transformation when he is suddenly hailed as Jewish, or African American, or Vietnamese; we understand him to be transformed because of the reactions of those around him. The quest for realism is abandoned, since the burden of seeing Bill Connor as "other" is placed on the viewer. In a way, Landis is faithful to Serling's vision, in which a protagonist who represents the norm in every way, but is close-minded toward those outside the norm, undergoes a change through contact with an alien dimension or alien way of life. Serling had neither the budget nor the inclination to strive for cinematic realism. Instead, he would usually reroute the vision of what was "alien" through his protagonists' perspective. But in the years between Serling's series and Landis's reenactment, the country came to a different understanding of racial and ethnic identity, and this change, too, makes Landis's segment seem anachronistic. The slippage from self to other, and from one other to the next, is too easy.

It is no accident that Smithee films are not about the Holocaust, Hiroshima, or any politically controversial (and not just sensational) topic. The Smithee movie cannot be a "history-changing movie," in which it might matter who wrote or directed what. How do we understand what a "history-changing movie" might be, either by Abraham Polonsky's definition, or by our own? I would reroute the question through a figure on the periphery of the *Twilight Zone* affair: Steven Spielberg. In the very early stages of the investigation, one of the witnesses (a truck driver) claimed that Spielberg had been on the *Twilight Zone* set on the day of the disaster. In a two-paragraph letter to the investigating bureau, Spielberg denied that he had ever even been to that location.[36] Indeed, Spielberg could not have been further from Landis's set, nor could he be further from the Smithee pseudonym. His name is essentially the negation of everything disastrous; he signifies success in every dimension of moviemaking, including, most recently, the history-changing one. With *Schindler's List* (1993), *Amistad* (1997), and *Saving Private Ryan* (1998), Spielberg has reached new heights of striving for cinematic realism: this is the history-changing element of his work on a formal level. In each film Spielberg approaches a historical subject in order to reinterpret it: his films are, literally, history-changing. Even though these three films share settings with Landis's segment of the *Twilight Zone*, they avoid his anachronistic adoption of the source television program's moralism; rather, each film resonates with its contemporary moment. And finally, in each film, Spielberg demonstrates how to take proper "responsibility" for one's directorial pursuits. In other words, Smithee cannot direct a history-changing movie, because in addition to its other absences, Smithee is the absence of Spielberg.

Smithee as a Trial of Authorship

> The spectacle is not a collection of images; rather, it is a social
> relationship between people that is mediated by images.
>
> —Guy Debord, *The Society of the Spectacle*

The trial of authorship that leads to taking a Smithee is a mundane event relative to the other trials encountered in the history of naming names. What the *Twilight Zone* credit reveals about the Smithee oeuvre is that its boundaries have been set by the much larger discursive logic of the pseudonym, and that the trial of Smithee authorship is really about what kind of responsibility a director assumes when he or she agrees to make a film. Smithee shares a "monopolization of the realm of appearances" with Debord's spectacle, but in the end it transcends that realm and manifests itself in a social space, much as the proceedings of the HUAC and the lists of names and pseudonyms that resulted from it could not fully account for the reality of Hollywood in the fifties. In the case of Anderson House, a Smithee credit on *Twilight Zone* dissociated him only from the finished film. He could not erase his testimony in the trial, or his role in the disaster. While Smithee is available to absorb failure, and make "[e]verything that appears ... good; [so that] whatever is good will appear," it can correct only the realm of appearances. Everything else remains known.

Notes

1. The variant spelling "Alan" Smithee is adopted in this essay, because that spelling is the one that appears in the credits of *Twilight Zone: The Movie*.

2. On the set of a film, the second assistant director answers to the production office, and not necessarily to the director. For this reason, the job serves more often as a path to a career in production than to a career in direction. The responsibilities of the second AD, as described by the Directors Guild of America in their training program, include the following tasks: "constantly communicate the on-going status of all elements of production to everyone associated with the production; distribute paperwork, schedules, scripts, and revisions; inform ADs constantly as to [each one's] location and the location of actors and crew; relay changes in schedule and plans to actors, crew, atmosphere [extras], and production office; help solve problems that interrupt actual shooting; monitor set safety and communicate safety problems; ensure the fulfillment of union and guild contractual requirements." Given these job functions, House could just as easily have been held liable for what happened on the set of this film as the director himself. See Directors Guild Producer Training Program, "Second Assistant Director Trainee Job Description," http://www.dgptp.org/jobdes.html.

3. For a detailed account of the incident and ensuing trial, see Stephen Farber and Marc Green, *Outrageous Conduct: Art, Ego and the* Twilight Zone *Case* (New York: Arbor House, 1988), or Ron LaBrecque, *Special Effects: Disaster at the Twilight* (New York: Scribner, 1988).

4. Paul Feldman, "Long-Delayed Trial in Three 'Twilight Zone' Deaths Opens," *Los Angeles Times* (4 Sept. 1986): I:3.

5. Aljean Harmetz, "Hollywood Ambivalent as Film Trial Nears End," *New York Times* (20 Apr. 1987): I:15:1.

6. For more on the relationships among the Directors Guild, the Motion Picture Production Code, and Smithee, see chapter 1 of the present volume.

7. Stuart Black, "Danger on the Film Set," *New York Times Magazine* 4 Dec. 1983: 124.

8. Randall Sullivan, "Death in the Twilight Zone," *Rolling Stone* 424 (21 June 1984): 33–41, 79–80.

9. Although the film was an anthology project, it was Landis who first took an interest in it, and steered the idea through the initial studio arrangements and preproduction. Landis even had a hand in "casting" the other directors, and saw the project as a whole as his creation (see Farber and Green).

10. Michael Apted et al., letter, *Rolling Stone* 432 (11 Oct. 1984): 7.

11. Farber and Green 199.

12. LaBrecque 10–11.

13. Feldman 3.

14. Farber and Green 129.

15. "Film Crew Reports Reprisals for Testifying" (AP), *New York Times* (12 Dec. 1983): I:30:6.

16. Equally relevant to Smithee, but unfortunately outside the scope of this essay, is the pseudonym in the context of censorship and dissident culture in Eastern Europe, especially in the period between the *Twilight Zone* series and the *Twilight Zone* movie. A longer project could draw interesting parallels between the highly politicized use of pseudonyms on the other side of the Iron Curtain and the development of the Smithee oeuvre.

17. See Kenneth Turan, "A Lean, Mean Machine," review of *Ronin*, dir. John Frankenheimer, *Los Angeles Times* (25 Sept. 1998): F:1+. "The other writing credit reads Richard Weisz, but figuring out that it's a pseudonym for David Mamet (who apparently no longer believes in using his name on shared writing credits) wouldn't have been difficult even if the situation hadn't become public knowledge" (F:19).

18. For two in-depth treatments of the blacklist era in Hollywood, see Victor Navasky, *Naming Names* (New York: Penguin, 1991), and Larry Ceplair and Steven Englund, *The Inquisition in Hollywood: Politics in the Film Community 1930–1960* (New York: Anchor, 1980).

19. Jeffrey Smith, "'A Good Business Proposition': Dalton Trumbo, *Spartacus*, and the End of the Blacklist," *The Velvet Light Trap* 23 (spring 1989): 75–100.

20. Frank Tarloff, "What's in a name?" *Written By* 10.10 (Oct. 1997) 25 May 1999, http://www.wga.org/journal/1997/1097/what.html.

21. Smith 82.

22. Smith 90.

23. LaBrecque 237.

24. J. Hoberman, "America's Twilight Zone," *Visions from the Twilight Zone*, ed. Arlen Schumer (San Francisco: Chronicle, 1990) 154.

25. See Jerry Roberts, "Alan Smithee," *Films in Review* 40 (Nov. 1989) 529. Both the pilot episode of *MacGyver* and the first season episode titled "The Heist" (1985) contain Smithee directing credits. John Rich is also one of those who is credited with christening the Smithee name.

26. Larry Ceplair, "Who Wrote What?" *Cineaste* 18.2 (1991): 21.

27. Peter Bart, "In Hollywood, the Name is the Game," *Variety* 21 (Mar. 1980): 3.

28. A brief look at this question in the context of Eastern European censorship: both Krzysztof Kieslowski and Krzysztof Zanussi were asked after 1989 if they would go back and reedit films that had pieces cut out by the censors. They both answered no, that the films as they exist now serve as historical testimony to what was or was not allowed under censorship. Krzyzstof Kieslowski, *Kieslowski on Kieslowski*, ed. Danusia Stok (London: Faber and Faber, 1993).

29. "Redone 'Dune,' Sans Lynch Sig, Will Work On Air, MCA TV Sez," *Variety* 1 June 1988: 83.

30. Judith Cummings, "Director Standing Trial For Deaths on Film Set," *New York Times* (23 July 1986): I:16:1.

31. Marcia Chambers, "'Realism at any Cost' Caused Movie Deaths, a Jury is Told," *New York Times* (4 Sept. 1986): II:12:1.

32. Cummings I:16:1.

33. From an interview with Lillian Gish on the subject: "This was the millennium, and we were taking the first baby steps in this great miracle. So, you see, when we went out and risked our lives, that didn't seem important. It

was only important what was up on the screen. That's all that mattered. So we wouldn't use doubles or fake anything because we were sure the audience would sense that something was wrong, it wasn't real. Everything had to be real!" See Ben Grauer, "Lillian Gish: Reflections," *The American Cinema*, ed. Donald Staples (Philippines: USIA Forum Reader Series, 1991) 67–68.

34. There is a further irony to unpack in this same comment. Even though Lillian Gish, Griffith, and crew did freeze on a real ice floe, it was in White River Junction, Vermont. The scene was intercut with footage of Niagara Falls, creating a seamless memory of cinematic realism for Judge Ringer.

35. In his review of *Twilight Zone: The Movie*, Vincent Canby understatedly leaves Landis for last, dismissing the individual failures of the other three segments to arrive at the following pronouncement: "John Landis, currently represented by the stylish 'Trading Places,' is responsible for the film's first segment, a muddled antibigotry lesson about a fellow who hates blacks, Jews and Orientals." Canby uses the cynical language of an unfavorable film review to account for every possibility presented in this essay with multiple meanings of "responsible" in his sentence. Vincent Canby, "Film: 'Twilight Zone' is Adapted to the Big Screen" *New York Times* (24 June 1983): III:16:1.

36. "Director Denies Presence at Fatal Movie Crash" (UPI), *New York Times* (12 Dec. 1982): I:30:6.

CHAPTER 6

Signateurism and the
Case of Allen Smithee

Christian Keathley

In a recent essay titled "The Unauthorized Auteur Today," Dudley Andrew suggests that, while it has once again become acceptable in film studies to discuss the *auteur*, what that term means has changed decisively. The contemporary director, he writes, is no longer "an individual with a vision or even a program" as the great classical *auteurs* were. If they once did so, Andrew writes, "auteurs today turn not away from the world but toward it.... Not long ago, one aptly referred to Fellini's 'world,' or Ingmar Bergman's or John Ford's.... But today, should we speak of Spike Lee's 'world,' when his is designed to fold itself into our world?"[1]

In this scenario, contemporary directors fail at that crucial level of cinematic authorship described by Andrew Sarris in his cornerstone essay, "Notes on the *Auteur* Theory in 1962."[2] That is, while many contemporary directors may display a consistent visual style from film to film, they fail to display, along with and through that style, an ethic, a worldview. What this failure points to, as Dudley Andrew concludes, is the extent to which contemporary cinema has become "part of the media economy that has reduced that auteur to a sign, indeed, precisely a signature."[3] That is, the received idea of "the *auteur*" that filmmakers, critics, and audiences now accept amounts to little more than a trademark, another commodity brand name displayed with pride even though there is no history of quality or distinction behind it. If we take this reduction that Andrew describes as the current state of affairs, then the *auteur* theory—which was so useful in the reevaluation of classical Hollywood cinema, and which was almost single-handedly responsible for the academic institutionalization of film studies—is no longer applicable. What is needed instead, as Dudley Andrew perhaps indirectly suggests, is a theory of the signature.

Fortunately, in a 1975 lecture on the works of the French poet Francis Ponge, Jacques Derrida offered just this: a theory of the signature. That lecture, which was later published in book form under the title *Signsponge*, provides us with a fully articulated program for *signateurist* criticism.[4] I believe that, given the situation described above, now is the perfect opportunity for a reconsideration of Derrida's project. Further, given the crisis that many scholars believe the discipline of film studies is now facing, *signateurism* may prove to be a productive way to open up for exploration new critical and theoretical ground.[5]

I would like to begin this essay by reviewing the basic tenets of the *signateur* theory and, in the process, by revisiting *auteurism* as outlined by Andrew Sarris. The two theories have some interesting points in common, and it is by such a comparison that we may begin to see more clearly the ways in which Derrida's theory is a complement to Sarris's. I will then suggest that perhaps the most fruitful place to begin the project of *signateurist* criticism is with the films of Allen Smithee. Finally, I will provide a brief *signateurist* reading of his 1981 film *Student Bodies*.

From *Auteurism* to *Signateurism*

Both the *auteur* and *signateur* theories identify three levels or modalities or registers. For Sarris, the three levels are linked to the *auteur*/director; for Derrida, they have to do more specifically with the signature. Sarris begins, "The first premise of the *auteur* theory is the technical competence of a director as a criterion of value. . . . A great director has to be at least a good director."[6] Derrida's theory provides something of a variant on this criterion. He notes that the first of the ways in which a writer signs her work is in the most literal sense—simply attaching (or signing) her name to the work in question. So in Derrida's theory, technical competence is also a given: an author must indeed be able to write in order to sign her name. But this process of signing for Derrida is not merely writing, it is the act of someone "engaged in authenticating (if possible) the fact that it is indeed he who writes."[7] This modality of the signature has to do both with claiming or accepting responsibility and with authorization: the signature marks the property in question (the text) as originating with its author/creator.

At the second level or register, Sarris and Derrida are in clear agreement. This level, Sarris writes, "is the distinguishable personality of the director as a criterion of value. Over a group of films a director must exhibit certain recurring characteristics of style which serve as his signature."[8] Derrida echoes Sarris in describing the second modality of the signature as "the set of idiomatic marks that a signer might leave by accident or intention in his product.... We sometimes call this the style, the inimitable idiom of a writer, sculptor, painter, or orator."[9] This characteristic is, of course, one that has been long and commonly valued in humanities studies.

It is at the crucial third level that Sarris and Derrida part ways. Sarris writes:

> The third and ultimate premise of the *auteur* theory is concerned with interior meaning, the ultimate glory of the cinema as an art. Interior meaning is extrapolated from the tension between a director's personality and his material. This conception of interior meaning comes close to what Astruc defines as *mise-en-scène*, but not quite. It is not quite the vision of the world a director projects, not quite his attitude toward life. It is ambiguous in any literary sense because part of it is imbedded in the stuff of cinema and cannot be rendered in non-cinematic terms. Truffaut has called it the temperature of the director on the set, and that is a close approximation of its professional aspect. Dare I come out and say what I think it to be is an élan of the soul?[10]

Interior meaning is thus not simply theme, or worldview, or personality, or vision, or *mise-en-scène*—but it clearly partakes of all of these. It is,

Sarris suggests in summing up, "that intangible difference between one personality and another, all other things being equal."[11] And it is only the clear presence of this indefinable quality throughout a set of works that can lift a director from the ranks of mere stylist (or *metteur-en-scène*) to that ultimate position of *auteur*.

For Derrida, the third level is equally crucial, but far more complex. Derrida first suggests that, at this third level, the name of the author is embedded within the text—in its imagery, its objects, its things—at what Derrida designates as a point or points of abyss. These points of embedding of the writer's name can be thought of as seeds "out of which the text has grown, by a process of metaphorical and intertextual development."[12] It is the critic's task to retrace this process, to locate the points of abyss via the process of antonomasia, the slippage from the proper into the common noun form. Derrida explains that this third modality can be understood as similar to the practice of heraldry, wherein a set of figures emblazoned on a shield references the name of the bearer; it references the name, its meanings, its associations, its functions. Thus, the images or figures that mark the points of abyss in the text also designate an association to the name of the *signateur*.

Next, once the name of the author has been transformed, worked over, and dispersed throughout the text, that common noun or thing becomes a metaphor for all compositional practice. The points of *mise-en-abyme* where the name is embedded thus evoke another function of heraldry, "the device whereby an image of a shield is represented on the surface of a shield,"[13] where the whole is represented in miniature in one of its parts. As Richard Rand explains, for Derrida this "placement in the abyss" is "meant to designate the way in which the operations of reading and writing are represented in the text, and *in advance*, as it were, of any other possible reading."[14] Derrida explains:

> Thirdly, and it is more complicated here, we may designate as general signature, or signature of the signature, the fold of the placement in the abyss where, after the manner of the signature in the current sense, the work of writing designates, describes, and inscribes itself as act (action

and archive), signs itself before the end by affording us the opportunity to read: I refer to myself, this is writing, I am a writing, this is writing—which excludes *nothing* since, when the placement in the abyss succeeds, and is thereby decomposed and produces an event, it is the other, the thing as other, that signs.[15]

In short, then, via this third modality, the *signateur* designates the way in which her texts are to be deciphered, and the key to this deciphering is in the author's name.

In reading the works of Francis Ponge, for example, Derrida found that, with a simple slip, Ponge became *éponge* (the French word for "sponge"), and with this slip Derrida discovered that Ponge's poetry is filled with spongelike images—images of soaking and wiping, drawing in, filtering and cleansing. Beyond this, the sponge also becomes the metaphor for a theory of writing:

> It loses and as easily recovers its form, which is neither proper nor im-proper, neither simply a thing, nor simply vegetal, nor simply animal. They call this thing either a *zoophyte*, an animal plant, or else the substance "deriving from a marine zoophyte" (Littré). Solid or plastic, full of air or water, what does the sponge resemble? An animal swollen with water, it is, in effect, a medusa. . . .
>
> Able to hold gases or liquid alternatively, "to fill itself with wind or water," the sponge is, above all else, writing.[16]

Elsewhere, Derrida applied the *signateur* theory to, among others, the works of Jean Genet (*genêt* = broomflower and horse), Hegel (which slips into *aigle* or eagle), and Kant (*Kante* = border or edge). From these slips, Derrida generated analyses and critiques of these authors' works, demonstrating the ways in which the authors' texts are extended mani-festations of the meanings and associations available in their names.

Derrida's preoccupation here with the proper name is an impor-tant element in his ongoing critique of logocentrism. As he has ex-plained, the logocentric tradition in Western philosophy—the tradition that subordinates writing to speech, and speech to thought—emerges with the development of the phonetic alphabet, the technology that brings speech and writing into accord; and it was above all the desire to memorialize the proper name that initiated this technological development. Thus, as the proper name was crucial in the consolidation of logocentrism, it is, for Derrida, to be equally crucial in its disruption, and in the development of an alternative compositional practice—one that returns to writing its original double value of graphic and phonetic elements. As one of his most explicitly articulated programs for such a transformation, the *signateur* theory is also part of Derrida's ongoing critique of logocentric notions of "origin" and "center," concepts commonly tied to, among other things, authorship. But here, Derrida's critique proceeds by taking the notion of author as origin to an absurd extreme. Like his model Francis Ponge, Derrida imagines an intimate, motivated relationship between a name and the thing it signifies—in this case, the name of an author and the works he signs; and like Saussure, who thought he had discovered anagrams of the names of the gods in Latin poetry, Derrida plays on the instability in language to prove the point. Putting his faith in what language knows, exploring what one scholar called "the traces left by meaning's adventures,"[17] Derrida shows how even (perhaps especially) the absurd results in the production of knowledge where it is least expected.

As Robert Ray has explained, in performing a *signateurist* reading, "Derrida assumes the roles of both the patient who generates an associative discourse and the analyst who reads it." He is both "performing a decipherment and producing the very enigma to be solved."[18] Thus, the reading the critic offers via this third modality is less a retrieval of meaning from the text than a projection of meaning into it, for while the first two levels of Derrida's *signateur* theory can indeed be said to originate with the author, the crucial third level marks a shift in the site of meaning production from author to reader/critic, from production to reception. But the reading the critic offers is not simply a freely projected one in the manner of reader-response criticism. Like a surrealist game, the *signateur* theory sets out in advance certain rules or parameters that must be adhered to, and the critic's analysis is both initiated by and limited to the meanings and associations available in the name of the author. By following this procedure, the reader is only bringing to light what was already present, but unrevealed: the ways in which the *signateur* has produced and organized her text out of her name. Though Derrida applied the *signateur* theory only to writers, he intended the practice to be used in other domains. In fact, Ray suggests, with its "representation of *diffusion*," *signateurism* "may be more appropriate to film study" than *auteurism*, for this strategy appropriately mimics the randomness and chance of the film production process.[19] This last point is a crucial one, for it points to the omission of a fundamental issue in Andrew Sarris's restatement of then-recent French film theory—an issue which is reintroduced with the *signateur* theory. That issue is automatism.

Automatism and the *Auteur*

Sarris is so often identified simply as the major American proponent of *auteurism* that it is often forgotten that his critical position was more complex, involving a combination of two different approaches, both associated with *Cahiers du cinéma*: *la politique des auteurs* (or *auteurism*) and Bazinian realism. These two positions are hardly the same. Although Bazin, as editor of *Cahiers*, served as a mentor to the young *auteurist* critics, providing them with a forum for their writings, it was Bazin himself who wrote the first critique of the *auteur* policy.[20] And Sarris's "Notes" essay was not merely an articulation of the *auteur* theory, it was also a review of Bazin's position *contra auteurism* and a response to it.

Otherwise, Sarris had been profoundly influenced by Bazin's realist argument, a theoretical and historical position articulated by the French critic most forcefully in the essays that open *What Is Cinema?*, the volume of his collected writings.[21] This position is one that rests on a fundamental assumption: that the production of a representation in photography (and thus, in cinema) is profoundly different from the production of a representation in the other arts, for with the photographic apparatus, the image is produced "by automatic means."[22] In "The Ontology of the Photographic Image," Bazin wrote,

For the first time, between the originating object and its reproduction there intervenes only the instrumentality of a nonliving agent. For the first time an image of the world is formed automatically, without the creative intervention of man. The personality of the photographer enters into the proceedings only in his selection of the object to be photographed and by way of the purpose he has in mind. Although the final result may reflect something of his personality, this does not play the same role as is played by that of the painter. All the arts are based on the presence of man, only photography derives an advantage from his absence.[23]

This position led Bazin to articulate an aesthetic that privileged not only the long takes and deep focus that respect the totality and continuity of space (the position for which he is most commonly recognized), but also the camera's ability to capture marginal, incidental details in the scene or object depicted. "The aesthetic qualities of photography," Bazin argued,

are to be sought in its power to lay bare the realities. It is not for me to separate off, in the complex fabric of the objective world, here a reflection on a damp sidewalk, there the gesture of a child. Only the impassive lens, stripping its object of all those ways of seeing it, those piled-up preconceptions, that spiritual dust and grime with which my eyes have covered it, is able to present it in all its virginal purity to my attention and consequently to my love.[24]

This sensibility occasionally led Bazin to focus on points of digression in the image. These points were to be found always at the surface, in the image as signifier, not as signified. For example, when describing a scene like the one of Susan Alexander's attempted suicide in *Citizen Kane*, Bazin is delighted to attend to the knob on the bedroom door behind which Kane is locked: "the color of the enamel, the dirt marks at the level of the hand, the shine of the metal worn away" are as important to him as the door's role in the dramatics of the scene.[25] This is the aesthetic sensibility Bazin most privileged, one in which the cinematic image is to be "evaluated not according to what it adds to reality but what it reveals of it."[26]

If Sarris chose to privilege the guiding hand of the director at the expense of the contingencies of the cinematic apparatus, this was perhaps due less to personal taste or critical conviction than to specific historical circumstances. In his review of Bazin's *What Is Cinema?*, Sarris wrote,

> I tend to agree with [*What Is Cinema?* translator] Dr. Gray when he agrees with Jean Mitry's challenge to Bazin's conception of the image "as being evaluated not according to what it adds to reality but what it reveals of it." Mitry contends that the camera reveals not reality itself but a new appearance correlated to the real, but restructured in a frame as arbitrary and artificial as the gilded frame of a painting. But if I agree with Gray and Mitry against Bazin, it is because too much of the modern cinema has abandoned its obligation to restructure reality into meaningful forms. Reality is too often flung in our faces like a dead mackerel to show that the artist is not interested in manipulating us.[27]

If I choose now to agree with Bazin against Gray, Mitry, and Sarris, it is because, at our present historical moment, the pendulum has swung to the opposite extreme. Today, the received idea of an *auteur* is one who controls as thoroughly as possible all the filmic elements available, manipulating the audience to the desired response—all as a sign of one's virtuosity.[28] Few contemporary filmmakers are modest enough to employ the camera's fundamental automatism as a means for discovery in the way Bazin valued it. So we must do it for them, and the *signateur* theory offers the means by which to do it, reintroducing the crucial component of automatism at the level of reception. The critic employing the *signateur* theory gives himself over to the name of the author, exploring its meanings, associations, and permutations, trusting the name to reveal marginal elements in the text as being the determining factors in the logic of its organization.

The Thing Is . . .

Jacques Derrida first proposed the *signateur* theory in 1975 at Yale University's inaugural seminar on "The Thing," that title referring partly to Martin Heidegger's concept of "the thing."[29] A brief review of some of Heidegger's philosophical ideas will be helpful in understanding why Derrida conceived of the *signateur* theory and what he believed its usefulness to be.

Heidegger believed that the essence of modern culture was found in a certain technological orientation which he called *Gestell*, or "enframing."[30] This tendency encourages us to see the objects in our world only in terms of how they can serve us or be used by us. The task Heidegger identified was to find ways to resituate ourselves vis-à-vis these "objects" so that we may see them as "things," pulled into relief against the ground of their functionality. While Heidegger's position sounds, on the one hand, similar to other early twentieth-century aesthetic philosophies that sought to reinvigorate our experience of objects in the world in a radical way (think, for example, of surrealism), it sounds, on the other hand, decidedly Platonic. Even though Heidegger had elsewhere criticized Plato for abandoning the consideration of Being, his position here clearly holds that there is some prior, originary state of objects that we must strive to (re)experience because objects as we encounter them via enframing are distorted or reduced at an essential level.

Quite unlike Plato, however, Heidegger believed that, rather than moving us farther away from this essence, art had the great potential to counter the technological orientation of enframing and reveal the thing-ness of objects. The work of art that reveals thing-ness is not just "the reproduction of some particular entity that happens to be present at any given time; it is, on the contrary, the reproduction of the thing's general essence."[31] The critique of this notion of an originary or essential status is, of course, at the very basis of Derrida's project.[32] But here, again, Derrida carries out his critique not in the conventional sense, but rather by taking the questionable assumption literally—absurdly literally. And again, in yet another radical inversion, Derrida shows that, even when pushing the assumptions beyond the margin of acceptable reason, knowledge is still produced, insight is still gained. Derrida begins by re-thinking Heidegger's basic insight. If, according to Heidegger, a work of art can re-thing the object it represents, what of the work itself? Is it to be relegated to a permanent object status, functioning only as a vehicle for re-vealing thing-ness? The *signateur* theory, Derrida suggests, is the method by which one can reveal the thing-ness of the text itself. He writes:

> by not letting the signature fall outside the text anymore, as an under-signed subscription, and by inserting it into the body of the text [via the third modality of the *signateur* theory], you monumentalize, institute, and erect it into a thing or a stony object. But in doing so, you also lose the identity, the title of ownership over the text: you let it become a monument or a part of the text, as a thing or a common noun.[33]

While Heidegger believed the essential opposition in modern cul-ture was between technology and art, he knew that this had not always been the case: indeed, the origin of the word "art" is found in the Greek *techne*—also the origin of the word "technology." What Derrida is show-ing us how to do, via the *signateur* theory, is to bring art and technology, things and objects, back into balance with one another. This is at the heart of Derrida's overall grammatological project: returning to writing its original double value; recovering a form of writing that combines phonetic and ideographic elements—that is, a writing practice that com-bines the features of technology and of art. Though certain literary and artistic texts (exemplified by those of Francis Ponge) offer a model of this double-valued writing, it is the cinema that enables the practice most thoroughly. With its mixture of words and images—indeed, with its grammar of images—the cinema offers the ultimate opportunity for a double-valued composition. The *signateur* theory, when applied to the cinema, can thus be seen to mimic its object of study, for it employs a critical approach that operates according to the same method or logic as the text it considers.[34]

What's in a Name?

The *auteurist* battle was fought primarily over the films and directors of Hollywood's classical period, and for many, the test case for *auteurism*, especially as it concerns this third level, would probably be Howard Hawks—a director who worked within the studio system for five decades, making films in virtually every one of the major genres, each of which, regardless of setting or story, revealed the same Hawksian world of professionalism and action, responsible men and strong women (or the crazy inverse). I would like to suggest that, just as *auteurism* had its test case in Howard Hawks, it is with Allen Smithee that the practice of *signateurism* finds its test case.

There are several reasons why Smithee is the ideal test case for *signateurism*. First, "Allen Smithee" marks the site of the motion picture industry's denial of automatism. Whereas removing one's name from a film may be an individual director's decision, offering the pseudonym Allen Smithee in its place is the decision of a professional organization (the DGA), one whose interests are, by extension, largely those of the film industry itself. The existence of Allen Smithee is a sign that the motion picture industry regards it as less risky to offer a film signed with a pseudonym, even one which everybody knows to be a mark of inferiority, than it would be to offer a film *sans* director credit. But why? What is the risk of the latter option?

First of all, because the industry's interests are, before anything else, economic, a film released without a director credit might be severely compromised at the box office. Used as we are to seeing credits at the start of a film or in advertisements, even the most casual, inattentive viewer might notice the absence of any acknowledgment of this centering presence and thus might be suspicious of the product. On the other hand, a "Directed by Allen Smithee" credit would more likely go benignly unnoticed by viewers unaware of the phantom director; in addition, those aware of what a "Smithee" designates might be inclined to seek out the film, even if only for its potential status as a camp curiosity. With a credit, then, less economic risk is taken.

Second, the aberration of a film without director credit might encourage in its viewers certain aberrant reading habits—especially those that recognize and are enabled by the cinema's fundamental automatism—and this is an inclination that the industry works hard to control, even in its most despised products. As the symptom of a denial, then, "Allen Smithee" marks a site that we, as film analysts, should immediately investigate.

Furthermore, with a figure like Smithee, one is in no danger of being distracted by the first two modalities of the signature, for they are simply not operative. Failure at the first level is due to the fact that the name attached to the work is not that of its actual director. By refusing to sign his true name, the director in question has refused to authorize and accept responsibility for the work according to Derrida's first principle (for the director does not regard the work as his). In addition, though a person may justify the use of a pseudonym in a variety of ways, it would seem that the main reason Smithee directors conceal their true identities is the fear that they will be regarded as technically incompetent, thus also failing at the first, most basic level of Sarris's criteria of the *auteur*. Regarding the second level, because each Allen Smithee refers to a different person, the likelihood of any stylistic consistency across the works is highly unlikely. With an Allen Smithee film, one is free to focus exclusively on the third level, that is, to concentrate on the name and how it is embedded in things of the text.

With the first two levels (those linked to the author) rendered inoperative, and only the third level (that linked to the reader/critic) functioning, the selection of Smithee most thoroughly and efficiently facilitates the crucial relocation of the site of meaning from author to critic. For if the *auteur* theory is no longer applicable, and meaning no longer finds its source in the director (especially not in this case), then the moniker "Allen Smithee" no longer designates the director of the film, but can now designate only its viewer, its critic. And as Smithee, it is the critic himself who, via the signature approach, embeds his name in the text.

As was explained earlier, a reading of the Smithee signature must begin with the move of antonomasia—the slippage of the name from the proper into the common noun form. The name Smithee, of course, derives from "blacksmith," a tradesman who works with hammer and anvil to shape hot iron; a man whose most common product, as we know from countless Westerns, is horseshoes—objects that can also be used for playing games, or for good luck. But since both the theories in question—*auteurism* and *signateurism*—originate in France, it might be more productive to follow the noun's slippage across languages. This proves to be a fruitful move, for in French, a blacksmith is known as a *forge*. With this, we see clearly why Smithee is appropriate for our study, for the meaning of the name both implicates the act of signing, and calls it into question: precisely the issues at stake in *signateurism*. Further, it is clear that no term could be more appropriately applied to the phenomenon of Allen Smithee, for every Smithee film must be recognized not for its status as authentic, but rather—in contrast to the values of *auteurism*—as a forgery. For even though they all bear the same name, every Allen Smithee film is signed by an impostor. The variation that a "Smithee" works on the process of forging is part of the inversion of values that occurs in the move from *auteurism* to *signateurism*: rather than signing a fraudulent work that he has produced with another's name that is itself associated with value, the Smithee forger offers an impostor's name to an authentic object, but one that is, according to the dominant system, without value.

The uncanny connection between the name Smithee and the act of signing/forging does not end there. For the word "forge" means not only to counterfeit or to reproduce for fraudulent purposes, but also refers to the productive process of giving form or shape to something: a blacksmith forges hot iron, a diplomat forges a treaty, a military leader forges a plan of attack. In all these senses, the term "forge" is a positive one of bringing order, organization, function, and identity to the object in question. This double, even contradictory, meaning of the word "forge"—which inevitably reminds one of the Derridean practice of deconstruction—is also at work in the *signateur* theory. For in applying that theory, the critic "forges" a reading of the text in the positive sense, showing how the text was given shape according to the meanings available in the name of the author. But because this reading is projected onto the text by the critic via the author's name, it is a reading that, according to more traditional critical approaches, would be considered a forged reading in the negative sense, for it points to places of meaning in the text and credits that meaning to the name of the author, even though that meaning was not consciously or explicitly assigned by her. Thus, with the *signateur* theory, the Smithee critic forges a reading of a text that implicates both the meanings of that term.

If the Shoe Fits . . .

As with any theory, the only sure way to know whether *signateurism* will prove useful or not is to try it out. But how will it be possible to determine the success or failure of the experiment? On the one hand, asking in advance what kind of results one should expect plays into the assumptions of the scientistic discourse that Derrida is critiquing. On the other hand, Derrida regularly carried out his critiques by taking up the discourse in question and pushing it past its apparent limits. After all, Derrida's argument is not that traditional doctrines don't result in knowledge, but that theirs are not the only methods that can produce it. Part of the conceit of Western philosophy is its belief that by reducing ornamentation in language—that is, by seeking to render the signifier invisible—one moves closer to truth. With the signature experiment and other of his experimental methods, Derrida seizes this despised ornamentation and makes it the center of his focus. The gamble is that even an approach that foregrounds those elements that traditional methodologies work to eliminate can result in an effect of knowledge.

In conclusion, then, I would like to provide a brief *signateurist* reading of Allen Smithee's *Student Bodies* (1981), a parody of the teen slasher movies that were so popular in the early 1980s. The script and direction of this film are credited to one Mickey Rose, and Allen Smithee is credited as the film's producer. But several sources reveal that Smithee not only carefully supervised the production of this film, he also directed large portions of it.[35] Thus, Smithee's role on *Student Bodies* is precisely analogous to that of *auteurist* test-case Howard Hawks on the 1951 sci-fi classic, *The Thing*. Though credited to director Christian Nyby, *The Thing* clearly bears the mark of Howard Hawks. Indeed, one sourcebook calls it "a Hawks film in all but director credit."[36] Thus, just as *The Thing* is the test case film for the test case director of *auteurism*, *Student Bodies* may be the test case film for the test case director of *signateurism*.

Like the slasher films it parodies, *Student Bodies* features a group of promiscuous teenagers who are successively knocked off by a mysterious, heavy-breathing killer at just the moment when they are about to satisfy their sexual longings. Our young heroine, whose chastity sets her apart from her peers, is hot on the killer's trail, but her proximity to each crime soon sets her up as the prime suspect. Locating a signature figure in *Student Bodies* was not a difficult task. As luck would have it, several people I spoke with who had seen the film before me had already, albeit unwittingly, located the same figure, something which is associated with the film's most memorable character, Mr. Dumpkin. Dumpkin is a monomaniacal high school shop teacher whose one project, which he assigns over and over, is to have his students construct what he describes as "perhaps man's highest cultural achievement": a set of horse-head bookends. When we remember the relationship of the third modality of the signature to heraldry, it becomes easy to imagine the horse-head figure emblazoned on a shield in order to herald its bearer as a blacksmith, a forger of horseshoes. In addition to claiming this as the embedded signature figure, I would like to suggest further that, just as the Smithee name, with its slip into *forge*, implicates the very act of signing, the horse-head bookends function in a similar way. For in them we find a chain of associations reminding us of various issues that come together in the *signateur* theory.

The fact that smiths and forges are known primarily for shoeing horses recalls that, in one of his most famous examples of an object being offered up in all its thingness, Heidegger pointed to a work by Van Gogh—his famous painting *Old Shoes with Laces*. In *The Truth in Painting*, however, Derrida suggested that, for Heidegger, the shoes were not a benign example, selected at random, but were, instead, a highly overdetermined choice, a projection of desire on the part of the philosopher/critic. Projection, Derrida writes, "operates in the choice rather than in the analysis of the model."[37] That is, under analysis, the object-example can easily be made to fit the metaphor or argument in question; it is the prior step, the selection of the object-example, that is the pure projection. As a projection of desire, then, Heidegger's selection of the shoes—indeed, anyone's selection of any object-example—is the selection of a fetish: an otherwise empty object that is then filled with meaning.[38] And for Freud, shoes were the fetish object par excellence.

The identification (or projection) of the horse-head bookends as a signature figure now appears appropriately overdetermined, for they reference not only forging, but also fetishizing; indeed, within the context of the movie itself, they exist as fetish objects for Mr. Dumpkin. More importantly, Derrida has explicitly linked the fetish to the signature effect: "The signature is a wound and there is no other origin for the work of art," he writes, referring to the fetish object's role as a protector against the acknowledgment that the woman bears the wound of castration.[39] The wounds in a work of art, then, are the points of abyss, the sites of the embedding of the signature, the places where the seed of the name is planted; but these wounds are unseen or unacknowledged until the critic/analyst locates them via the *signateur* theory.

As Gayatri Spivak has confirmed, there is a variation of the Oedipal scenario played out in Derrida's concept of signing. "I can read . . . the insertion of the signature," she writes, "as an ancestral rite—counterfeiting the countersignature of the fathers, so that the contract which is the book may be validated."[40] Here, Spivak acknowledges first that the placing of the signature is linked with ancestral riting/writing: it is the ancient performance of a double-valued compositional practice. Second, she explicitly associates the placement as an act of forgery, of counterfeiting; but it is this act that, paradoxically, results in the production of the text. In addition, it should be noted that there is something of the Oedipal scenario in *Student Bodies* as well, for just as in Freud's reading of Sophocles' play, one can easily read Smithee's film as being about the dangers that accompany the awakening of sexual desire. Also, the most common objective shots we see of the killer in *Student Bodies* are low angle close-ups of his feet in heavy boots, slogging along in much the same way that Oedipus, the club-footed king, might have done. (Or, following the association with mythology, as the lame Hephaestus might have. Hephaestus—Vulcan in Roman mythology—was the Greek patron god of smiths who was known for forging, among other things, the shield of Heracles.)

In the same way that the fetish holds a double, explicitly contradictory meaning—it designates both the castration and the noncastration of the mother—the horse-head bookends are similarly doubled and contradictory: they come in pairs, identical but opposed, facing in opposite directions but possessing the same function. This double status also marks the reintegration, the bringing into balance of the opposites with the same origin: art and technology. The trade of ironworking (blacksmithing)—and that of woodworking (the bookends are carved in wood)—straddles the two domains. On the one hand, reference books repeatedly refer to ironworking as an ancient, lost art; on the other, they regularly designate it as a crucial technological development in the civilization of mankind. The practice of woodworking, at least as it is offered in countless high schools across America, is regularly referred to as an "industrial art"; thus, Mr. Dumpkin himself is an embodiment of the balance sought by Heidegger.

In addition, the horse-head figure also implicates Heidegger's notion of "enframing" in both its figurative and literal senses. Its status as a bookend is crucial, for in *The Question Concerning Technology*, Heidegger explained that, "According to ordinary usage the word *Gestell* means some kind of apparatus, e.g., a bookrack."[41] And indeed, if there is one technology that has most perpetuated the practice of enframing, it is the technology of alphabetic writing—the paradigmatic case of an invention credited with bringing about a fundamental shift in our perception of, and relationship to, the world—reducing as it does things to objects.[42]

The horse-head bookends function in other ways as a device for "enframing." They both support and mark the opposite ends of a line of books, clearly separating what is contained within from that which lies without, while existing themselves in both realms simultaneously (like the signature in its multiple modalities). But the bookends that frame are themselves framed—in the cinema screen—and this frame returns us again to *Gestell* and the question of technology. Whereas Heidegger was suspicious of the cinema, Bazin saw it as the ultimate device for re-thinging the world. And it was the directors who embraced the cinema's automatism who realized this potential most effectively. For example, in making an argument for the importance of Roberto Rossellini and Italian neorealism, Bazin offered an explanation of how this sensibility operates. When one approaches a river, he wrote, one may find that, by chance, several stones are positioned as a makeshift bridge, allowing one to cross the river without getting one's feet wet. The greatness of the neorealist aesthetic, Bazin argued, was that it enables us to see the stones not only as objects, enframed for use as a bridge, but also as things whose existence preceded any such use.[43] Our experience of these most ordinary objects is thus reinvigorated.

Finally, the horse-head bookends refer us to the fact that *Student Bodies* is itself enframed, and this enframing references both the meaning of our *signateur*'s name, and the critical approach's origins in French theory. At the film's conclusion, we learn that the film itself has been enframed; that is, in narrative terms, it has a framing device that reveals that the story that has been set up to involve us was, in fact, phony. In the tradition of *The Wizard of Oz*, the film ends with our protagonist awaking to find that her unconscious has projected a false tale, and that her nightmares were in fact just that—nightmares. And in this safer, saner world to which she has returned, Mr. Dumpkin is no longer a shop teacher, but is, in reality, a French instructor.

Notes

1. Dudley Andrew, "The Unauthorized Auteur Today," *Film Theory Goes to the Movies*, ed. Jim Collins, Hilary Radner, and Ava Preacher Collins (New York: Routledge/AFI, 1993) 81.

2. Andrew Sarris, "Notes on the *Auteur* Theory in 1962," *The Primal Screen* (New York: Simon and Schuster, 1973) 38–53.

3. Andrew 82.

4. Jacques Derrida, *Signsponge*, trans. Richard Rand (New York: Columbia University Press, 1984).

5. For one discussion of the crisis afflicting film studies, see Robert B. Ray, *The Avant-Garde Finds Andy Hardy* (Cambridge: Harvard University Press, 1995).

6. Sarris, "Notes" 50.

7. Derrida, *Signsponge* 52–54.

8. Sarris, "Notes" 50.

9. Derrida, *Signsponge* 54.

10. Sarris, "Notes" 50–51. See Sarris's foreword to this book for Astruc's definition of *mise-en-scène*.

11. Sarris, "Notes" 51.

12. Robert Scholes, Nancy R. Comley, and Gregory L. Ulmer, *Text Book* (New York: St. Martin's, 1988) 261.

13. See translator Richard Rand's introduction to Derrida's *Signsponge*, ix.

14. Rand ix.

15. Derrida, *Signsponge* 54.

16. Derrida, *Signsponge* 70.

17. Ray 136.

18. Ray 181.

19. Ray 182.

20. André Bazin, "On the *politique des auteurs*," trans. Peter Graham, *Cahiers du Cinéma, the 1950s: Neo-Realism, Hollywood, New Wave*, ed. Jim Hillier (Cambridge: Harvard University Press, 1985) 248–59. Bazin's critique was originally published in *Cahiers du cinéma* 70, April 1957. For a discussion of Bazin's critique in the context of Smithee, see the introduction to this book.

21. André Bazin, *What Is Cinema?* vol. 1, ed. and trans. Hugh Gray (Berkeley: University of California Press, 1967).

22. André Bazin, "The Ontology of the Photographic Image," *What Is Cinema?* vol. 1, 13.

23. Bazin, "Ontology" 13.

24. Bazin, "Ontology" 15. Bazin's position here is remarkably similar to that expressed by Walter Benjamin in "The Work of Art in the Age of Mechanical Reproduction," *Illuminations*, ed. Hannah Arendt, trans. Harry Zohn (New York: Schocken, 1969): "[B]y focusing on hidden details of familiar objects,... [the camera] extends our comprehension of the necessities which rule our lives....

It reveals entirely new structural formations of the subject" (236). "The camera introduces us to unconscious optics as does psychoanalysis to unconscious impulses" (237).

25. André Bazin, "An Aesthetic of Reality," *What Is Cinema?* vol. 2, ed. and trans. Hugh Gray (Berkeley: University of California Press, 1971) 37–38.

26. André Bazin, "The Evolution of the Language of Cinema," *What Is Cinema?* vol. 1, 28.

27. Andrew Sarris, "The Aesthetics of André Bazin," *The Primal Screen* (New York: Simon and Schuster, 1973) 89–90.

28. James Bernardoni has dubbed this valuing of control and manipulation "The Hitchcockian Fallacy." See his *The New Hollywood: What the Movies Did with the New Freedoms of the Seventies* (Jefferson, NC: McFarland, 1991).

29. "The Thing" that Derrida explores in *Signsponge* is not only Heidegger's, but also Freud's. Space will limit me to a consideration of only the former.

30. Martin Heidegger, *The Question Concerning Technology*, trans. William Lovitt (New York: Garland, 1977).

31. Martin Heidegger, "The Origin of the Work of Art," *Poetry, Language, Thought*, trans. Albert Hofstadter (New York: Harper and Row, 1971) 36–37. A good discussion of Heidegger's position on art, technology, and equipment can be found in Jospeh J. Kocklemans, *On the Truth of Being* (Bloomington: Indiana University Press, 1984).

32. In *Signsponge*, Derrida plays with the concept of an originary or prior state in a variety of ways. First, via Heidegger's concept of the thing and the object; but also via Freud's theory of the infant's concept of the thing (*das Ding*), which finds ultimate (but indirect) objectification in the body of the mother. Further, Derrida plays with the different meanings in the title of Ponge's exemplary text, *The Pré*, which translates as "meadow," but which can also be read, without the accent mark, as "pre"—as in "previous," something that comes before.

33. Derrida, *Signsponge* 56.

34. Mimicry/miming/mimesis are important issues for Derrida. See, for example, *Dissemination*, trans. Barbara Johnson (Chicago: University of Chicago Press, 1981), which includes two essays offering a new theory of mimesis. For an explanation of Derrida's "new mimesis," see Gregory Ulmer, "The Object of Post-Criticism," *The Anti-Aesthetic*, ed. Hal Foster (Seattle: Bay Press, 1983) 83–110.

35. See the entries on Michael Ritchie in *American Directors*, ed. Pierre

Coursodon with Jean-Pierre Sauvage (New York: McGraw-Hill, 1983), and in the *Cinemania 96* CD-ROM.

36. Tom Milne, ed. *The Time Out Film Guide* (New York: Penguin, 1989).

37. Jacques Derrida, *The Truth in Painting*, trans. Geoff Bennington and Ian MacLeod (Chicago: University of Chicago Press, 1987) 420–21.

38. Gregory L. Ulmer, *Applied Grammatology* (Baltimore: The Johns Hopkins University Press, 1985) 111-17.

39. Jacques Derrida, *Glas*, trans. John P. Leavey Jr. and Richard Rand (Lincoln: University of Nebraska Press, 1986) 202.

40. Gayatri Spivak, "*Glas*-Piece: A *Compte Rendu*." *Diacritics* 7.3 (fall 1977): 23. Spivak goes on to argue that Derrida ultimately offers a critical approach that is other than Oedipus-centered.

41. Heidegger, *The Question Concerning Technology* 20.

42. See, for example, Walter J. Ong, *Orality and Literacy: The Technologizing of the Word* (New York: Routledge, 1982).

43. Bazin, "An Aesthetic of Reality" 35–37.

CHAPTER 7

Smithee's Incorporation

Jeremy Braddock

> Before the law, the man is a subject of the law in appearing before
> it. This is obvious, but since he is *before* it because he cannot enter it,
> he is also *outside the law* (an outlaw). He is neither under the law nor
> in the law. He is both a subject of the law and an outlaw.
>
> —Jacques Derrida, "Before the Law"

It is a felicitous function of the unconscious, as Christian Keathley points out at the end of the previous chapter, that reveals the sinister shop teacher who lurks within the French instructor. In its final movement, we learn that the mayhem of Allen Smithee's *Student Bodies* has been entirely motivated by the heroine Toby's fearful suspicion that the culturally legitimated discipline of French bears a family resemblance to the (apparently) horrifyingly mechanical qualities of high school shop class. This hackneyed narrative device that concludes *Student Bodies* also neatly condenses, in an image, a fundamental issue in the discourse of *auteurism*. In its very inception the *auteur* was defined against the more technical abilities exemplified by the *metteur-en-scène*, who was understood to be merely "the gentleman who adds pictures" to a preconceived "scenario."[1] The most lasting effect of the *politique des auteurs*, however, is the way in which it has persuaded audiences to imagine films to be the purely artistic creations of directors, the greatest of whom, in turn, are granted the status of genius in the tradition of all the fine arts. This interpretation of the *auteur* theory has itself been reified, as Craig Saper and Tom Conley remind us, to the status of a highly successful marketing strategy in Hollywood and elsewhere.[2] But what tends to be forgotten is that the *auteur* theory refuses to allow the cinemagoer to separate the French instructor from the shop teacher, the visionary from the technician. Wheeler Winston Dixon's 1993 collection of François Truffaut's early criticism, for example, contains a series of reviews in which the critic evaluates films almost entirely on their employment of Cinema-Scope. In one such piece, Truffaut concludes his consideration of Henry Koster's biblical extravaganza *The Robe* (1953) by insisting, "It needs also to be admitted that, if CinemaScope is a commercial REVOLUTION, it is also an aesthetic EVOLUTION."[3] Even as the *auteurist* critics demanded that Hollywood directors be considered anew as great artists, what was of equal importance was the implication that art could itself no longer be considered a realm forever divided either from its commercial or its technical dimensions. Indeed, it would prove unavoidable that it was precisely through such commercial and technical revolutions that *auteurs* had left authorial signatures on their films in the first place.

According to the guidelines of the *politique des auteurs*, and in the spirit of this volume, can it also be said that Allen Smithee, who himself embodies a commercial revolution, could also signal an aesthetic evolution? Smithee might have provided a clue for answering this question by titling his 1981 film *Student Bodies*. What initially appears to be a crass joke about the spectacle of the corpses filling the halls of his film also suggests a way of interrogating the cinema's problematic relationship with individual and corporate identities. A student body is a collective identity, or, to be more faithful to the term, an *incorporated* identity. However, Smithee's film becomes a spectacle at the moment at which this "body" is made into individuated subjects (its dead bodies), each of which then becomes emblematic of the student body as a whole insofar as that collective identity is endangered (in this case because of a psychopathic shop teacher/French instructor). The work of Smithee as a director likewise reminds us of the way cinema is beset by the desire to attribute meaning alternatingly between collective and individuated identities, each of which must invoke and occlude the another.

Some Window Dressing

As Keathley points out, the final revelation in *Student Bodies* appears as a heavy-handed reference to the closing scene of *The Wizard of Oz*. Using

Smithee's allusion as the starting point of this essay, I want to suggest that L. Frank Baum should be a figure of consequence in cinema studies for a reason not immediately related to *The Wizard of Oz*. As recent studies of the department store and American commerce have noted, before he settled into a career of writing political allegories for children, L. Frank Baum played a key role in pioneering the modern technique of department store window display. He published the first issue of *The Show Window* ("a monthly journal of decorative art") in 1897, and founded the National Association of Window Trimmers a year later.[4] Drawing from his early professional experience both in the theater and in commercial marketing, Baum emphasized the important role that the show window could play in creating the desire of possession within the heart of the consumer. As William Leach describes,

> Baum exhorted merchants not to crowd goods in the windows, as in the past, but to single them out. Don't let the lamps and tin pots sit there, Baum said; make them "come alive" as if they were figures on the stage. *The Show Window* dwelled repeatedly on theatrical themes. Look for the "possibilities lying dormant in the beautiful goods." "Tastefully display a single apron." Adjust the electric lighting and widen and deepen the show windows.[5]

Breaking with the earlier method of filling windows with large stacks of the goods for sale, Baum drew on his theatrical background and employed technical innovations to present commodities in an unexpected way. Each object was uncannily individuated, but still representative of the identical objects that were grouped collectively within the store. In attempting to produce the effect of animation (to have them "come alive"), Baum understood that one "possibilit[y] lying dormant in the beautiful goods" was the opportunity to make them stars.

Baum's innovations lend a surprising historical justification to the familiar analogy of the Hollywood cinema as a kind of department store window display, even though the comparison has never required this kind of contextualization. It is not likely, for example, that Orson Welles had the author of the *Oz* books in mind when he described the classic Hollywood style as if it replicated a "merchant's eye ... lovingly evaluating texture, the screen being filled as a window is dressed in a swank department store."[6] Welles's observation has nevertheless become a useful reference point for critics of the Hollywood style,[7] and it provides James Naremore with a useful way to begin his study *The Films of Vincente Minnelli*. The connection here is especially poignant for Naremore, since Minnelli's first professional employment came as window decorator for Marshall Field in Chicago (the city in which Baum had reinvented the discipline a generation earlier). For Naremore this detail acts as a cipher for Minnelli both thematically and stylistically, accounting equally well for Minnelli's portrayal of and participation in American commercialism, and for his "signature style" of shot composition.

Although Naremore's book operates within the discourse of *auteurist* criticism, his argument is also in many ways a recuperative one on behalf of Minnelli, a director who did not reap the critical acclaim that Alfred Hitchcock or Howard Hawks received following the *auteurist* reevaluation of cinema history, and who became the subject of debates about the relationship of art and commerce as *auteurism* entered its second decade. François Truffaut, writing some time after his initial celebration of Hollywood directors, dismissed Minnelli as *un esclave*.[8] In his measured consideration of the younger *Cahiers du cinéma* critics, André Bazin called the American director "a director of filmed ballets."[9] And on the other side of the *auteurist* ocean, Andrew Sarris alloted Minnelli a place among the second tier of directors, but argued that Minnelli was wrong to assume that style could determine substance, adding by way of conclusion, "Minnelli believes implicitly in the power of his camera to transform trash into art, and corn into caviar. Minnelli believes more in beauty than in art."[10]

Stressing from the very beginning the importance of window dressing to Minnelli's directorial style, Naremore argues that Minnelli treats the contradiction between his commercial work and his aspirations to artistry in a much more reflexive fashion than Sarris would have admitted possible. For example, the conclusion of *Father of the Bride* (1950) appears to portray the wedding of Kay Banks (Elizabeth Taylor) and Buckley Dunstan (Don Taylor) as a happy triumph of show business and consumerism, those two themes L. Frank Baum had united in the modern show window. But the climactic moment is preceded by numerous scenes that depict Kay's father (Spencer Tracy) aghast at the consumerist frenzy of his daughter and wife, thus confirming that the context of the film is, as Naremore points out, an era "when a popular daytime TV show was broadcasting live marriage ceremonies of real couples, showering them with gifts from sponsors."[11] Even as the pivotal scene that precedes the wedding involves Mr. Banks warmly admiring his daughter in her wedding dress, thereby paving the way for the real-life wedding dress product tie-in (Naremore's book reprints the magazine advertisement for the dress), the moment has already been undercut elsewhere in the film. Naremore explains:

> The image of Taylor standing in front of the mirror, admired by her fictional father, is therefore evidence of the film's cunning and almost irresistible duplicity. Minnelli and his writers have satirized women for reading *Vogue*, and now they invite those same women to stand in breathless awe of a star in the latest wedding gown. They have treated females as consumers, and now they construct a female image that can be lovingly consumed through a man's eyes. In fact, they have done this throughout the film, as we can see from the special care MGM took with all of Taylor's costumes.[12]

One could again invoke L. Frank Baum and go on to say that the gown is itself presented as a unique and glamorous object, and is, like Taylor, a star of the scene.

Although Naremore does not see Minnelli as a radical, he does cite one critic who does. The *Cahiers* critic Jean Domarchi, writing from Paris in 1956, commented: "If the Hollywood [sic] un-American Activities investigation had had any sense [it would have blacklisted Minnelli instead of] those admirable but infinitely less dangerous directors like Dassin, Losey, or Berry."[13] Naremore and Domarchi both recognize that whatever disruptive function Minnelli's films may possess operates by way of those stylistic elements that only appear to present those films as pieces of consumerist mass culture, as films ideologically consistent with the tactics of modern window display by which they are stylistically marked. For Domarchi, the cinematic critique of what he calls "a serious crisis in the American economy's system of purely material values" is most extensive in those films that outwardly present themselves as having no "social preoccupation," that is, in films whose pretensions to "meaning" are necessarily mediated by their unabashed status as commodities.[14] Put another way, what may be "lying dormant in *these* beautiful goods" (both the films and the objects within them) is the possibility of their being readily interpretable as fetishized commodities.

Domarchi's reference to the HUAC does not fail to remind his reader of the pseudonyms that blacklisted writers, actors, and directors were forced to assume because of the blacklist in 1950s Hollywood.[15] On first glance, such a claim may seem out of balance with Domarchi's larger argument about Minnelli's lack of "social preoccupation." Particularly when paired with Sarris's dismissal of the former window dresser's belief "in the power of his camera to transform trash into art," Domarchi's insight could apply equally well to apparently equally disengaged Andy Warhol, whose work also depends upon its apparently easy consumption, and whose most famous film is, of course, called *Trash* (1970). Pseudonyms and window dressing also play roles in Warhol's own career, however, and a closer look at Warhol may add a further dimension to Domarchi's argument. Beginning in the mid-1950s Warhol, Jasper Johns, and Robert Rauschenberg all found employment as window display designers for a number of New York department stores.[16] Of these three artists, however, only Warhol refused to take a pseudonym for this commercial work; Johns and Rauschenberg worked collectively under the pseudonym Matson Jones.[17] Warhol, on the contrary, advertised his belief that his commercial work was continuous with his painting, to a degree that must have astonished even the department stores that employed him. In April 1961 Warhol used a number of pop pieces as a backdrop to a series of female mannequins in the windows of Bonwit Teller, thereby equating his paintings with the displayed fashions, while perhaps also making a sly reference to Marcel Duchamp's appropriation of the term *readymade* from the world of mass-produced fashion attire.[18] This not only had the effect of obviously situating his paintings as commodities, each painting being of equivalent value in the artistic marketplace, but the viewer was also reminded of the individuated identity, heretofore associated more properly with a work of art, that was conferred upon a commodity when it was displayed as a unique object.

On the other hand, when Johns and Rauschenberg disassociated themselves from their commercial work, it indicated a desire not to implicate their legitimate work with the commercialism and commodification represented by the medium of the show window. Such a strategy, however, would be compromised from the start by the department store's assumption that display windows should be "signed," since the necessity of having a name to place on the decorative work presumes that the work in some sense originates from an author or artist. But is it enough simply to dismiss Johns and Rauschenberg for being naive about the marketplace of fine art within which they hoped to be (and of course soon were)

Figure 7.1. Bonwit Teller, New York City, April 1961. Photograph courtesy of the Andy Warhol Museum. Copyright 2000 Andy Warhol Foundation for the Visual Arts/Artists Rights Society (ARS), New York; reprinted with permission.

rewarded? Warhol was able to flaunt the commerciality of his work because, as with Minnelli, the inevitably commercial function of art was already a prominent theme within his work. For Johns and Rauschenberg the problem was always going to be more vexed, largely because the marketplace in which their art was to be received was one that had come to require the artist's name to exist beyond the realm of commerce. In fact, it was not long after Warhol's Bonwit Teller "show" that Leo Steinberg published the monograph that marked the watershed of Jasper Johns's career. In contrast to Warhol's installation, and because of the success of the Matson Jones pseudonym, Steinberg's essay did not connect Johns's window display work to his paintings.[19] Quite the contrary, Steinberg averred that Johns was not even to be compared to celebrated writers from the era of modern capitalism, like "O. Henry or Somerset Maugham," but that he rather belonged among those eternal icons of the Western canon, "Homer and Shakespeare."[20]

Steinberg's essay went on to reveal in greater detail the degree to which the marketplace into which Johns's art was circulated was still organized around the valorization of the Romantic male genius that was evidently represented by "Homer and Shakespeare." Perceptively noting the "non-hierarchic" quality of Johns's paintings, Steinberg substantiates his interpretation with this telling anecdote:

> A young woman wrote to me in June 1960: "When I saw Jasper Johns's paintings I wondered why he wasted these beautiful Chardin-like whites and greys on flags and numbers." It was the classic feminine disapproval—like the familiar "I-don't-know-what-he-sees-in-her!"—of a man's love that seems misdirected.[21]

Although Johns and Rauschenberg have more recently been understood to have presented sustained critiques of the masculinist, Romanticized expressivity that characterized abstract expressionism (see, for example, Johns's *Painting with Two Balls*, 1960), Steinberg sought to situate Johns as an artist whose genius needs no context other than the continuum of genius itself.

Jonathan Katz's essay "The Art of Code: Jasper Johns and Robert Rauschenberg" presents another context that informs the employment of the Matson Jones pseudonym, and one that throws into further relief Steinberg's comment about Johns's "misdirected" love. As was first implied by Calvin Tomkins, and later more fully confirmed elsewhere, Johns and Rauschenberg were lovers for the six years that coincided with their commercial partnership (1955–61). As Katz points out, this partnership also occurred against the backdrop of the Red Scare, during which homosexuality was associated with communism and suspected "deviants" were persecuted similarly.[22] Seen in this light, the name Matson Jones could be seen to cover over both their commercial and sexual relationships. In masking these contexts, the artist's name (Jasper Johns) becomes a signifier that is ironically similar to Matson Jones in that it points to a banal concept (in this case, "genius") and to a specific series of works (those produced for gallery display), rather than to the complex identity that produced those works, and that the pseudonym helped to obscure.

From Steinberg's perspective, the most valuable proper name was one that could be thought to exist outside of, at the very least, an economic context. But the economic contexts that are pertinent to the present discussion employ proper names in ways that both mimic and complicate the paradigm that Steinberg invoked. The corporate identities that have dominated the retail and cinematic industries contrast tellingly on this point. Every major American department store operating during the Studio Era was named for its owner (Macy's, Hudson's, Marshall Field, Bloomingdale's, etc.), not in an expression of signing a work, of course, but instead as a gesture of accountability, to put the suggestion of a human face upon a commercial experience. Of Hollywood's original Big Eight studios, on the other hand, the names of only four contained proper names in any form, and those were often in some way occluded (as in the "Twentieth Century" that precedes "Fox" or the "Radio-Keith-Orpheum" concealed within RKO Radio Pictures). But just as Rauschenberg and Johns may have been expected to lend a human face to the commercial enterprise of window display, so too did Hollywood studios recognize in *auteurism* the opportunity to personify their commercial endeavors. In the latter instance, however, the singular identity of the director does not obviously refer to the corporate machinations of the studio (accountable or not), but rather to a Romanticized *auteur* appropriated from an image of the artist which the Matson Jones pseudonym sought to protect.

It is here that we must reintroduce Allen Smithee, the cinematic analogue of Matson Jones and the director who stands most evidently for corporate interests, even if he is less evidently incorporate. The Smithee and Matson Jones pseudonyms share the assumption that a name has the potential of bearing exchange value by itself, an assumption long supported by the fine arts marketplace, but one that has mattered for directors only palpably since the invention of the category of the *auteur*. But whereas Johns and Rauschenberg were allowed the freedom to choose their own pseudonym, and thereby ensure the obscurity of their commercial work, Hollywood directors must apply to the Directors Guild of America to have their names removed from a film, and, if approved, they must use the name Allen Smithee. The DGA has in recent years attempted to withhold and suppress information about the production of Smithee films by forbidding directors to discuss the production of those films, an edict that has brought upon itself increasingly noisy repercussions, from the disastrous irony that visited the Joe Eszterhas-penned *Burn Hollywood Burn: An Alan Smithee Film* (1998) to the lawsuit filed by Tony Kaye against the DGA after they ruled out his use of the pseudonym for *American History X* (1998).[23] It is the secrecy that surrounds Smithee that has lately served to confirm his status as an authentic celebrity.

Indeed, Smithee appears to insist upon being recognized far more than does any other pseudonymous persona. When Johns and Rauschenberg worked as Matson Jones, the odds of there being an actual person with that name (one living in New York, even) would have seemed pretty good, and such a confusion would have been desirable to them. On the other hand, the name Allen Smithee was chosen precisely for the unlikelihood of anyone else's having it; it was altered from the originally proposed "Alan Smith" for precisely this reason. Strikingly, however, an

Internet search produced more than two hundred people named Matson, none of whom could claim the common last name Jones, while there are at least two Americans named Allen Smithee. I have, in fact, received a letter from Mrs. Nellie Smithee, Allen Smithee's widow. According to her letter, she had been aware of the odd circumstance that links her to Hollywood filmmaking; her nephew listed a note to this effect on his Web site at Syracuse University. Allen Smithee was born the grandson of a full-blooded Cherokee Indian in Swifton, Arkansas, in 1918, served in the Marines in the Second World War, and retired after forty-two years of service from the Laclede Steel Company in Alton, Illinois (which is itself a pseudonym for East St. Louis). He died 26 July 1988, after a lengthy illness.[24]

Because of the success of the *politique des auteurs*, this insistence on recognition extends even more emphatically to Smithee's own films. Here, however, the authorial mark we are compelled to recognize does not represent Smithee's personal history so much as his professional identity. Since Smithee's primary function seems to be, as Jonathan Eburne argues, to "complete" a film, thereby allowing it to make whatever money it can, in the theaters or (more often these days) on videotape, his work, like Minnelli's and Warhol's, makes no bones about its primarily commercial function.[25] And just as these two figures' creative work can be read against the grain, in the service of producing nuanced critiques, like Naremore's, that invoke artists' experience as window dressers, so too can Smithee's oeuvre be seen to reveal and comment upon his own commercial function. To effect this kind of reading will require a use of *auteurist* criticism that takes, to borrow Andrew Sarris's phrase, the "distinguishable personality of the director as a criterion of value." But rather than dismiss out of hand what Sarris calls "a badly directed or an undirected film,"[26] we will find that even these movies bear the signature marks of their nominal director. The aim of using an *auteurist* technique is not to measure the "value" of Smithee's oeuvre, but must instead be in the first case hermeneutic. Where does Smithee place himself in his films? In order to answer this question, we must find out who Smithee is.

Smithee's Other Biography

The first chapter of this volume presents most of what is known of Smithee's historical biography. There are, however, other ways of locating his identity. If we were to present Smithee's *literary* biography, we should attend to him in a more textual fashion, beginning with the document that determines his existence. This document, the *Directors Guild of America Basic Agreement of 1996*, posits Smithee as the antithesis of each statement that describes the position of the director. According to Article 7 of the *Basic Agreement*:

> The Director's professional function is unique, and requires his or her participation in all creative phases of the filmmaking process, including but not limited to all creative aspects of sound and picture.

> The Director works directly with all of the elements which constitute the variegated texture of a unit of film entertainment or information.

> The Director's function is to contribute to all of the creative elements of a film and to participate in molding and integrating them into one cohesive dramatic and aesthetic whole.[27]

Particularly with respect to this last "function," two things are clear. The first is that whereas the DGA seeks in the broadest sense to protect the conditions under which a director's name can carry value, in short, to provide insurance for the name of the *auteur*, the legalized definition of the director is much more Foucauldian, even to the point of refiguring Michel Foucault's "author-function" as the "Director's function," rather than simply as the "Director." In each case, the author/*auteur* restricts meaning, either by "molding and integrating" "elements" "into one cohesive dramatic and aesthetic whole" (as the Directors Guild of America states), or by limiting "the cancerous and dangerous proliferation of significations within a world where one is thrifty ... with one's discourses and their significations" (as Foucault has it).[28] The more important point here is that, despite the DGA's best intentions, Allen Smithee is the director who best exemplifies theses guidelines, for each description refers completely to the work done by the name and in the name of Allen Smithee.

As a way of illustrating this basic point, consider a candid scene from the 1989 film *Backtrack*, which starred Dennis Hopper, and was released in Europe under Smithee's name. Following Hopper and his saxophone, the camera pans ninety degrees left, passing from a Jenny Holzer piece that reads "Even your family can betray you," to an enlarged reproduction of Hieronymous Bosch's *Garden of Earthly Delights*. Once in front of the famous triptych, the audience experiences nearly a full minute of Hopper's caricature of avant-garde jazz before the shot eventually dissolves into the next scene. As the director of *Easy Rider* (1969) and *The Last Movie* (1971), films of great importance to second-generation *auteurs* like Martin Scorsese and Francis Ford Coppola, Dennis Hopper occupies an important place in the current myth-history of American cinema. He is also the original director of *Backtrack*.[29] The use of Smithee's name precludes the *auteurist* line of inquiry that would hold Hopper responsible for a shot that combines Holzer, Bosch, and a toothless Pharaoh Sanders impersonation. This line of inquiry could, in turn, have the effect of devaluing Hopper's good name as a director. Instead, it is Smithee who assumes the responsibility for the scene.

Foucault's argument turns on their head what even today are accepted ideas of what constitutes authorship, and it is important to note that this is precisely what the DGA's *Basic Agreement* does as well. Its entire set of laws and conditions is haunted by the unnamed, yet everywhere implicit, specter of Smithee. Herein lies the paradox of Smithee's instrumentality, for just as Smithee strips bare—more economically than Foucault could have hoped to do—the "author-function," he also serves to protect the very illusion of the *auteur* that Foucault demystifies. By far the most substantive items accessible from the DGA's Web site, the *Basic Agreement* and its accompanying *Creative Rights Checklist* open with a series of questions, including:

Figure 7.2. Even your family can betray you.

Figure 7.3. The garden of earthly delights.

Were you notified of the date, time, and place of every postproduction operation?

Did you receive a shooting script with your name on it?

Was there a reasonable purpose for each of the people present at the casting session to be there?

Did all notes to cast and crew come directly from you?[30]

The *Checklist* in no way concerns itself with communicating "interior meaning," "the distinguishable personality of the director," or even "technical competence" (taken in reverse order, the three basic criteria Sarris proposed in 1962 for identifying an *auteur*).[31] Rather, it stresses the profoundly managerial, bureaucratic function of the director, a function that every myth of cinematic artistry tries hard to suppress. But because the DGA is the institution that creates and legitimates Smithee, and also the one that requires that the original director be obstructed before Smithee is activated, every question here is clearly also a call for Allen Smithee. The director is therefore not only the person who "integrat[es]" "elements" "into one cohesive dramatic and aesthetic whole," but is also legally defined by those events that did not occur in the process of making the film. The director is an *auteur* insofar as he or she is not Allen Smithee.

Smithee is, for these reasons, considerably more than a legal fiction. Indeed, Smithee's "distinguishable personality" can be said to embody the paradox of law itself. To justify this claim, I want to invoke two points made by Jacques Derrida in his essay concerning Kafka's story "Before the Law," the essay from which this chapter's epigraph is taken. As Derek Attridge points out in introducing the piece, Derrida's interest in Kafka's parable consists in its treatment of "the problematic relation between the singular and the general," a problem that marks the relationship of the individual subject to the universal expression of law.[32] In Derrida's words, "There is a singularity about relationship to the law, a law of singularity which must come into contact with the general or universal essence of the law without ever being able to do so."[33] This insight is perhaps illustrated even more elegantly by the case of Allen Smithee than it is by Kafka's parable.[34] A director who wishes to be disassociated from his film comes before the DGA as an individual agent, seeking from the law redressment for an infringement of his rights as a singular director/artist. Only if he is turned down, as was Tony Kaye, only if he is denied access to the activity of the law, does he maintain his singular identity. In being granted access to the law of the DGA, the director must then assume the collective, generalized identity of Allen Smithee. Herein lies a telling point of contrast between Smithee and Matson Jones. Matson Jones is a name that requires no act of legislation to be accessed, and as such stands for nothing more than the desire to effect a value-based distinction between two genres of creative work, one genre receiving the authentic, individuated name (Jasper Johns), the other a collective, incorporated pseudonym (Matson Jones). Smithee, on the contrary, is a figure who indicates the inability of the individual director to authorize a work within the generality of the law, to effect the impression that he has succeeded in "molding and integrating" "elements" "into one cohesive dramatic and aesthetic whole." However, it is also implied that had the "molding and integrating" been performed successfully, the director would have succeeded in securing the preserve beyond commerce that is the artist's true domain. Smithee is the crucial functionary here, for he enables a similar division between authentic and inauthentic work to be drawn, but this time it is within the single genre of film.

In discussing Kant's categorical imperative, Derrida points out that for Kant the moral law (and what is the *Creative Rights Checklist* if not an instance of moral legislation?) must be by definition "without history, genesis, or any possible derivation."[35] This is why the categorical imperative insists that one must "act *as if* the maxim of one's action were by one's will to turn into a universal law of nature" (my italics).[36] By contrast, Derrida turns to Freud's attempt to trace to its origins the concept of moral law, in order to show the logical inconsistency that necessarily marks attempts to historicize law such as Freud's. In *Totem and Taboo*,

Derrida writes, Freud thought he had discovered that the history of the law "refers back to the unique historicity of an event, namely the murder of the primeval father":

> The murder fails because the dead father holds even more power [than did the living father]. Is not the best way of killing him to keep him alive (and finite)—and is not the best way of keeping him alive to murder him? Now, failure, Freud specifies, is conducive to moral action. Thus morality arises from a useless crime which in fact kills nobody, which comes too soon or too late and does not put an end to any power; in fact, it inaugurates nothing since repentance and morality had to be possible *before* the crime. Freud appears to cling to the reality of an event, but this event is a sort of non-event, an event of nothing or a quasi-event which both calls for and annuls a narrative account.[37]

The institution of Allen Smithee similarly invokes a history, in this case the history of Hollywood-as-factory, the studio system that impersonally employed directors as if they were of only slightly more importance than the cinematographers, writers, editors, casting agencies, and so forth, all of them equally and relatively anonymously involved in the making of the same movies. This factory, the myth would go on to say, was designed only to produce commodities for profit, not art. In collecting themselves as the DGA, scripting the *Creative Rights Checklist*, and creating Allen Smithee, Hollywood directors similarly posited the "quasi-event" which was the primeval slaying of the *auteur* at the hands of the Hollywood machine.[38] The positing of this quasi-event, as well as the moral rights it has sought to legislate, is necessarily anachronistic, not least because it depends on the category of the *auteur*, an idea that can clearly be traced to its origin in 1954, the year Truffaut published "A Certain Tendency of the French Cinema" in *Cahiers du cinéma* (the DGA would purchase its first home building one year later). Moreover, the studio system through its very machinery enabled the category of the *auteur*, as its impersonal style produced a wealth of B-movies, which, Truffaut said, "are often better than important films because they are made so fast."[39]

This biography reveals the way in which Smithee stands before the law, tricking it into thinking he is an individuated subject, like Joseph K. or even Orson Welles (and it is to be remembered that Welles filmed a version of this very scene in *The Trial*). It is through this trickery that he is able to confront the universality of law, and thereby liberate those *auteurs* for whom he stands from the contingency that would mark their status as subjects under the law: Smithee enters the law so that the directors may remain Romantic outlaws. Looked at another way, invoked by the shameful memory of the murder of the originary *auteur*, Smithee both preserves the possibility of the director's status as *auteur* (by protecting his name) and maximizes the commercial potential of the film (by allowing it to be distributed as an "authorized" film), all the while pretending to keep these two categories, art and commerce, separate. We will see, however, that Smithee's films of the law undo this fictive separation.

Smithee and the Law; or, Three Films about Smithee

Smithee's first film, *Death of a Gunfighter* (1969), is a Western set in a moment of historical change that marks it as being the last chronologically possible Western. This moment is signaled in the film by, to name just two examples, rather pedantic shots of lightbulbs and of automobiles. Marshal Frank Patch (Richard Widmark), the gunfighter whose death is foretold in the film's title, embodies a paradox. As one citizen puts it, "We don't have any law in this jerkwater town. He's the law." The marshal, then, is given straightaway as the embodiment of a law that does not exist. More to the point, whereas a Leone Western (clearly a formal antecedent of Smithee's film, as Laura Parigi points out) always analogizes historical conflict as a conflict between or among men (cf. Henry Fonda and Charles Bronson in *Once upon a Time in the West*), in *Death of a Gunfighter*, Patch is brought down by a council of commercial authorities who seek to replace him with a figurehead who will act in their name, while remaining powerless himself. The vision of the new lawman is an anticipation of Smithee, the problem-solving director-lawman. This new lawman nominally holds the traditional sheriff position, while actually acting on behalf of an abstracted, collective interest whose principal concern is not so much that maintenance of the law, but the maximizing of the commercial potential of the town. Fittingly, then, *Death of a Gunfighter* rehearses neatly the primeval *Death of the Auteur* discussed above, complete with all the paradoxes attendant to that killing. The murder of Frank Patch does not fail to create in the spectator a sense of nostalgia for the days in which the director-lawman was a *real* director-lawman, when of course these days never existed. Important, too, is the scene in which Will Oxley, the boy who is set up by the council of authorities to bring down the gunfighter-*auteur*, learns in his dying moments that he is an orphan. This lack of a father is especially crucial to the argument here, as the word "paternity" is the DGA's predominant metaphor for the director's relationship to his film. The tragedy of Will's death is therefore emblematic of the general concern for films separated from their father-directors by the obscene and invasive bureaucracy of the Hollywood system.[40]

But this is only a way of setting the stage for a more thorough consideration of *Backtrack*, a film that might once, before Smithee's involvement, have wanted us to believe that its theme could be rendered by the following reading of the scene described in this chapter's previous section: Milo (Dennis Hopper) is a hitman for the Mafia who is not so much trapped in his profession as he is trapped between, on the one hand, the faceless and technologized "conceptual art" represented by the Holzer piece, and, on the other hand, the perverse and archaic carnality represented by Bosch. When Dennis Hopper is situated as the focal point of an *auteurist* reading of *Backtrack*, this scene helps to articulate a theme of a foundational *ur*-text of art, wherein Bosch, Holzer, Hopper's saxophone playing, and, inevitably, Hopper's film are harmoniously united as fruit of mankind's essential creativity. Viewed from this perspective, the same theme is also *biographically* supported by the eventual meeting between Milo and Anne Benton (Jodie Foster–as–Jenny Holzer). By locating their meeting in Taos, New Mexico, Hopper links his film to his own purchasing of the Mabel Dodge Luhan house in 1970, a house that since its construction in 1918 had been conceived as "an alternative creative space that would transform American culture," while remaining consistent with its location in Taos, a city whose citizens were imagined "to live in peace and harmony with the land."[41] The house had been a site of pilgrimage for such figures as Willa Cather, Jean Toomer, Georgia O'Keeffe, Carl Jung, Martha Graham, and D. H. Lawrence, seemingly demonstrating their belief that an abstracted, collective author ("the land") was to underwrite their individual creative endeavors. To make the reference to the Luhan house clear, Lawrence in fact appears in *Backtrack* by way of a cameo by the director Alex Cox. Such a contextualization of the scene also encourages an *auteurist* reading that situates *Backtrack* as continuous with Hopper's experimental film of 1971, *The Last Movie*. The films' locations are meant to invoke one another, they share similar obsessions with primitive cultures, and D. H. Lawrence is an anachronistic presence not just in *Backtrack*, but in *The Last Movie* as well.

An *auteurist* reading of *Backtrack* that privileges Allen Smithee, on the other hand, promotes a very different, and I would argue more compelling, interpretation. This reading foregrounds the character of the conceptual artist Anne Benton (the name that "Smithees" Jenny Holzer until the closing credits), who appears to be the film's central character until the scene in Taos. Benton is introduced in the film as an artist now successful enough to be enjoined by the major media to explain how her work can justify itself as "art." Driving home after a long day of studio- and publicity-work, Benton catches a flat tire, and this misfortune causes her to witness a gangland execution performed at the hands of Leo Carelli, John Luponi, and "Pinella" (Joe Pesci, Dean Stockwell, and John Turturro). Benton then becomes the key witness in an investigation that aims to bring down the infamous mob boss Mr. Avoca (Vincent Price). In her interview with Detective Pauling (Fred Ward), Anne realizes that her obligation to the law has forced her into a Smitheean situation:

PAULING: When it's all over, we'll put you in the FBI program for witnesses against the mob. They'll relocate you. You can start a whole new life—with a new name.

ANNE: I don't want a new name!

PAULING: Look, you'll have the best.

What Pauling fails to realize (and what Milo will later betray) is that for Anne Benton even to "have the best" name will nevertheless have serious consequences for her career as an artist, a field in which she has only just begun to "make a name for herself." Indeed, the commercial success of Holzer's art, which could be said to have possessed (by reappropriating) a technology at least as much as it possesses a *style*, depends especially upon the public's association of that technology with the name Jenny Holzer. Hence, in *Backtrack*, the motivating commercial concerns are not fundamentally a *collective* interest, as they were in *Death of a Gunfighter*. They instead belong to the individuated artist-*auteur* represented in the figure of Anne Benton, an artist who has succeeded in establishing a signatory relationship between her name and the LED technology that constitutes her medium. However, the textual messages of Holzer's

Figure 7.4. I walk in and out the cracks of my skull.

(Benton's) pieces are effective primarily because they appear to be spoken neither by an individual or collective subjectivity, but by the actual machines that are programmed to reiterate them ad infinitum.

Again Smithee appears before the generality of the law (here represented by Fred Ward's Pauling), but in this case (s)he has the effect of suggesting that there is no authentic artistic subject to be protected.

Backtrack can now usefully be read as Smithee's meditation on the commercial function of the *auteur*, in the sense that the term is everywhere silently privileged by the DGA. Smithee elaborates on the sequence in Pauling's office by countering the DGA's trope of paternity, the social relationship that traditionally mediates the inheritance of property, with the trope of prostitution. Smithee's insight here is that prostitution, like Smithee himself, brings to light the commercial function of an area (either sex or authorship) that many would wish to keep sacred and uninterrogated, and in each case the law is invoked to protect sacred categories (female sexuality or art). Anne terminates her interview with Pauling when she catches sight of John Luponi, one of the assassins, whom she immediately recognizes to be an "inside man" working for Mr. Avoca within the L.A. Police Department. Rejecting Pauling's offer to "Smithee" her, Anne hurries out of the office and attempts to elude Luponi by walking into the women's restroom. Here she encounters a prostitute who has evidently just made bail. Anne offers the prostitute forty dollars in exchange for her blonde wig and overcoat, an offer to which the prostitute agrees after a fleeting moment of skepticism. Assuming this absurd disguise (whereby the audience is encouraged to view Foster's character as "prostituting herself"), Benton is able to evade the gaze of the law and escape. Smithee portrays this commercial exchange as a moment of identification between the two women in an effort to stress that the prostitute's divesting herself of the tools by which she makes a living will mirror Anne Benton's ensuing loss of her name, a tool by which *she* makes her living. Assuming the name Katherine Louise Marks (a name she has taken from a gravestone), Anne escapes to Seattle where she prostitutes herself in a different way—by writing slogans for an advertising firm.

Figure 7.5. "I been there, but it's gonna cost you fifty bucks."

Figure 7.6. "OK, so you owe me ten."

The audience's sympathies now firmly on the side of the artist formerly known as Anne Benton, Smithee re-deploys Dennis Hopper, the initial *auteur* of *Backtrack*, as a figure whose primary concern is to render Anne Benton's name bereft of its commercial function. Hopper's character Milo, who has been hired by Carelli and Avoca to find and kill Anne Benton, has in the process of his investigation become a kind of *auteurist* critic himself. In the only scene from *Backtrack* in which Hopper's character wears scholarly eyeglasses, Milo recognizes Benton's signatory mark in a magazine advertisement for lipstick: its slogan, "Protect me … from what I want," repeats, with the addition of an ellipsis, the slogan from one of Benton's LED pieces. Tracing the ad to the agency that produced it, Milo narrowly misses killing Anne in Seattle, but then tracks her to Taos, abetted by the unwitting assistance of the chainsaw-sculptor (Bob Dylan) who is Anne's former mentor. By this time, Milo has become obsessed with Anne's art, despite his skepticism about its technological form ("Your art," he later says to her, "don't exist without a wall socket to plug it into!"). Instead of killing her, an act that would increase exponentially the commercial value of those pieces connected to the Anne Benton name, Milo abducts the artist in an attempt to refigure her as an artist in the Romantic image he feels is attendant upon all proper creative activity.

Since it takes place against the backdrop of reactionary gender politics, this final movement of *Backtrack* could be described as an act of *repatriation*, reestablishing as it does the DGA's trope of paternity by making it the primary cause of both creativity and procreation. In an early scene, Milo has read aloud an essay on "conceptual art," repeatedly mispronouncing "concept" by putting a heavy accent on the second syllable, as if to stress the importance of the word's archaic connotation of insemination,[42] while declining to emphasize the prefix that would imply that the man and woman are (at least) mutually active in the process of conception. As if in response to Milo's influence, Benton remarks into her dictaphone that taking the pseudonym Katherine Louise Marks is "kind of like being a baby and coming into the world." The child in this case is not Anne's, but is rather Anne herself, implying that Milo might imagine himself both as her father and her lover in this arrangement. Milo makes this point even more clearly when he informs the abducted Anne, "I loved you before you was even born," and when Anne makes one last protest for her status as individuated subject, she learns that her hopes are in vain:

ANNE: Look, you can't be thinking that I'm going to do anything you want, because I'm not. It's not fair, it's not right. This is my life, not yours.
MILO: No, this is not your life. This is not my life either. This is our life.

There is nothing for it, then, but for Anne to surrender her identity to Milo, and, in an eerie restaging of 1980s exploitative romance fantasies like *Romancing the Stone* (1984), the film closes with a shot of Milo leading a boat to sea, as Anne is finally able again to work in her electronic medium. This time, however, there is no audience for the art, and the LED sign reads "THE END," blinking repeatedly in various configurations.

Milo's heavy-handed reinscription of paternity (and patriarchy) helps to enunciate within the film's cinematic context the Romantic concept of authorship against which Smithee stands. "Art," as Milo loudly proclaims, "is Charlie Parker. Art is Hieronymous Bach or whatever-his-name-is." Milo understands art to be something that must possess a technique irreplaceable by technology. In thirty short minutes, Hopper's Milo supplants Anne Benton both as the film's main character and as the figure most evidently identifiable as the *auteur* figure within it. *Backtrack* is, therefore, Smithee's darkest film, for it is not acceptable even to allow Anne Benton the Smitheean position of pseudonymous production. Instead, Milo seeks to absorb the commercial possibility of any creative work. In the end, Hopper's character reunites Anne with the technology by which she once made a living as an artist, but he continues to deny the public circulation of her name and of the work that depends on its public display to solicit meaning. The last of Anne's pieces that we see in the film, "THE END," can be seen to comment on the end of the status of those pieces as art and the end of Benton as an artist, as it draws the trajectory of Holzer's work neatly to a close within the diegesis of *Backtrack*, her art now repatriated within the creative vision of Milo. *Backtrack* can also be read as Smithee's most self-pitying film; everywhere calling for his own presence, Smithee invokes throughout the film a series of devices that both remind the viewer of the powerful hold that Romantic ideas of authorship still possess, and frustrate Smithee, the true *auteur* of this film, from becoming corporeally represented within it. Fittingly, the only version of the film available for study on videocassette is Hopper's restored "Director's Cut."

Smithee resolves these problems in his film from the following year, *Solar Crisis*. From the Smitheean perspective, *Solar Crisis* is a more optimistic film than *Backtrack*, because it is able to implicate the paternal metaphor through which the DGA bastardizes Smithee with the kind of naive humanism upon which that metaphor depends. Charlton Heston appears only briefly as Admiral "Skeet" Kelso, the figure of patriarchal authority both within the narrative of the film and within the hierarchy of its actors, since he is the film's only authentic star (Peter Boyle and Jack Palance also appear, but are understood in the film to be, respectively, a minor character actor and a renegade lunatic). Heston's major scene is the one in which he demands the tribute of affection ("Hold it, damn it! Tell me you love me before you leave this room!") from his son Steve Kelso (Tim Matheson), who is the commander of the spaceship in which they are traveling. The Admiral returns to Earth on a Romantic quest to find his lost grandson, who is suggested to be a King Arthur–figure, born to establish order and save civilization from chaos. The Earth is a lawless postapocalyptic desert, savagely run by corporate interest, and as such would appear to be waiting for such a humanistic triumph. But the incompleteness of *Solar Crisis*, an incompleteness Smithee celebrates while allowing it to present itself as a self-contained narrative, prevents any such triumph from occurring.

The unredeemed anarchy on Earth contrasts with the relatively utopian situation on the spaceship, to which the audience's attentions are unavoidably drawn, partly by its slightly more focused plot, but mainly because of the film's superb special effects. Here, the principal romantic

Figure 7.7. Tell me you love me before you leave this room!

interest is a woman conceived in a test tube, without the necessity of the paternal function that comes to organize *Backtrack*. What strikes the viewer is not the humanist ideology we associate with traditional *auteurism*, but rather the positioning of Freddy the computer within the collective workings of the ship. No longer the devious and messianic HAL of Stanley Kubrick's *2001*, upon whom Freddy is clearly based, this computer earnestly represents himself by saying, "I want to thank you for taking me seriously." Freddy is more than the minor comic character that he surely would have been in a legitimately authorized and completed version of the film. By thanking (and gently mocking) Steve Kelso for generously paying him the tribute of obeisance that Kelso has already grudgingly paid to his father, Freddy both demystifies the Romantic technophobia attendant upon cinematic on-board computers since HAL, and assumes a nonpatriarchal position of authority within the ship's collective interests. Freddy, of course, is a figure of Smithee, for it is in his name that the film draws to an unexpected close, as the ship careens into the heart of the sun in an empty heroic gesture. Because the incompleteness of the film provides no substantial narratological support for this final moment in *Solar Crisis*, we are compelled to read it as an appeal to the aesthetic spectacle of special effects technology. Smithee thus succeeds in uniting within a single film the singular and collective interests contained by his name, while also plainly staging the conflicts between the hero-artist and the technician that his name was invented to suppress.

Notes

I am grateful to Christian Keathley for his valuable comments that helped me think through this essay's introduction, and to Gregor Kalas for his insights about my section on Warhol, Johns, and Rauschenberg.

1. François Truffaut, "A Certain Tendency of the French Cinema," *Movies and Methods*, vol. 1, ed. Bill Nichols (Berkeley: University of California Press, 1985) 233. As with his appropriation of the term *auteur*, Truffaut's use of the word "gentleman" is ironic if not sarcastic.

2. See chapters 2 and 11 of the present volume.

3. François Truffaut, "En avoir plein la vue" ["On Being Dazzled"], trans. Sonja Kropp, Wheeler Winston Dixon, *The Early Film Criticism of François Truffaut* (Bloomington: Indiana University Press, 1993) 26.

4. William Leach, *Land of Desire: Merchants, Power and the Rise of a New American Culture* (New York: Pantheon, 1993) 59–60. See also Bill Lancaster, *The Department Store: A Social History* (London: Leicester University Press, 1995), and Susan Porter Benson, *Counter Cultures: Saleswomen, Managers and Customers in American Department Stores, 1890–1940* (Urbana: University of Illinois Press, 1986).

5. Leach 60.

6. Quoted in James Naremore, *The Films of Vincente Minnelli* (Cambridge: Cambridge University Press, 1993) 1.

7. See, for example, Jane Gaines's study of the marketing in show windows of motion picture product tie-ins in "The Queen Christina Tie-Ups: Convergence of Show Window and Screen," *Quarterly Review of Film and Video* 11.1 (1989): 35–60.

8. A longer discussion of Minnelli's critical history can be found in Naremore 45–47.

9. André Bazin, "On the *politique des auteurs*," trans. Peter Graham, *Cahiers du Cinéma, the 1950s: Neo-Realism, Hollywood, New Wave*, ed. Jim Hillier (Cambridge: Harvard University Press, 1985) 249.

10. Andrew Sarris, *The American Cinema: Directors and Directions 1929–1968* (New York: E. P. Dutton, 1968) 102.

11. Naremore 106.

12. Naremore 108.

13. Jean Domarchi, "Knife in the Wound," trans. Diana Matias, *Cahiers du Cinéma, the 1950s: Neo-Realism, Hollywood, New Wave*, ed. Jim Hillier (Cambridge: Harvard University Press, 1985) 244. Quoted in Naremore 45.

14. Domarchi 246, 243.

15. For a more thorough consideration of Smithee in the context of blacklisting, see Jessie Labov's chapter in the present volume.

16. Bill Lancaster's book on department stores notes that before coming to New York, Willem de Kooning also worked as a window display artist in Utrecht (68).

17. David Bourdon, *Warhol* (New York: Harry N. Abrams, 1989) 65. The name "Matson Jones" did not cover over shoddy work, however. As Calvin Tomkins notes, Johns and Rauschenberg were serious about their commercial work, and made a name for Matson Jones with their memorable renderings of swamps, highways, and winter scenes. Their cover design for a medical journal won an industry award, which further necessitated the pseudonymous arrangement (their photographer accepted the award as a proxy). By 1958 they had become so successful as commercial artists that they were able to sponsor, along with Emile de Antonio, a retrospective concert held at New York's Town Hall in honor of their friend John Cage. Calvin Tomkins, *Off the Wall: Robert Rauschenberg and the Art World of Our Time* (Garden City, NY: Doubleday, 1980) 113–14, 147–48.

18. See Jonathan Eburne's chapter in the present volume for an extensive discussion of Duchamp and the Smithee readymade.

19. The first printed acknowledgment of Johns's commercial work appears to have been the entry on the artist in *Current Biography* (May 1967), which suggests that Johns's identity as an important artist was by then safely a matter of record.

20. Leo Steinberg, *Jasper Johns* (New York: George Wittenborn, 1963).

21. Steinberg.

22. Jonathan Katz, "The Art of Code: Jasper Johns and Robert Rauschenberg," *Significant Others: Creativity and Intimate Partnership* (New York: Thames and Hudson, 1993) 189–207.

23. See chapter 1 and chapter 2 for discussions both of the DGA's policy and these two related controversies.

24. Nellie Smithee, letter to the author, 27 June 1997.

25. It is important to remember the obvious point that Warhol never directly indicated that his work intended any critique of consumerism. An exemplary instance of his (dis)ingenuity appears on the CD that accompanies the *Andy Warhol Museum* book. In an excerpt from his 16 July 1965 tape recording, Warhol and a friend can be heard to peruse the aisles of Gristede's, waxing rhapsodic about packaging and logos, most notably The Jolly Green Giant. Andy Warhol, "Andy in a supermarket, July 16, 1965," *Andy Warhol from Tapes: Sounds of his Life and Work* (Pittsburgh: Andy Warhol Museum, 1994).

26. Andrew Sarris, "Notes on the *Auteur* Theory in 1962," *Film Theory and Film Criticism*, ed. Gerald Mast and Marshall Cohen, 2d ed. (New York: Oxford University Press, 1979) 662.

27. "Directors Guild of America Basic Agreement of 1996," *DGA 1996 Creative Rights Handbook*, Directors Guild of America, 5 Sept. 1997 <http://www.dga.org/dga-info/dga_creative_rights_handbook.htm>.

28. Michel Foucault, "What Is an Author?" trans. Joseph V. Harari, *Modern Criticism and Theory: A Reader*, ed. David Lodge (London: Longman, 1988) 209.

29. Smithee's European release was entitled *Catch Fire*. Hopper's restored "Director's Cut" of *Backtrack* is easily found in video stores today.

30. "Creative Rights Checklist," *DGA 1996 Creative Rights Handbook*, Directors Guild of America, 5 Sept. 1997 <http://www.dga.org/dga-info/dga_creative_rights_handbook.htm>.

31. Sarris, "Notes on the *Auteur* Theory in 1962," 662–63. See Christian Keathley's chapter of the present volume for a discussion of Sarris's criteria in the context of Jacques Derrida's *signateur* theory.

32. Jacques Derrida, "Before the Law," trans. Avital Ronell and Christine Roulston, *Acts of Literature*, ed. Derek Attridge (New York: Routledge, 1992) 181.

33. Derrida 187.

34. In Kafka's story, a "countryman" comes to stand before the door of the Law, begging to be allowed admittance to the Law. The doorkeeper acknowledges that "'It is possible … but not at the moment.'" The doorkeeper then postpones admittance seemingly indefinitely, until the countryman is so old that he is physically incapable of entering the doorway. At the moment of his dying, it occurs to him to ask the doorkeeper why "'no one but myself has ever begged for admittance?'" The doorkeeper responds, "'No one else could ever be admitted here, since this gate was made only for you. I am now going to shut it.'" The story is reprinted in full within Derrida's essay. The translation printed by Attridge comes from *Wedding Preparations in the Country and Other Stories*, trans. Willa and Edwin Muir (Harmondsworth: Penguin, 1978).

35. Derrida 191. See, for comparison, Lesley Ellen Harris, "Just What Are Moral Rights, Anyway? A Primer for Directors," *DGA Magazine*, 9 July 1999, http://www.dga.org/magazine/v21-2/moralrights.html.

36. As quoted in Derrida 190.

37. Derrida 197–98.

38. In the first chapter of this volume, it is suggested that this primeval *auteur* may be Orson Welles.

39. Quoted in Dixon 3.

40. Donald Pease discusses *Death of a Gunfighter*'s "excluded narratives" in chapter 4 of the present volume.

41. Lois Palken Rudnick, *Utopian Vistas: The Mabel Dodge Luhan House and the American Counterculture* (Albuquerque: University of New Mexico Press, 1996) 4–5.

42. *OED*, "concept," v. Obs. To conceive (in the womb).

CHAPTER 8

This Is Too Big for One Old Name: Hitchcock and Smithee in the Signature Centrifuge

Stephen Hock

The Two Als

Part of the problem facing any student of Alan Smithee[1] films is the difficulty of locating the objects to study. Smithee films do not receive the gift of rerelease either in theaters or on special collector's edition videocassettes; the home-video versions of the films appear on few video store shelves; and, perhaps most telling of all, no professors devote the valuable resource of a semester's class to studying the films of Alan Smithee, as they might devote a class to studying the works of, for example, Alfred Hitchcock. The Smithee scholar must not limit him- or herself to the confines of film studies as that discipline generally defines itself and the limits of its objects of study. Instead, the Smithee scholar must choose to take on a perambulatory perspective, walking outside the patterns of viewing prescribed by video store displays and film studies syllabi. In preparing to write this essay, for instance, I went to three video stores— all franchises of national chains—before finding one that had a copy of Smithee's 1994 made-for-TV movie *The Birds II: Land's End*. Even at this store, I noted that, whereas the store's management had placed the videocassette of Alfred Hitchcock's 1963 film *The Birds* toward the front of the store, in a special "Hitchcock" subsection of the "Suspense" section, the videocassette for *The Birds II* occupied a place near the rear of the store, in the somewhat less prestigious "Horror" section. There was, of course, no "Smithee" subsection anywhere in the store. Given that the store's management had seen fit to mark *The Birds* as the product of a featured director, while burying *The Birds II* in a distant aisle, there seemed little danger of confusing the film with its sequel. The casual renter of video-cassettes, walking through the store on a path guided by the markers of genre and *auteur*, markers that mirror those that shape the dimensions of film studies, would have little reason to think of the Hitchcock original and the Smithee sequel as being linked to one another. Only when we learn to walk in a different way, to see around the distance that commercial considerations impose between the works of Hitchcock and Smithee, and to use our perspective to create connections where, ostensibly, none exist, can we begin to understand the relation of Smithee to Hitchcock. My purpose in writing this essay is to question the separation of film and sequel, in order to set the two Als—Hitchcock and Smithee—side-by-side and see what connections this juxtaposition can both reveal and create.

Beyond the problem of locating Smithee films lies the question of what critical apparatus best serves to make texts that yield productive information out of these otherwise forgotten films. The student of Smithee learns early on that modes of criticism based on the two classificatory schemes common to video stores and film studies—genre and *auteur*—cannot apply to Smithee films, since the only feature those films share is that their directors abandoned them and signed the films not with their own names, but with "Alan Smithee." The Smithee signature covers films across many genres and directors, and no critical apparatus can hope to unite these wildly divergent texts. Instead, the scholar's attention loses its focus as the critical gaze wanders from text to disparate text. The Smithee scholar needs a perspective that takes this diffusion of attention into account, one that scatters its interpretive energies even as the films that constitute the Smithee oeuvre remain scattered throughout video store shelves.

The Smithee scholar whose attention threatens to spin out of control when trying to track Smithee films across video store aisles, genres, and styles might do well to keep in mind that cinema, according to André Bazin, operates as a sort of centrifuge. Whereas theater centripetally concentrates its action into a limited space, Bazin argues, "the space of the screen is centrifugal,"[2] always suggesting a space beyond that which is shown on the screen. In a similar manner, the Smithee signature always gestures beyond the space of the screen, reminding viewers of the missing directorial signature, the lack around which the film and the film scholar's attention begin to fall apart. Robert Ray, in *The Avant-Garde Finds Andy Hardy*, advocates a model of film studies that takes into account this Bazinian centrifugal dynamic of film. Ray also focuses on the signature itself, which is felicitous since the signature is all that the scholar studying Smithee has to work with. Ray locates his model in the Derridean signature experiment:

> the signature experiment, with its representation of *diffusion*, may be more appropriate to film study than its opposite, *auteur* theory. While *auteurism* centripetally (and misleadingly) gathers filmmaking's disparate work into one proper noun ("Hitchcock," "Capra"), a book like *Signsponge* works centrifugally, amending structuralism's "death of the author" by perversely using the author's name to scatter his effects.[3]

"If names are the raw material," Ray notes, "then a film scholar faces an overabundance of riches,"[4] including the names of directors, actors, characters, and scriptwriters. A method that diffuses the signature of the director seems the most appropriate one for Smithee, since the films that bear the mark of his signature owe their very status as Smithee films to their original directors' refusals to lend their names as the films' organizing principles. Indeed, the method of the signature experiment seems particularly suited to Smithee, since Smithee's signature, like the signature experiment itself, owes its existence to a willingness to accept that factors of chance can and often do remove a film from the control of its *auteur*.[5] The Smithee signature, as revealed in my signature experiment, poses a disruptive threat to the *auteurist* valorization of the director in general, and Hitchcock's *auteurist* aura in particular. The Smithee signature experiment becomes the centrifuge in which we put the two Als, spin them apart, and see what results.

Building the Brand Name

As a centrifuge tearing Hitchcock's name apart, my Smithee signature experiment mounts an attack on Hitchcock the *auteur*, especially the *auteur* of *The Birds*. Today, Hitchcock's reputation as one of Andrew Sarris's Pantheon directors has permeated our culture. Sarris's view of Hitchcock as "the supreme technician of the American cinema,"[6] a director whose films "operate on ... many levels," and whose style is one of "beauty," as well as "speed and efficiency,"[7] seems enshrined in the minds of generations of moviegoers and critics. Four Hitchcock films, for instance, appear on a 1998 American Film Institute list of the top one hundred American films of all time;[8] likewise, a recent Internet Movie Database[9] survey ranked Hitchcock as the fourteenth-best director of all time. Similarly widely accepted is Sarris's praise of *The Birds* as a film that "reveals a rigorous morality coupled with a dark humor."[10] Though *The Birds* does not appear on the American Film Institute's list, an ongoing Internet Movie Database survey, as of June 1999, ranked the film as the 239th-best film ever made,[11] while *The Birds II* was tied with ten other films as the forty-fifth-worst film ever.[12] In short, Hitchcock has become more than a director, more even than an *auteur*. His name has become, as Ray suggests, a sort of brand name, a name that produces instant recognition among audiences and critics who know what to expect from any film authored by Hitchcock.

As Michel Foucault reminds us, however, an author, or an *auteur*, "is not defined by the spontaneous attribution of a discourse to its producer, but rather by a series of specific and complex operations,"[13] operations of constructing identities and excluding facts that disrupt those identities. "[T]hese aspects of an individual which we designate as making him an author," Foucault argues, "are only a projection, in more or less psychologizing terms, of the operations that we force texts to undergo, the connections that we make, the traits that we establish as pertinent, the continuities that we recognize, or the exclusions that we practice."[14] Indeed, as Robert E. Kapsis demonstrates in his *Hitchcock: The Making of a Reputation*, Hitchcock's reputation as *auteur* depends greatly on such operations. "Prior to the 1960s," Kapsis observes, "most American film critics and scholars did not rank Hitchcock's films as 'serious art.'"[15] Kapsis goes on to describe in great detail how, although "[b]etween 1960 and 1964, Hitchcock himself made a concerted effort to reshape his reputation among the serious journalistic critics" (73), it was "[n]ot until the early 1970s, when the auteur theory became the dominant aesthetic discourse among journalistic and academic film critics, [that] his reputation improve[d]" (70). In fact, Kapsis characterizes *The Birds* as "the first, the most ambitious, and certainly the most expensive project the filmmaker undertook for the purpose of reshaping his reputation among serious critics" (74), a project undertaken simultaneously with those *auteurist* critics like Sarris and François Truffaut who felt what Kapsis describes as an "infatuation with Hitchcock" (91). Indeed, Kapsis notes that Hitchcock regarded Truffaut's well-known book of interviews with Hitchcock as "a vehicle for promoting not only himself but also *The Birds*" (142), so much so that he "was prepared to charge all of Truffaut's travel-related expenses ... to the publicity account for *The Birds*" (91). In the figures of Hitchcock and Truffaut, then, we see a director searching for critical acclaim, and a younger critic and director perhaps seeking to make a name for himself not unlike that which the object of his veneration also desires. Controlling both the production of films and the interpretation of those films, the marketing team of Hitchcock and Truffaut contributed mightily to the creation of the Hitchcock brand name as a marker of critical, as well as commercial, successes.

Despite Hitchcock's efforts, *The Birds* received a decidedly mixed early set of reactions. *Time* magazine's review held that "the movie flaps to a pointless end."[16] One of Hitchcock's own fans wrote him a letter criticizing the film for not explaining why the birds attack; in an uncanny bit of foreshadowing, the fan closes the letter by asking Hitchcock if he will put the explanation in the sequel.[17] James Watters, later entertainment editor of *Life* magazine, wrote a critical memo to Richard Griffith, then director of the Museum of Modern Art's film program, which was about to hold a retrospective on Hitchcock's work at the suggestion of *auteurist* critic (and later filmmaker) Peter Bogdanovich. Not coincidentally, as Kapsis notes, this retrospective was to be paid for by the public relations firm promoting *The Birds*.[18] Watters cautioned Griffith:

> This film is a humorless and contrived tale based on a gimmick with a weak, unresolved ending. The audience hissed at the conclusion of the showing. No matter how well-conceived and executed, the special effects are obvious and thus destroy the illusion of reality and negate the terror. Not since the films of the 40's have I seen so much process photography. The actors excepting Jessica Tandy are one-dimensional and unconvincing. Tippi Hedren, Hitchcock's "new personality," is a cold, shallow nonprofessional who belongs on the cover of *Vogue*. She is so icy the audience last night mistaked [sic] her for a figure of evil—quite the contrary to Hitchcock's concept of the junior sophisticate Miss Hedren plays. She is his worst leading lady since Priscilla Lane. This is minor Hitchcock for the emphasis is on design details for production values with a complete disregard for developing depth of character and atmosphere and for doing anything with an ineffectual and undeveloped plot line.[19]

For the purpose of juxtaposing the two Als, compare these reactions to this not entirely dissimilar review of *The Birds II* from *Daily Variety*: "Script ... would have been sharper if characters were smarter; if there's a wrong turn to be taken here, somebody takes it. . . . At any rate, the results are routine and acting is pedestrian, but high marks go to the avian villains—real, animatronic and (it appears in some scenes) animated. . . . Story is left open-ended."[20] Likewise, *New York* magazine's John Leonard writes of the sequel: "Director Alan Smithee, with the help of trainer Gary Gero and many puppets, dummies, and stunt birds from the folks at Animatronics, gets more emotion from the bloodshot sky than he does from Brad [Johnson, who plays the protagonist] and Chelsea [Fields, playing his wife]."[21] Initial critical reactions to the two films, then, place *The Birds* and its Smithee sequel far closer to one another than either film scholars or video store clerks would do.

Hitchcock, however, has to his advantage over Smithee a group of *auteurist* critics dedicated to working in opposition to the critics quoted above, in order to build up his reputation. Bogdanovich prepared a monograph for the MoMA Hitchcock retrospective in which he argues that *The Birds* "is ... an excellent blending of character and incident, of atmosphere and terror. If he had never made another motion picture in his life, *The Birds* would place him securely among the giants of cinema. And that is where he belongs."[22] Likewise, Sarris's review describes *The Birds* as "a major work of cinematic art," one that "finds Hitchcock at the summit of his artistic powers," and concludes by proclaiming, "If formal excellence is still a valid criterion for film criticism ... then *The Birds* is probably the picture of the year."[23] Truffaut praises the film as follows:

> what an injustice there is in the generally bad reception. I am so disappointed that no critic admired the basic premise of the film: "Birds attack people." I am convinced that cinema was invented so that such a film could be made. Everyday birds—sparrows, seagulls, crows—take to attacking ordinary people, the inhabitants of a seacoast village. This is an artist's dream.[24]

Truffaut further declares, "the special effects are realistic. In fact, Hitchcock's mastery of the art grows greater with each film and he constantly needs to invent new difficulties for himself. He has become the ultimate athlete of cinema."[25] Seen through the adoring lens of these and other *auteurist* critics' viewpoints, Hitchcock appears as one of the "giants of cinema"—indeed, "the ultimate athlete of cinema"—"at the summit of his artistic powers"; he becomes, in short, an Olympian figure: heroic, athletic, even virile, a veritable god of artistic creation. That is to say, he does not at all resemble an all-too-human aging director engaged in a late-career effort to salvage his critical reputation, a transformation these critics willingly abetted.

In addition to their roles as promoters of the virtues of Hitchcock and his films, these and other *auteurist* critics also served to exclude from the critical discourse those traits that might damage the reputation they and Hitchcock had worked to build. Kapsis cites Sarris in particular as one of those critics who "attempted to protect [Hitchcock's] public image" from allegations concerning the director's "dark side" contained in works such as Donald Spoto's 1983 biographical exposé *The Dark Side of Genius*. Kapsis describes Sarris as taking the occasion of the 1983 re-release of *Rear Window* as an opportunity "to denounce Richard Grenier for using Spoto to attack Hitchcock," making an effort to "deflect the Hitchcock debate away from Spoto's 'revelations' about Hitchcock's questionable conduct to the strength of the films themselves."[26] Of course, the "strength of the films themselves," as the early critical reaction to *The Birds* shows, far from being a self-evident property of the films, remains dependent upon the image of Hitchcock that these critics had developed in terms almost of hero-worship. As protectors of that image, Sarris and his fellow *auteurist* critics serve as the guarantors of the quality of the Hitchcock brand name, thereby securing an image of Hitchcock the *auteur* fit for public consumption. In so doing, they protect not only the continued revenues of Hitchcock's films, but also their own status as marketers and, indeed, creators, of the privileged Hitchcock brand name.

Today, of course, the Hitchcock brand name has established itself as an unqualified success. The name has, over the course of its lifetime (a lifetime that shows no signs of being limited by Alfred Hitchcock's own mortality), appeared not only on Hitchcock's films, but also on those films' numerous theatrical and videocassette rereleases, three television series,[27] and various periodicals and books. In 1998 Hitchcock even received validation from the United States Postal Service, which issued a Hitchcock stamp bearing a photograph of the director, as well as the instantly recognizable stylized silhouette of Hitchcock that appeared at the introduction of the *Alfred Hitchcock Presents* television series. As the Associated Press article on the stamp's issue reports, "Alfred Hitchcock, whose profile became as famous as his skill directing such films as *Psycho* and *The Birds*, is making a cameo nearly two decades after his death. A 32-cent U.S. postage stamp honoring Hitchcock goes on sale nationwide today, part of the Postal Service's Legends of Hollywood series that includes Humphrey Bogart, Marilyn Monroe and James Dean."[28] The report goes on to quote Hitchcock's daughter Patricia as saying, "My father's legacy will be preserved forever in American film and of all the awards he has received for his work, he would be most honored to be immortalized through America's stamp program." One interesting fact the Associated Press report fails to mention is that each sheet of twenty Hitchcock stamps (the twenty-stamp sheet being the only form in which the Postal Service sells such special commemorative stamps) bears, in addition to the Postal Service's standard notice that the stamps themselves are copyrighted by the United States Postal Service, the notices "Alfred Hitchcock™ & © The Alfred Hitchcock Trust" and "Alfred Hitchcock Presents© Universal Studios." Like his fellow subject of postal immortality, Elvis Presley, Hitchcock, in death, has left not only the realm of the living. He has also left the realm of the individual. Instead of a person, Hitchcock—or, as I should perhaps, for legal reasons, refer to him, "Hitchcock™ & © The Alfred Hitchcock Trust"— has become a commodity, trademarked and copyrighted by "The Alfred Hitchcock Trust," easily reproduced and sold, provided, of course, that the Trust approves of and is properly compensated for each use of the director's trademarked likeness and brand name.

What to make, then, of the fact that the Hitchcock brand name, like those of Kleenex and Xerox before it, has, in a somewhat perverse way, become the victim of its own success? As noted above, the image of Hitchcock the *auteur* of, among other films, *The Birds*, has become part of the common cultural literacy of contemporary American society. A *New York Times* story of 5 July 1998, describing an infestation of vultures in a New York state property, quotes one of the property's owners, Carol Ann O'Byrne, as remarking, "But it was the scariest thing, one day I was coming home and they were all flying above my house. It was like the movie 'The Birds.'"[29] In a similar display of the pervasiveness of knowledge of *The Birds*, NBC's Katie Couric, at the beginning of the 6 October 1998 *Today* show, commented on an upcoming segment featuring wildlife expert Jim Fowler with some birds: "Yow! We need Tippi Hedren for that spot."[30] Invoking not the name of *The Birds'* star, but rather its *auteur*, a 4 October 1998 *Philadelphia Inquirer* article on swarming blackbirds refers at one point to its subject as "Hitchcockian swarms."[31] Herein lies a problem: where does the proper, and in fact trademarked and copyrighted, name, "Hitchcock," yield to the public-domain adjective, "Hitchcockian"? Texts such as news reports and academic publications may refer to Hitchcock without fearing legal consequences. When the *Philadelphia Inquirer* invokes the name of Hitchcock on a front-page story, however, underneath a photograph of a menacing-appearing swarm of blackbirds, we might wonder whether commercial considerations are not also at work in the reference to Hitchcock. If so, is the *Philadelphia Inquirer* illegally benefiting from the intellectual property of the Alfred Hitchcock Trust?

Like the brand names "Kleenex" and "Xerox," "Hitchcock" has transcended the specific product to which it originally referred. Today, as the Katie Couric example shows, any variety of references to birds—whether menacing or not—can call to mind thoughts of Hitchcock and his film; the meaning of the name has become diffuse, scattered. Like the uncapitalized word "kleenex," which today can refer to any sort of facial tissue, or the similarly uncapitalized "xerox," which has become both a common noun referring to any photocopy as well as a verb designating the act of photocopying, "Hitchcock" has in a way ceased to be a brand name and become instead a generic name. It is to counter the specifically economic aspect of this process, of course, that the Alfred Hitchcock Trust has trademarked and copyrighted Hitchcock. When the Hitchcock name becomes generic, it serves, on one hand, as the greatest possible advertisement for Hitchcock products, since the connection between birds and Hitchcock becomes universal. At the same time, however, the process by which a brand name becomes a generic name also represents a process of economic loss for those who control the brand name. The name begins to seem less like the property of a corporate entity, and more like common property available to anyone. This process of antonomasia—the same process that Derrida puts at the heart of works such as *Signsponge*[32]—by which a proper name becomes a common noun, is the greatest threat both to Hitchcock the *auteur* and to Hitchcock the registered trademark of the Alfred Hitchcock Trust.

Of course, antonomasia is something that the other Al—Smithee, that is—has never needed to fear.

"I Am The/A Lens"

Alan Smithee, instead of being a director who fears antonomasia, is a director whose name embodies a sort of antonomasia. The Smithee name remains, of course, the intellectual property of the Directors Guild of America; only the Guild may sanction a director's substitution of the Smithee pseudonym for his or her own name. In this sense, then, "Alan Smithee" is and remains a proper name. By virtue of its very status as the generic pseudonym by which directors disassociate themselves from films over which they have lost control, however, the Smithee name loses any ability to refer to films directed by any specific individual. Rather than serving as a director's brand name, as Hitchcock's does, the Smithee name instead serves as a kind of generic brand name. The Smithee name stands for the principle of antonomasia, the surrendering of a name's specificity and its status as the property of an individual or an individual's trustees. Indeed, as much as the guardians of the Alfred Hitchcock Trust might resist the very idea, Smithee represents what could happen to Hitchcock as the name slowly but surely transforms from a proper name referring to a man and his films to a common word referring to a broad variety of works reflecting a "Hitchcockian" sensibility. The name will lose its value, both aesthetically, and, should the copyrights on Hitch-cock's films and Hitchcock himself ever expire, economically.

Smithee, then, stands for the loss of set values, the opening of a space for the creation of new meanings. This is the point at which I would like to bring my signature experiment to bear on Hitchcock and Smithee. The Smithee name's role in this experiment will be to break down the Hitchcock brand name, to scatter its value by turning the brand name—as well as various assorted names associated with *The Birds* and its sequel—against itself, in order to uncover precisely those sorts of distracting and detracting details about Hitchcock that Hitchcock, the *auteurist* critics, and other interested parties such as the Alfred Hitch-cock Trust would prefer to suppress in their attempts to build up the brand name. The particular detail I will attempt to use Smithee to high-light is the obsession Spoto describes Hitchcock as having with the actress Tippi Hedren, what Spoto terms a "strange fixation."[33] At various points, Spoto claims, Hitchcock attempted to control Hedren: he advised her what to wear both on and off the set (451); "recommended that she gain weight, and one afternoon there were two bushels of potatoes delivered to her doorstep with a written reminder that in sufficient amounts they were rich in calories" (452); gave Hedren's daughter Melanie Griffith (on the future actress' sixth birthday) "a strange and somewhat frightening gift: an elaborate and expensive doll of her mother dressed as the character she played in *The Birds*, complete with minia-ture green suit and elegant coiffure—but the doll was packaged in a tiny pine box" (467); and, "under pretext of a complicated makeup session, . . . made a life mask of his actress, and for a long time jealously guarded her delicate features, captured forever in perfect repose" (467). As Spoto notes, "Another devotee might have cherished a photograph or a ring or a garment, but Hitchcock had already designed her pictures, jewelry, and wardrobe" (467–68). In short, Hitchcock exerted a proprietary control over Hedren, turning the actress herself into a product—a brand name. Of course, as the creator and maintainer of the Hedren product, Hitch-cock expected to reap all of the product's profits, economic and other. Indeed, all of these efforts culminated in what Spoto refers to as "an overt sexual proposition" during the making of *Marnie* in 1964, which Hedren declined (475). Afterward, Spoto claims, Hitchcock significantly "never even uttered her name, referring only to 'that girl'" (476). Since he could not control Hedren as a product, he determined to efface her name value, just as the protectors of Hitchcock's legacy seek to efface these and other instances of what Spoto terms the "dark side of genius."

As many critics have noted, sex in general is one of the more prev-alent themes running through Hitchcock's films. Nonetheless, Hitch-cock himself offered the disclaimer to Truffaut, "I never have any erotic dreams!"[34] perhaps as another one of the exclusions necessary to con-struct his valuable identity as dignified and respected *auteur*. This effaced sexuality will serve, as it does in Hitchcock's films, as a running theme of my signature experiment. Text printed on the Hitchcock stamp sheet comments: "No other filmmaker has so successfully and subtly blended private concerns with themes of universal significance." As my signature experiment will show, the blending of Hitchcock's private obsession with Hedren with the universal theme of sexuality, while successful, need not be subtle at all. The very names of those involved in the making of *The Birds* and *The Birds II: Land's End*, when spun properly in the centrifuge of the signature experiment, separate Hitchcock's "private concern" for Hedren from the "themes of universal significance" of the text, and make Hitchcock's "private concerns" clear for all to see. That these concerns are resolutely masculinist can hardly be surprising, given both Hitchcock's position relative to Hedren and also the masculinist rhetoric that has often marked the critical statements of the *auteurs* and their defenders; as Barton Byg has noted, "The 'camera-stylo,' 'auteur theory' and the new wave impulse are typified by language redolent of masculine rejuvenation."[35] Just such a framework of masculinist power not only underlies the plot of *The Birds*, but also appears from within the play of signatures associated with the film. As my signature experiment will also show, however, Hitchcock's appropriation of a particular position of sexual power need not go unchallenged. Instead, the Smithee name can turn the same metaphors of sexual power back on Hitchcock as tools in *The Birds II*'s attack on the heroized position of the masculinist *auteur*.

In making use of Smithee's signature, I take as my guide an anagram that can be made from his name as it is spelled in the credits of *The Birds II*: "I am the/a lens."[36] The anagram Smithee's name lends itself to wavers on the question of whether he is "the" lens, or merely "a" lens, through which we can view his and Hitchcock's films. In this undecidability about which sort of lens his name provides, Smithee allows for the possibility of meanings that the *auteurist* critics' acceptance of the name "Hitchcock" at face value does not allow. Unlike the *auteur* theory that holds that the director's personality is the dominant factor through which we must view films, a focus on Smithee's signature allows other factors—such as the factors of chance that constitute a necessary element of all filmmaking and that the signature experiment makes use of—to enter into the interpretation of his films, thereby helping to undo the "principle of thrift in the proliferation of meaning" that Foucault locates in the figure of the author.[37] Smithee's is no brand name that requires its adherents to view the world through only the consumerist lens provided by product placement, advertisement, and other promotions. Instead, the Smithee name, in its anagram, identifies itself as the generic equivalent to an *auteur*'s brand name: not necessarily "the" lens providing definitive meaning, but at least "a" lens, providing, if nothing else, a meaning that is perhaps as valid as any that results from operations—like Hitchcock's—aimed at creating a brand name out of a director's signature. Since the Smithee name refuses to be the only lens through which we can view Smithee films, a signature experiment based on the Smithee signature allows us to consider multiple names—not only the director's, but also those of the cast, crew, and characters, among others—as lenses through which to read the film. My signature experiment considers precisely such names, in a variety of associative chains they suggest, to come to a reading of *The Birds* and *The Birds II: Land's End* that refuses to follow the path of brand-name loyalty and instead plays with the very stuff of the brand name, namely, the signature.

To begin with the original Hitchcock film, I observe that a number of critics have noted the similarity between the first name of the male protagonist of *The Birds*, Mitch Brenner, played by Rod Taylor, and Hitchcock's nickname, Hitch. In fact, David Sterritt argues that the film "pivots on the simplest and most revelatory of equations. Mitch = Hitch."[38] I would like to introduce into this discussion another word, one which Theodore Price contends was one of "Hitch's favorite words": bitch, the word that Price argues sums up Hitchcock's feelings toward a type of woman embodied by Hedren's character in *The Birds*, Melanie Daniels.[39] As important as the bitch-Mitch-Hitch axis in this associative chain is the second half of Hitchcock's last name: cock. The two syllables come together when we remember a comment Price quotes Hitchcock as making to describe Hedren's character in *The Birds*: "The whole performance, the whole shape deals with the smug American girl who talks sex, lives sex, but won't go to bed. We have a vulgar phrase for that: they are what are called cockteasers."[40] Taken by itself, cock, as a designator of the phallus, relates to the first name of the actor playing Mitch Brenner: Rod Taylor. The Rod, as the erect phallus, would be the result of the action described by Hitchcock's last name in its entirety: the hitching of the cock. In *The Birds*, then, we have the story of Melanie, the bitch who teases Mitch—that is to say, Rod—who stands for Hitch, he of the hitched cock. As the hitched cock, Hitchcock's name reflects the carefully crafted image of his brand-name identity as the director who exerts control over his film and the actors and actresses in it, albeit in a more vulgar tone than Hitchcock or his trustees might generally like to project. Taken in conjunction with these other names, however, "Hitchcock" can call up a far different story, one in which Hitch/Mitch remains the victim of the cockteasing bitch played by Hedren.

Other signatures among the various credits of *The Birds*, however, show that Hedren's position as cockteasing bitch is perhaps not entirely free from Hitchcock's domination. For example, I turn to Mitch's last name: Brenner, the German word meaning "burner." Putting "Mitch" and "Brenner" together, we can identify this character as the bitch-burner, the torturer of the bitch Melanie Daniels played by Hedren. Mitch's role as Hedren's torturer further strengthens the identification between Mitch and Hitch when we remember the torture Hedren went through at the hands of Hitchcock in the filming of *The Birds*' climactic attic attack scene, a scene the filming of which, as Spoto relates, involved actual birds being "hurled" at Hedren, "as she defended herself against the gulls and crows with wild, increasingly honest and unacted gestures of terror."[41] Eventually, Spoto notes, "one bird became particularly agitated and went for her left eye. A catastrophe was avoided, but a deep gash appeared on her lower lid. At that point she became hysterical and suffered a complete collapse,"[42] a collapse that closed down production of *The Birds* for a week. Rather than being simply an old man teased by a bitch, the director exerted a control over his actress that, in the case of the attic attack scene, bordered on the sadistic. Of course, the sadism this associative chain ascribes to Hitchcock depends on his first being entranced by Hedren. Accordingly, to look at the director's surrogate's name through a different lens, "Mitch Brenner" designates "Mitch burner," thereby indicating the burning desire Mitch feels for the bitch played by Hedren. The associative link between fire and sexual desire, in this context, calls to mind another of Price's comments on Hitchcock, in which he remarks that Hedren, as seen through Hitchcock's director-ial lens, perfectly fills the role of "Hitch's well-known Nordic blonde, who looks cool and calm, but who (as Hitch feels) smoulders within, with sex."[43] As the name of Mitch Brenner indicates, Hitch, too, feels the burning power of Hedren's sexuality. Similarly indicative of Hitchcock's relation—real or perceived—to Hedren is the last name of the actor playing Mitch, Taylor. Rod Taylor, the name of the actor who incarnates Hitch in the film, indicates the power and desire of the one wielding the phallus—that is, Hitchcock—to control Hedren by becoming her tailor, dictating the clothes she would wear, and, generally, attempting to tailor her life and career to fit his needs. On just the level of the names of

Figure 8.1. Tippi Hedren under attack in *The Birds*.

Hitchcock and his on-screen surrogate Taylor/Brenner, then, we can see an associative chain that suggests the dynamic of the relationship between Hedren and her director, the controlling but frustrated Hitchcock.

As my signature experiment turns from Hitchcock and Taylor to Hedren, a number of new possibilities suggest themselves. Melanie, besides being the first name of Hedren's character, is also the name of her real-life daughter Melanie Griffith, who was a child at the time of the making of *The Birds*. Melanie, then, serves as the name of an infantilized, easier-to-control version of Tippi, one whose sexuality has not yet emerged to turn her into the cockteasing bitch Hedren plays in the film. On this level, Melanie Daniels's first name serves to neutralize her dangerously independent sexuality. The connection on the level of the name between Melanie Daniels and Melanie Griffith also calls to mind a similarly nominal link to Richard Griffith, director of the MoMA's film department at the time of its Hitchcock retrospective, and a man who, according to Kapsis, was no fan of Hitchcock or of *The Birds*. In the range of real-life figures suggested by this associative chain proceeding from the name "Melanie Daniels," we can see incarnated a number of persons who could serve as targets for the anger that Hitchcock's film demonstrates toward the character Melanie Daniels. Melanie's relation to Annie Hayworth, Mitch's jilted former lover who still pines for him, played by Suzanne Pleshette, further indicates Melanie's status as seen through the lens of Hitchcock's sexual morality. In this lens, it becomes all too easy to read Melanie as *mal* Annie, bad Annie. Annie's last name is Hayworth—she still, perhaps, finds Mitch worth a roll in the proverbial hay. In contrast, the bad Annie's last name is Daniels, and, like the biblical Daniel's three friends Shadrach, Meschach, and Abednego, she does not burn for Mitch/Hitch as Brenner and Hitchcock burn for her.[44] In short, Melanie Daniels's name indicates her place in the film as a character whose sexuality Hitchcock views as something to be controlled, something that should serve his desire but, because of its "badness," remains coldly unresponsive to his advances, just as Hedren asserted her independence from Hitchcock by refusing his sexual advances during the making of *Marnie*.

Hedren is the only actor from *The Birds* to appear in *The Birds II*, though her name, significantly, appears differently in the credits of each film. Spoto observes that Hitchcock insisted that Hedren's first name, Tippi, appear in single quotation marks in the credits of *The Birds*—and, in fact, "in every connection with Alfred Hitchcock and his films"[45]— even though she had long since adopted the childhood nickname as her preferred first name over her given first name, Nathalie. By enclosing Hedren's chosen first name in quotation marks, Hitchcock foregrounds the name's status as a nickname, and, in so doing, reminds the audience of *The Birds* that 'Tippi' Hedren is in some sense an assumed and created persona. The fact that the full credit reads "And Introducing 'Tippi' Hedren" further works to create the perception that Tippi Hedren is a product, a new model that Hitchcock unveils, as it were, for public consumption in *The Birds*. Notably, the credits do not identify the 'Tippi' nickname as one that preceded Hedren's career as an actress. From the very introduction of Hedren's name in the opening credits of *The Birds*, then, Hitchcock works to craft a perception of 'Tippi' Hedren as a subsidiary of the Hitchcock brand. In *The Birds II: Land's End*, on the other hand, Tippi appears without quotation marks. Instead of the new product presented in *The Birds*, the Hedren of *The Birds II: Land's End* is an actress who needs no introduction, and whom the Smithee film allows to reclaim her name from Hitchcock's proprietary control.

Hedren appears in the sequel as one of the few characters who understands what is going on with the birds of the town of Land's End. Even though she plays a different character in the sequel from the one she did in the original, it is almost as if Hedren's new character some-how draws on the knowledge of her old one to interpret the film's events for the new male protagonist, Ted Hocken, played by Brad Johnson. Hedren's character's name in the sequel—Helen Matthews—indicates her position as interpreter. As Helen, Hedren becomes an interpreter of the film's events just as another Helen—Helen G. Scott—served as the interpreter between Hitchcock and Truffaut in the interviews that went into the famous book that Hitchcock saw as a publicity tool for *The Birds*. Here, however, Helen does not serve Hitchcock's interests, but

Figure 8.2. Hedren as object of desire in *The Birds* . . .

Figure 8.3. . . . and as interpretive confidante in *The Birds II*.

rather those of Smithee, the principle of dissolution of the very directorial control Hitchcock attempted to exert over Hedren. Accordingly, Hedren's Helen displays a knowing sympathy for Ted Hocken, at one point coyly telling him that, no matter what others say, "You and I both know there's something going on around here, don't we?" Since, as the signature experiment will show, I view Hocken as a surrogate for Smithee, the fact that Hedren's Helen displays such a friendly, confiding attitude toward Hocken is perhaps the Smithee film's way of highlighting that Hedren appears in it as a sympathetic and wise interpreter and confidante, while she remained for Hitchcock an uncontrollable and unreachable object of sadistic desire.

In this signature experiment, Hocken's name reveals his role as Smithee's on-screen avatar. "Hocken" is the German verb meaning "to squat." The Hocken family, appropriately enough, are squatters, occupying for the summer a house that, while it cannot be the Brenner home from *The Birds*, is obviously designed to be reminiscent of the earlier house. Smithee, of course, is also a squatter, taking over the director's chair formerly occupied by Hitchcock, not to mention that of the sequel's original director, Rick Rosenthal. Accordingly, *The Birds II* is Smithee's assertion of his squatter's rights. Significantly, Smithee's opening credit as the film's director appears in the film at the precise instant that Ted approaches the house his family has rented for the summer. Indeed, the Smithee credit appears superimposed over an image of Ted himself, as if announcing the identification of Hocken with Smithee.[46] Notably, the actor standing in for Smithee bears a phallic name: Brad Johnson, with "Johnson," of course, being a slang term for the penis. In this cluster of signatures and meanings generated by those signatures, then, an image emerges of Smithee linked to Johnson's Hocken as a squatter bearing his own phallus not controlled by that raised by Hitchcock in the original film.

In addition to its indication of squatting, however, the German verb "hocken" also has the meaning "[to] set up (*sheaves*) in piles *or* stooks."[47] "Hocken" is to construct an alternative to challenge that cock hitched up by Hitchcock, but a more diffuse, organic alternative, rather than the rod Hitchcock appropriates through his on-screen surrogate Rod Taylor. Similar organic imagery permeates *The Birds II*'s various signatures: the screenplay was written by Ken and Jim Wheat, and Ted's wife May is played by Chelsea Fields. Smithee, accordingly, works with a diffuse organic flexibility that draws on the names of women as well as men for its meaning, in a way that Hitchcock's rod, which cannot bend, but only break, cannot, as it attempts to subsume all male names into itself, even as it attempts to force women and their names to submit to its control.

The Death of the *Auteur*

More than simply offering Smithee and Johnson/Hocken as alternatives to Hitchcock, *The Birds II* provides its audience with no fewer than three characters who, much like Rod Taylor's Mitch Brenner in the original, serve as on-screen avatars of Alfred Hitchcock, each of whom challenges Ted in various ways, focusing on his sexual prowess. Somewhat unsurprisingly, each of these Hitchcock surrogates dies in *The Birds II*, each death playing out an on-screen enactment of the Barthesian death of the author, here the death of Hitchcock the *auteur* at the hands of the film signed by Smithee.

The first of the Hitchcock surrogates whom I consider in this experiment also poses the most explicit challenge to Ted's sexuality, as it manifests itself in his relation with his wife. Ted's wife's name is May Hocken, and, unlike Hedren, whose career and life Hitchcock attempted to control, May's life in Smithee's film remains her own; she "may" accept or reject the men who compete for her attentions as she pleases. She is not a blonde like Hedren and other Hitchcock heroines, but she does attract the attention of Frank Irving, the newspaper editor and photojournalist played by James Naughton. Frank's status as a voyeuristic photojournalist who would rather flirt with and take pictures of May than work on his newspaper should speak for itself in identifying him with Hitchcock; as Laura Mulvey has noted, "Hitchcock has never concealed his interest in voyeurism, cinematic and non-cinematic.... The power to subject another person to the will sadistically or to the gaze voyeuristically is turned on to the woman as the object of both."[48] As one of *The Birds II*'s avatars of Hitchcock, Frank poses a direct challenge to the authority of Smithee and Ted. In fact, Ted is more or less a failure in his role as a father and a husband throughout most of *The Birds II*. Unable to finish his graduate thesis, he is stuck at an unglamorous job, and has been unable to fulfill his paternal and conjugal duties properly since the death of his son two years earlier. Ted is further emasculated by the appearance of a rival for May's affections in the form of the apparently virile Frank, who at one point, in an act of proprietary misnaming, addresses Ted as "Fred," a diminutive form of "Alfred." Like Hitchcock's enframing of Hedren's first name in quotation marks, Frank exerts his power over Ted's name as a sign of sexual aggression, aggression that directs itself both at May and at Ted himself.

Various factors contribute to a sense of identity between Ted and Hedren. As mentioned above, Hedren's Helen shares a confidence with Ted, a confidence reflected in the fact that Ted Hocken and Tippi Hedren share the same initials. Indeed, the very name "Ted" sounds almost like a contraction of "Tippi" and "Hedren." Ted, then, does not merely stand as an on-screen surrogate for Smithee; he also represents Hedren herself, further indicating the degree to which Smithee aligns himself with Hedren against Hitchcock's attempted control. This identity on the level of the signature later manifests itself in the plot of *The Birds II* when Frank, in the company of May, comes upon Ted after Ted has been injured by a bird, in a scene that bears an obvious resemblance to that of the initial attack of a seagull on Melanie Daniels in *The Birds*. If, as Price argues, the birds of *The Birds* "are phallic symbols, flying phalluses, whose aim is to rape the life out of" Hedren,[49] then we could say that Ted is raped in the scene of his being attacked by the bird, as Hedren is throughout the original. In the scene in which he encounters the freshly injured Ted, then, Frank comes to assume a position of masculine strength above the victimized and feminized Ted, a position from which he hopes to supplant Ted as husband to May and father to the Hocken children. In Smithee's film, though, Frank, as played by Naughton, remains simply naughty, a dirty old (or at least middle-aged) man whose advances toward May, like Hitchcock's toward Tippi, eventually come to naught. Naughton's phallus, as far as May Hocken is concerned, remains not on; for Naughton's Frank, the "may" in May Hocken becomes a definite "may not/naught," as she rejects him. Eventually, in a literal enactment of the death of the author, Frank becomes a victim of his voyeuristic tendencies as he ignores the general rush to flee Land's End and stays behind, like a good director, to "try to get the best shots" of the attacking birds. Unfortunately for Frank, the birds of the sequel are unleashed by Smithee, not Hitchcock, and Frank dies in an explosion set off during the birds' attack, a victim of the sequel's revenge on the original's *auteur*.

I now turn my attention to the second of Hitchcock's three surrogates in *The Birds II*: the Hocken family dog, Scout. The identification of Hitchcock with Scout works on various levels. On the level of Hitchcock's own self-identifications, it is useful to remember that Hitchcock, as part of the directorial product placement that he exercised to promote his brand name, made cameo appearances in most of his films. This act of visibly inserting the director's presence into his films operates, in the words of Thomas M. Leitch, "as if the film were a mass-produced Christmas card on which the cameo were a scribbled personal message."[50] In fact, the Hitchcock cameo serves as an on-screen enactment of Hitchcock's signing his films with his brand name; if the cameo represents a personal message, it remains a personal message reproduced on a mass scale, designed to heighten consumer loyalty to the Hitchcock brand name. Obviously, this sort of product placement—with the product being the director's universally recognized face—cannot work in a Smithee film. Instead of presenting a counter-cameo of Smithee, *The Birds II* works to take Hitchcock's proprietary and identificatory cameo in *The Birds* literally, to appropriate that cameo appearance as a starting point for further attacks on Hitchcock. Notably, Hitchcock's cameo appearance in *The Birds* shows him walking a pair of dogs, an identificatory appearance that provides one ground for the associative link between Hitchcock and Scout. Moreover, on the level of the name, Scout is identified as the one who runs ahead to see what lies ahead, and as such resembles the voyeuristic Hitchcock, whose obsession with Hedren renders him a dirty old dog.

Instances in which Scout appears to stand in for Hitchcock, in the director's battle with Smithee and his surrogate Hocken, abound in *The Birds II*. Price contends that the bird—and specifically, in Hitchcock's films, the chicken—can serve not only as a phallic symbol but also as "vagina or girl symbols."[51] If we accept this link, we can read the scene in which Scout takes advantage of a momentary distraction to consume a chicken that was to serve as dinner for the Hocken family as an instance in which Ted is unable to keep his family—a family that, notably, contains no males other than himself, and, by extension, Scout—from being collectively ravished by the "bad dog." Later, when Ted and May begin to rediscover their sexual attraction to one another in fairly graphic terms (in direct violation of Hitchcock's dictum that "[s]ex on the screen should

Figure 8.4. Hitchcock's proprietary cameo in *The Birds*.

be suspenseful.... If sex is too blatant or obvious, there's no suspense"[52]), Scout begins barking excitedly, distracting Ted and thereby separating the conjugal pair in accordance with Hitchcock's directive. The fact that this near-fulfillment of May and Ted's sexual desire for each other appears intercut with shots of birds gathering on a swingset, a scene that calls to mind the original film's scene of birds gathering on a jungle gym while Melanie Daniels seductively smokes a cigarette, only further exposes to the audience the "private concerns" that were on Hitchcock's dirty old mind while he was shooting Hedren in the original scene. As such, May and Ted's momentary sexual empowerment represents a direct challenge to Hitchcock's failure to have his way with Hedren. Still, Scout is present in this scene to cut short this momentary victory, so in order for Smithee's challenge to Hitchcock to succeed, Scout must be eliminated. Accordingly, Scout, like Frank a surrogate for Hitchcock, later dies a victim of Smithee's birds. Notably, a hawk, a bird linked phonetically to the last name of the Hockens, leads the attack on Scout. We could consider Scout's death Smithee/May and Ted Hocken/Tippi Hedren's revenge on that dog Hitchcock.

The Birds II provides us with one other avatar of Hitchcock, in the form of the old lighthouse keeper Karl, played by Jan Rubes. Karl is, aside from Hedren's character, the only town local who recognizes the menace the birds pose. As such, Ted goes to him for advice; he becomes an authorial oracle of the type that Hitchcock's fans often supposed him to be, but a failed one, since Karl, like Hitchcock, ultimately gives no explanation for the birds' attacks. Given Karl's status as a Hitchcock surrogate appearing to possess privileged knowledge, it seems a true turning point of the film when he presents Ted with a blatantly phallic fish he has caught, a fish that provides the Hockens' dinner in a symbolic reversal of Scout's earlier ravishing of the chicken. Explaining, "This is too big for one old man," the Hitchcock surrogate Karl gives up the larger-than-life phallic role he has assumed and passes it on to the squatters—Ted and Smithee—who have taken over his role. Later, Karl confesses to Ted the great regret of his life, "I ended up alone," thereby reminding us

Figure 8.5. The jungle gym scene in *The Birds.*

Figure 8.6. The intercut action in the analogous scene from *The Birds II* . . .

Figure 8.7. . . . . reveals the "private concerns" of the original.

of Hitchcock's status as a dirty old man separated from Tippi Hedren. The name Karl is, of course, an anagram for "lark," a type of bird, hence the hint of Hitchcockian menace that surrounds Karl's appearances. Taking the lark as an example of the phallic bird symbolism Price describes, we can link this hint of menace to Karl's possible status as a dirty old man, and from there to Hitchcock. In the end, Karl dies falling from his phallic lighthouse residence, a fall that comes as a result of the birds' attack on the lighthouse. Perhaps had Karl not hitched his cock so high, the film seems to be saying, he might have survived, along with those squatters Hocken and Smithee. Like his fellow Hitchcock stand-ins Frank and Scout, Karl dies as a result of the Smithee sequel's reappropriation of the birds that Hitchcock uses as symbols of his phallic power in the original film. Like the deaths of Frank and Scout, Karl's death appears, in the centrifuge of this signature experiment, as another instance of *The Birds II*'s staging of the death of Hitchcock the masculinist *auteur*.

Figure 8.8. "This is too big for one old man!"

Signing Off

No signature experiment would be complete without a consideration of the signature of the one who conducts the experiment. In my last name, Hock, there appears an indication of my own place in the associative chain that links Alan Smithee and the Hockens as the squatters who unleash a hawk to kill Scout. The willingness on the part of the experimenter to subject his or her own signature to the centrifuge of the experiment, rather than being a superfluous flourish, is in fact a necessary part of the signature experiment. Whereas Hitchcock and the *auteurist* critics offer a valorized image of the director as *auteur*, emphasizing his control over every aspect of the film, this signature experiment replaces Hitchcock's strong directorial presence with a subversion and diffusion of the guarantor of that strength, namely, the director's name. The diffusion of this experiment, of course, is itself occasioned by the signature that stands for the subversion of the director's authority, namely, Alan Smithee.

Accordingly, the signature experiment must reflect on itself, refusing to take its own author's name as a guarantor of the experiment's value, and instead playing with that name as surely as it does with Hitchcock's. In the end, my signature experiment definitely turns on itself, for "Hock" links not only to Smithee in the forms of "Hocken" and "hawk," but also, as a contraction, to "Hitchcock," the very name my experiment works to diffuse. Apropos of this reflexive return of the signature of the *auteur* at the culmination of my signature experiment, I would end simply by observing that, in the context of this signature experiment, it seems noteworthy that Andrew Sarris and Alan Smithee—one the signature of a defender of the name of the *auteur* and the other the signature of the scatterer of that name—share the same initials.

Notes

1. Throughout this essay I use the "Alan Smithee" spelling of the name, since that is the spelling that appears in the credits of *The Birds II: Land's End*.

2. André Bazin, "Theater and Cinema, Part Two," *What Is Cinema?*, vol. 1, ed. and trans. Hugh Gray (Berkeley: University of California Press, 1967) 105.

3. Robert B. Ray, *The Avant-Garde Finds Andy Hardy* (Cambridge: Harvard University Press, 1995) 182.

4. Ray 182.

5. For a detailed theorization of the signature method, particularly as it relates to Smithee, see Christian Keathley's "*Signateurism* and the Case of Allen Smithee," chapter 6 in the present volume.

6. Andrew Sarris, *The American Cinema: Directors and Directions, 1929–1968* (New York: E. P. Dutton, 1968) 57.

7. Sarris, *The American Cinema* 60.

8. The four films are *Psycho* (number eighteen), *North by Northwest* (forty), *Rear Window* (forty-two), and *Vertigo* (sixty-one). The list is reproduced, among other places, in Carrie Rickey, "Film List Overlooks Much That Is Worthy," *Philadelphia Inquirer* 21 June 1998: E4.

9. *Internet Movie Database*, 20 Sept. 1997, http://www.imdb.com.

10. Sarris, *The American Cinema* 57.

11. *Internet Movie Database*, 22 June 1999, http://www.imdb.com/top_250_films.

12. *Internet Movie Database*, 22 June 1999, http://www.imdb.com/bottom_ 100_films. Notably, *The Birds II*, as of this writing, was the only Smithee film on the IMDB list of the one hundred worst films ever.

13. Michel Foucault, "What Is an Author?" trans. Josué V. Harari, *The Foucault Reader*, ed. Paul Rabinow (New York: Pantheon Books, 1984) 113.

14. Foucault 110.

15. Robert E. Kapsis, *Hitchcock: The Making of a Reputation* (Chicago: University of Chicago Press, 1992) 1.

16. Quoted in Kapsis 94.

17. Quoted in Kapsis 66.

18. Kapsis 87.

19. Quoted in Kapsis 260–61.

20. Todd Everett, review of *The Birds II: Land's End*, *Daily Variety*, 17 Mar. 1994: 25.

21. John Leonard, review of *The Birds II: Land's End*, *New York*, 21 Mar. 1994: 66.

22. Quoted in Kapsis 140–41.

23. Andrew Sarris, review of *The Birds*, reprinted in *Confessions of a Cultist: On the Cinema, 1955–1969* (New York: Simon and Schuster, 1970) 84–86.

24. François Truffaut, review of *The Birds*, reprinted in *The Films in My Life*, trans. Leonard Mayhew (New York: Simon and Schuster, 1978) 87.

25. Truffaut, review of *The Birds* 87.

26. Kapsis 121.

27. The three television series were *Alfred Hitchcock Presents* (1955–1965), *The Alfred Hitchcock Hour* (1962–1965), and a revived *Alfred Hitchcock Presents* (1985). Hitchcock served as the host of the first two series, and archival footage of Hitchcock was used to make him the posthumous host of the third.

28. Associated Press report, 4 Aug. 1998.

29. Debra West, "Vultures on the Roof, in the Trees, Around the Dog," *New York Times*, 5 July 1998, Metro sec.: 17.

30. Katie Couric, *Today*, National Broadcasting Corporation, 6 Oct. 1998.

31. Monica Yant, "Feathers Fly over Swarms in Pa. Towns," *Philadelphia Inquirer* 4 Oct. 1998: A1.

32. Jacques Derrida, *Signsponge*, trans. Richard Rand (New York: Columbia University Press, 1984).

33. Donald Spoto, *The Dark Side of Genius: The Life of Alfred Hitchcock* (Boston: Little, Brown, 1983) 461.

34. Quoted in François Truffaut with the collaboration of Helen G. Scott, *Hitchcock*, rev. ed. (New York: Simon and Schuster, 1983) 261.

35. Barton Byg, "Nazism as *Femme Fatale*," *Gender and Germanness: Cultural Reproductions of Nation*, ed. Patricia Herminghouse and Magda Mueller (Providence: Berghahn Books, 1997) 180.

36. Jonathan Eburne's essay in the present volume argues for the central position of anagrams within Smithee studies.

37. Foucault 118.

38. David Sterritt, *The Films of Alfred Hitchcock* (Cambridge: Cambridge University Press, 1993) 143.

39. Theodore Price, *Hitchcock and Homosexuality: His 50-Year Obsession with Jack the Ripper and the Superbitch Prostitute—A Psychoanalytic View* (Metuchen, NJ: Scarecrow, 1992) 187.

40. Quoted in Price 187.

41. Spoto 458. Notably, Hedren's character in *The Birds II* never comes under direct attack by the birds.

42. Spoto 460.

43. Price 187.

44. Camille Paglia offers another reading of Melanie Daniels's last name, identifying Melanie's entrance into the Brenners' attic as an instance of her "living up to her name—a Daniels who enters the lions' den." Camille Paglia, *The Birds* (London: BFI, 1998) 82.

45. Spoto 456.

46. The image of this credit is the second from the left of five Smithee directorial credits reproduced in John Waters's "Despair." John Waters, *Director's Cut* (New York: Scalo, 1997) 66–67.

47. "Hocke," *Cassell's German-English/English-German Dictionary*, rev. Harold T. Betteridge (New York: Macmillan, 1978) 315.

48. Laura Mulvey, "Visual Pleasure and Narrative Cinema," *Screen* 16.3 (autumn 1975): 15.

49. Price 191.

50. Thomas M. Leitch, *Find the Director, and Other Hitchcock Games* (Athens: The University of Georgia Press, 1991) 3.

51. Price 198.

52. Quoted in Truffaut, *Hitchcock* 224.

PART III
SMITHEE SUGGESTS

The Fake Americans of the Italian Cinema: A Marketing Strategy or a Strategy for Interpretive Cooperation?

Laura Parigi
Translated by Thomas Kelso

Spaghetti Western

In 1969 Universal released to American movie screens a low-budget Western called *Death of a Gunfighter*. As has been described elsewhere in this collection, controversies that arose during production of this film led to the creation of the Smithee pseudonym. After its release *Death of a Gunfighter* received reviews as controversial as the production problems that led to the birth of Smithee, but perhaps it is worth recalling, among the various comments, those of Gary Arnold in his merciless tirade in the *Washington Post* in May 1969:

> What "Gunfighter" really seems to be about is the death of Western genre. This film is simply a reprise of every cliche in the "adult" Western catalogue, and the static direction and simplified color mark it even more as fodder for television. The studio doesn't have its eyes on either Greek tragedy or the Old West; it's looking ahead to "Monday Night at the Movies" a few seasons from now.[1]

Arnold's review predicts accurately both the reputation Smithee was to acquire and also the medium in which his films would find their prevailing audience. Indeed, even in Italy, Allen Smithee is the undisputed king of afternoon television.

In Europe, only five years before Allen Smithee's sheriff wound up

defeated by time's usury, and as the rustproof formula of the classic Western began to show signs of imminent crisis, a mysterious and unknown
director called Bob Robertson beat all the box office records with the
first episode of a series of Westerns that would be remembered as the
trilogy of "the man with no name," a lonely, vagabond gunslinger who
roamed the territories of the Mexican-American border.

Bob Robertson abandoned the themes that had made the Western
an epic genre, such as the frontier myth, and replaced its heroic pioneers
and upholders of the law with cynical characters in a struggle of all
against all in a world as arid and raw as the landscapes of the West. He
thereby managed to revitalize a genre that seemed already to have ridden
into the sunset. It was 1964, the man with no name had the impassive
face of Clint Eastwood, the film was *A Fistful of Dollars*, and in reality
Bob Robertson was a director named Sergio Leone. Though *A Fistful of
Dollars* was an Italo-Spanish coproduction, the names of the entire crew
had been americanized in order to guarantee the operation's credibility.
Thus, the director of photography, Massimo Dallamano, assumed the
name of Jack Dalmas; the cameraman's name, Stelvio Massi, was literally
translated into the improbable Steve Rock; Ennio Morricone, composer
of the film's musical theme, became Leo Nichols; and even the set designer, Carlo Simi, figured in the credits as Charles Simons.

The strategy did not spare the film's actors. The villain, or to be
more precise, Eastwood's antagonist, was played by the almost-unknown
John Wells, aka Gian Maria Volonté, an actor with a solid theatrical
background who would go on to become the symbolic face of the politically engaged cinema of the decades that followed (from Elio Petri's
Investigation of a Citizen above Suspicion in 1970 to 1990's *Open Doors* by
Gianni Amelio).

Although such a concentration of pseudonyms might seem out of
the ordinary, the case of Leone's film was neither unique nor infrequent
in the Italian cinematic production of those years. At the end of the
1950s neorealism was entering into a phase of decadence after having ex-
ported a style and an idea of cinema that were destined to extend their
influence well beyond Italy's borders. But the era of great creativity on

the part of directors like Roberto Rossellini and Vittorio De Sica did not leave behind a heritage that could easily be appropriated, and the end of this era coincided with the aftermath of the market crisis that had stricken Hollywood at the end of the fifties.

Italian audiences began to forsake the movie theaters. They were distracted by television, which had only then become a common household appliance in Italy, despite having served for some time as a status symbol in the immediate postwar context. Furthermore, when Italians went to the movies in the early sixties, they tended to prefer films from Hollywood, specifically, the spectacular entertainment films that were the strong point of the American industry. There was no industry in Italy that could be counterposed to Hollywood, and the only indigenous genre that caught the attention of the public was the *commedia all'italiana*, a group of popular films that used the neorealist mode as a sort of façade, often built entirely around the persona of a comic like Totò (Antonio de Curtis).

Italian cinema had neither the experience nor the productive resources that would have been necessary to create a cinematic genre like the Hollywood movies that had conquered the public, but already in the 1950s some producers intuited that it was possible to imitate the Hollywood model while radically reducing costs, and that they could win a slice of its market by disguising films produced in Italy as American films.

The first fruit of this situation was *peplum* cinema,[2] which was inspired by the Hollywood epics of DeMille and Wyler and by the mythological films that, at the century's beginning, had well served the chauvinistic tendencies of fascist propaganda, as was the case with *Cabiria* (1914), directed by Giovanni Pastrone with a screenplay from the writer Gabriel D'Annunzio. In 1958 *Le fatiche di Ercole*, the film by Pietro Francisci that inaugurated the *peplum*'s most fortunate season, reinvented mythological cinema without paying too much attention to historical coherence or iconographic sources. Slaves, gladiators, and gods all had rigorously Yankee faces, and the sets and costumes seemed to have been inspired more by comic strips than by historical reconstructions. Steve Reeves was called upon to interpret the role of Hercules. This former

Mr. Universe, who reached the height of popularity in the garb of the mythic hero, was only the first of a small group of American actors who found their fortune in the *peplum*, among whom it seems worth recalling at least Brad Harris, whose face was loaned to the "proletarian" characters in the sagas of Maciste and Ursus.[3]

Foreign protagonists constituted a first step taken by producers in order to capture the public's approval. The only Italian Hercules was Sergio Ciani, who acted the role in *Ercole contro Roma* (1964) by Piero Perotti and in *Ercole, Sansone, Maciste, e Ursus* (1965) by Giorgio Capitani, but in both cases he adopted the pseudonym Alan Steele. Notwithstanding a few exceptions, such as the case of Riccardo Freda, who filmed *Spartaco* (1953) and *Teodora imperatrice di Bisanzio* (1953) as Robert Hampton, directors who worked on *peplum* films hardly ever used fictitious names. The advertising strategy, if it can be called such, limited itself to choosing actors who were foreign or who had at least chosen anglophone stage names. For a short period this must have been enough to attract spectators. There were a good number of Italian actors who began their careers under false names and then, once the *peplum* was exhausted as a genre, reappropriated their own identity. After the first half of the sixties, the fortunes of mythological film began to decline rapidly, in part because of the competition from American epics like *Cleopatra* (1963) by Joseph L. Mankiewicz. But the *peplum* was an indispensable training ground where some of the best directors of Italian B-movies mastered their trade. Mario Bava, Sergio Leone, Riccardo Freda, Antonio Margheriti, and Lucio Fulci are only a few of the directors whose names recurred in the credits of mythological films and who would become prolific creators of genres and subgenres of Italian cinema. When the cycle of mythological films ended, the majority of these professionals redirected their talents toward the Western, a trend inaugurated by Sergio Leone.

In the beginning of the sixties some German production houses had outfitted sets in Spain, exploiting the arid and barren hinterland plains in order to simulate the landscape of Texas or Arizona. The German Western was an experiment that had concluded without much success, but the sets that had been built in Spain were recycled by Leone and his emulators, who replaced Maciste, Hercules, and Ursus with Sartana, Sabata, and Django, the antiheroes of the spaghetti Western.

From 1962 until the end of the 1970s more than 475 films were made. Most were of extremely low quality, produced in series, and filmed in approximately the same manner, in the wake of the success of *A Fistful of Dollars*. Leone's success was so unforeseen that before the film was distributed on the Italian and European market the producers decided to change the names of the entire technical and artistic cast to make it seem as if the film were "made in the USA." But Bob Robertson/Sergio Leone had not limited himself to cloning the American Western; he had transformed its aesthetic and had invented a style that was destined to become his personal signature, a style that alternated between extremely long shots of silent landscapes and extreme close-ups of Eastwood's impassive face.

When the film came out in the United States, Bob Robertson had disappeared from the opening credits, along with the rest of the cast of "fake Americans." On the strength of the profits obtained in Italy and Europe, and aware that he had made more than just a B-movie, Leone finished the trilogy of the man with no name (*For a Few Dollars More* in 1965, *The Good, the Bad, and the Ugly* in 1966), and continued his career without adopting other pseudonyms. The life and death of Bob Robertson showed the way to many other directors, who proceeded to imitate Sergio Leone, but with far more limited talents and ambitions. Signing one's films with an American pseudonym became the practice of dozens of directors. Gianfranco Pannone, the director of *L'America a Roma*, a documentary on the spaghetti Western that was presented at the 1998 Locarno film festival, maintains that there were also political reasons for these disguises: "Directors hid behind American names for shame; filming Westerns meant being branded, especially by the left." The political connotations of the spaghetti Western, considered "rightist" by many intellectuals of the period, as well as the attitude of critics with regard to genre films, surely contributed to the birth of the various Anthony Ascotts, Frank Garfields, and Sidney Leans, whose signatures accompanied productions that were sometimes of the lowest quality. But this is not sufficient to justify the phenomenon. It is an incontestable fact that the anglophone pseudonyms were often associated with awful, even embarrassing, films, but if the principal exigency of these professionals was the necessity of defending their reputations as "serious and committed" filmmakers by separating their own work from their commissioned work, one must wonder why a director like Giuliano Carmineo went to the trouble of coining the pseudonym Anthony Ascott in order to sign films like *Sono Sartana, il vostro becchino* (*I'll Dig Your Grave*, 1968) or *Lo chiamavano Spirito Santo* (alias *Blazing Guns*, 1970), only then to own up to soft porn comedies like *Prestami tua moglie* (*Loan Me Your Wife*, 1980).

The production of spaghetti Westerns was heterogeneous: among the 150 films produced in 1967 and 1968 there were absolutely forgettable films such as *Sette pistole magnifiche*, by Rod Gilbert, aka Romolo Girolami, or *Adios Gringo* (1967) by George Finley/Giorgio Stegani, but also some attempts to politicize the Western, as in *Requiescat* (1967) by Carlo Lizzani, in which Pier Paolo Pasolini, left intellectual and director of the masterpieces *Mamma Roma* (1962) and *Accattone* (1961), had a cameo role. It is not easy, therefore, to discover a criterion that explains why some of the directors and screenplay writers of this consumer cinema invented an American alter ego, often coined on the basis of a translation of or an assonance with their original name, while others, like Duccio Tessari and Sergio Corbucci, two of the most prolific creators of spaghetti Westerns, never felt a need to hide themselves behind fake names, and still others started their work in Westerns with a pseudonym only to later abandon it, like Franco Giraldi, formerly Leone's assistant, who directed *Sette pistole per i McGregor* in 1966 as Frank Kramer, and two years later signed the sequel, *Sette donne per i McGregor*, with his real name.

If the "fakery" accomplished through the use of pseudonyms was initially meant to fool audiences, the consecration that box office receipts and critics gave to Leone allowed the spaghetti Western greater autonomy with respect to its original model, the American Western. By the end of the decade Italian spectators no longer expected a title like *Django*

(1966) to be a Western by John Ford, but were aware that they were choosing a Sergio Corbucci film. Nevertheless, the pseudonyms did not disappear from the credits of these films. Instead, they often remained as the sole guarantee of survival for the weakest and least credible products.

The phenomenon not only involved directors and screenplay writers, but also some Italian actors. Giuliano Gemma debuted as Montgomery Wood in *Una pistola per Ringo* (*A Pistol for Ringo*, 1964) by Duccio Tessari, but continued to be successful after he left the pseudonym behind. Few later Westerns would actually end up diminishing their gunslinger's credibility by dropping his former pseudonym. Gemma's is an exemplary parable of the fate of many of his colleagues who made their fortune in Cinecittà in those years. As soon as the public associated a face with the "man with no name" of the moment, the pseudonym became superfluous. Whether it was Lee Cliff playing Sabata or Franco Nero in the role of Sartana, spectators recognized a "character" and an image that the spaghetti Western had already accustomed them to: the gunslinger with quick reflexes and an impenetrable gaze, born on the set of *A Fistful of Dollars*. It was an icon that represented the maximum distance of the Western *all'italiana* from its "made in the USA" progenitor, the model that had invigorated a ballet of names and faces that gradually weakened the trend.

From Spaghetti Horror to Sci-Fi

While the Western *all'italiana* went out of style, the habit of using American names survived, and even had a prolific new season following the success of what historians of the Italian cinema would later define as "spaghetti horror." Almost contemporaneously with their appropriation of the Western, Italian producers discovered that horror was a genre that guaranteed sure box-office success and that could be realized without committing the capital required by epics. Even in this case the model was imported from abroad, more precisely, from England, where Hammer Studios, in collaboration with the American producer Robert L. Lippert, had invaded the movie market with B-movies that ranged from science fiction to gothic, all produced at the lowest costs. Hammer Studios had been able to count on a team of genre film professionals. The likes of director Terence Fisher and director of photography Jack Asher produced dozens of films such as *The Curse of Frankenstein* (1957) and *The Brides of Dracula* (1960), which, through worldwide distribution, greatly increased the popularity of their protagonists, Christopher Lee and Bela Lugosi, and made Hammer Studios a trademark guarantee for horror fans.

The first spaghetti horror films appeared on the market at about the same time as those of Hammer Studios. *Caltiki il mostro immortale* (*Caltiki, The Immortal Monster*) dates to 1959. Inspired by one of H. P. Lovecraft's stories and set in the Mexican jungles, the film came out under the name of Robert Hampton/Riccardo Freda, who had already directed several *peplum* films. In the credits, which are rigorously anglophone, Mario Bava hid behind the pseudonym John Foam. He was the director of special effects, which, according to a production note, were so homespun that some were actually produced with tripe. The collaboration of Freda and Mario Bava, who also worked as director of photography, was renewed again in 1959 on the set of *Agi Murad il diavolo bianco* (*The White Warrior*), but while Riccardo Freda would sign all his gothic films, including the greatest work of his career, *L'orribile segreto del dottore Hitchcock* (*The Horrible Secret of Doctor Hitchcock*, 1962), with the name of Robert Hampton, Mario Bava would forgo the embarrassing pseudonym of John Foam ("foam" being the literal translation of the word "bava") and with films like *La maschera del demonio* (*Black Sunday*, 1960) would, together with Lucio Fulci, one of the few Italian B-movie directors never to have employed a pseudonym, become known the world over as a cult filmmaker of the gothic cinema. Curiously, the only subsequent film that led Bava again to take recourse to a false name was a spaghetti Western titled *La strada per Fort Alamo* (*The Road to Fort Alamo*, 1964), distributed under the name of John Old. Twenty-two years later, Bava's son would use the name John Old Jr. to sign *Shark—Rosso nell'oceano*, a horror film very freely inspired by Spielberg's *Jaws*.

The sixties and the first years of the seventies brought the era of American pseudonyms to a close with science fiction films—still more B-movies, strictly low-budget productions, still imitating the science fiction of Hammer Studios. The sci-fi films represented a handcrafted cinema that constructed for itself a system of genres (or better, subgenres) on a track parallel to that of the "A-movies," a cinema of pseudofilmmakers versus that of filmmakers. Anthony Dawson, born Antonio Margheriti, confirmed himself as a genre specialist by directing four films in 1965 alone, including *Il pianeta errante* and *I diafanoidi vengono da Marte*. Margheriti, who is still considered, both in Italy and abroad, one of the indisputable masters of nondigital special effects, stuck with his pseudonym even in the credits to his collaboration with Andy Warhol, which produced *Andy Warhol's Frankenstein* (1974) and *Andy Warhol's Young Dracula* (1974), both filmed in Italy for producer Carlo Ponti. Surviving until 1991, Anthony Dawson proved to be the last of the great "fake Americans." He, along with the other minor filmmakers of science fiction *all'italiana* (Al Bradley/Alfonso Brescia, Vincent Dawn/Bruno Mattei) can be seen as closing the epochal cycle of Italian B-movies.

From Mondo Movies to the
Passing of the Fake Americans

After this phase, pseudonyms did not entirely disappear from the credits of films on the Italian market. In Italy, as opposed to the United States, movie directors are neither restricted nor protected by any organization that could be compared to the Directors Guild of America, and the decision to use a fictitious name is subordinated only to obligations stipulated by the production contract. Using a pseudonym was a choice that directors continued to make with a certain nonchalance, despite the fact that the conditions and motivations for this choice had changed.

In the latter half of the seventies, cinema audiences began to thin out, and the incumbent crisis diminished the number of B-movies produced, so the pseudonym phenomenon was not only reduced in proportion, but was transformed into something else. Directors like Ruggero Deodato or Aristide Massaccesi (a fictitious name record-holder, given that he signed films with almost thirty different aliases) gave the pseudonym a more conventional function, namely, that of hiding the real identity of the creators of scabrous and compromising films, who not only ran the risk of embarrassment but also could attract censorship in more or less direct forms. Deodato (alias Roger Rockefeller) was the most prolific director of Mondo movies, a series of pseudodocumentaries set in exotic locales whose common denominator was an extreme sadism, just a step shy of both the porno film and the snuff movie. *Cannibal Holocaust* (1978) by Deodato, *Doctor Butcher M.D.* (1982) by Frank Martin/Marino Girolami, and Umberto Lenzi's *Cannibal Ferox* (1972) rapidly took over a semiclandestine market that crossed international borders but regularly encountered censorship problems. Some of Lenzi's splatter films included the torture and killing of animals and were banned by more than twenty states in the United States. The pseudonyms that concealed the real authors of Mondo movies gave the lie to every hypothetical strategy, except that of protecting persons and commercial operations at the limits of legality. We must also consider that many of these directors switched back and forth from the savageries of Mondo movies and a more innocuous career, recycling themselves as directors of miniseries for family television. For example, Ruggero Deodato directed *Noi siamo angeli* (*We Are Angels*, 1996) for TV. For them it became indispensable to maintain their credibility and keep their "double" professional life hidden. The case of Aristide Massaccesi, better known as Joe D'Amato (the pseudonym he used most frequently), belongs to the same category. Massaccesi is simply the most prolific living director of porno films in Italy, with more than seventy-five titles to his credit, a small part of which, especially at the beginning of his career, were intended for theaters not part of the pornography circuit.

Anglophone names continued to be chosen, more from habit than from an effort to involve the public, which had become more discerning in the interim. The deceit of masking oneself as an American in order to attract audiences had not worked for some time, and the genres and the filmmakers with whom spectators had established a relation of complicity and "trust" were slowly disappearing. Italian audiences of the seventies and eighties certainly did not desert B-movie cinema, but they were drawn more by sexy comedies with popular TV comics and successful starlets than by clonings of successful American films. The few commercial endeavors that exploited the old strategem of the anglophone pseudonym did not aim to reinvent genres, but limited themselves to exploiting the success that some American films left in their wake. John G. Advilsen's saga of the Karate Kid "inspired" to the limits of plagiarism the film series of *Il ragazzo dal kimono d'oro*, directed by a certain Larry Lundman, who was in reality Fabrizio De Angelis. Umberto Lenzi, Fabrizio Lenti, and Claudio Fragasso, under the pseudonyms of, respectively, Humphrey Humbert, Martin Newlin, and Clyde Anderson, directed three fake sequels to Sam Raimi's *Evil Dead* (1987).[4] Even Lucio Fulci got himself involved in the production of these cloned films with *Murderock—Uccide a passo di danza* (1983), which was nothing other than a horror caricature of the then-famous *Flashdance* by Adrian Lyne. In truth, these films were destined more for export than for Italian audiences. The production of B-movies sought to conquer a share of the market in the Third World and in Eastern Europe. By this point they would have had difficulties not only "convincing" spectators, but also acquiring adequate distribution to movie theaters. The only alternative market for these products was public and private television, interested above all in filling up the "difficult" segments of their programming, for example, late-night TV. These cloned films were qualitatively distant, not only from the "*auteur* fakes" of a Bob Robertson or an Anthony Dawson, but also from the B-movies produced by dozens and dozens of minor "craftsmen" who had carved out a market for themselves and had helped to vitalize all of Italian cinema, including the A-movies.

In the eighties and nineties the "fake Americans" progressively vanished. With the exception of a few sporadic episodes, the directors of the last decade have abandoned the habit of adopting pseudonyms, and at the same time the presuppositions that were at the origin of this phenomenon have given way. Many historians of Italian cinema tend to dismiss these pseudonyms by considering them the "vice" of a few filmmakers or, at most, an expedient for capturing the interest of ingenuous spectators. Nevertheless, for more than thirty years there were dozens of directors who translated their names into English, and were imitated by actors, screenplay writers, set designers, and photography directors, all of whom contributed to the realization of hundreds of films and succeeded, irrespective of the quality of their films, in drawing audiences back to movie theaters. Taken alone, the numbers and the box office receipts of the "fake Americans" can, for good reason, be considered significant.

Extrafilmic Fiction and Interpretive Cooperation

But what were the presuppositions and the conditions that favored the development of this phenomenon? Was it really just a brilliant intuition about how to market most successfully grade-B cinematic products by exploiting the Italian public's "xenophile" tendencies? Or were there really deeper cultural motivations behind the tastes and the demands of the spectators? Were the "fake Americans" created by an improvised, but effective, marketing strategy, or were they a necessary invention insofar as they satisfied the exigencies of the Italian cinematic imaginary, an imaginary that had undeniably evolved through the importation of Hollywood models?

This is not to dispute the fact that "Bob Robertson" was created to make *A Fistful of Dollars* more "realistic," just as it was, for the same reason, an American actor, and one as recognizable as *Rawhide*'s Clint Eastwood, who played the role of the man with no name. No complicated analysis is required to intuit that Italian audiences would have received a Western created at Cinecittà skeptically, that they would at least have perceived it as an improbable endeavor. The Western, perhaps more than any other genre, was extremely representative of U.S. culture, or better, of the self-image that the United States transmitted through cinema, an image that was extremely well diffused, that was consumed daily by Italian spectators, and that gradually entered into both their field of cultural reference and their behavioral models. The idea of an Italian Western, directed by professionals who had seen the frontier only at the movies, would have encountered the skepticism of the public. Bob Robertson was born to keep this skepticism from undermining the film's capacity for turning a profit—a margin of profit that was unforeseeable precisely because that which should have been the weakness of a Western *all'italiana* was transformed into its strong point. Sergio Leone's

Western, which had in fact seen the frontier only at the movies, was a "second-hand" Western, born from the cinematic imaginary of its author. But that imaginary was by now the patrimony of many spectators, who were perhaps less "ingenuous" than one tends to imagine. If Bob Robertson was indispensable as a "compromise for the sake of authenticity" between Sergio Leone and his audience, the relation between the makers and the spectators of spaghetti Westerns was too prolific and long-lasting to have been based on the "trick" of pseudonyms.

The "*auteur* fakes" and, to a lesser extent, all the "fake Americans" had such a long successful season because they showed in their cinema what Italians had already seen of the United States on the big screen: the landscapes, the lifestyle, the linguistic expressions of the overdubbing on the model of prior translations, the narrative structures, the "myths" and the traditions. Literally thousands of pages have been written on the influence of American culture on Italy immediately after World War II, and the subject is still current in historical and cultural debates. Remaining within a strictly cinematic ambit, at the war's end Italy escaped the autarchic, fascist politics that had involved the arts and other public spectacles. In the fifties the Italian cinema worked under precarious economic conditions and was not capable of competing with the flood of American products that were present *en masse* in the world market. American cinema was often more sophisticated, more spectacular, and produced with more resources. It was, moreover, sustained by an industry with decades of experience, which was particularly capable when it came to managing the aspects of distribution and advertising, as compared to Italy's impoverished, handcrafted, and disorganized cinema. Italian spectators began to "consume" American films, and Hollywood sent an image of America to Italy. Perhaps it was a cinematic America, a fictional geographical space that furnished an ideal portrait of the "American way of life," but the Italian public appropriated this image, often without worrying about verifying how truthful Hollywood's stereotypes were.

The "fake Americans," even when they limited themselves to dishonest imitations of American-made movies, had the function of bringing to the screen those images and stereotypes in precisely the form that

they had been imported into Italian culture. These images and stereotypes were filtered, translated, and adapted through Italian culture. This
process sometimes deformed them and subjected them to the restrictions of production. But the "fake Americans" always could count on the
complicity of spectators, who would recognize in these films, despite
their quality, something familiar.

It would be extremely interesting to discover how many of these
spectators were really convinced that Anthony Ascott or Robert Hampton were American directors. Even on the hypothesis that the pseudonym trick worked for a few years, it is still hard to believe that the
Italian public continued to go to the movies to see spaghetti Westerns
without becoming aware of what they were watching. Many of these
films were recognizable aesthetically, without having to go to the lengths
of Leone's hieratic gunslingers or Fulci's *auteurist* splatter films. The B-
movies distinguished themselves from Hollywood films by using inferior
equipment, the slenderest of plots, makeshift sets, and improbable scripts,
which were then often recycled by other productions. One could recognize the actors, who were always the same. Little by little, it was discovered that Montgomery Wood, really Giuliano Gemma, did not hail
from Texas, but from Ciociaria (a rural area between Rome and Naples).
The B-movies were such garish falsifications of their original models
that there was no need for a refined cinephile to unmask them. Even
admitting that at the beginning the pseudonyms could have fooled some
inexpert spectators, if the "fake Americans" were only a marketing strategy, they would have been much more short-lived. Once the public had
discovered the trick and, in spite of it, continued to go to the movies, disguising oneself as an American would have been superfluous for directors
and screenplay writers. Instead, "fake Americans" survived for more than
thirty years.

A clue for explaining this longevity can be found in the words
of the ex-stuntman Franco Daddi, alias Frank Daddy, as quoted in Pannone's documentary, regarding the locations used for exterior shots in
Westerns: "We were filming in the suburbs of Rome, in a place called the
Tolfa Ravine. Said like that, one imagines something kilometers long,

but it was only a canal a hundred and thirty meters long which by framing it from every direction and connecting the pieces seemed endless."
Whether one speaks of the Tolfa Ravine or a valley in the Sicilian hinterland, the spaghetti Western twisted the landscape and changed its
connotations to the point of rendering it as similar as possible to the
image of the American West that the public was accustomed to perceiving. Certainly, the transformation of geographic spaces is one of
cinema's typical procedures, but that which particularizes the work of
the makers of spaghetti Westerns on the landscape is the fact that they
had as their referent another cinematic image, which was so recognizable for spectators that it became significant on its own. The Tolfa
Ravine in the Roman suburbs, dismantled and reassembled in order to
resemble some corner of Texas, aspired to the same identity counter-
feited by the "fake Americans," and like those pseudonyms it was con-
fident in the complicity of a public that probably knew, but pretended to
know nothing.

Even outside of the phenomenon of anglophone pseudonyms,
the americanization of the landscape in Italian genre film is a tendency
with its own autonomous life. In the seventies, detective film arose, and
unlike the other genres of spaghetti cinema, it attempted to reconcile its
intent to espouse social causes with a spectacular style based on American detective movie models. In films such as *La polizia incrimina, la Legge
assolve* (1973) by Girolami, *Milano odia; La polizia non può sparare* (1974)
by Umberto Lenzi, and *Napoli serenate calibro 9* (1978) by Alfonso Brescia,
the directors and protagonists abandoned the pseudonymic strategy. The
stories were bound up with Italian current events, with the Mafia, with
the terrorism and corruption of big cities, but while on the surface the
films sought to indict the social realities of Milan, Naples, and Rome,
which were in fact recognizable as such, they also wound up transformed
cinematically into something new. The chases, shoot-outs, and police
actions were scrupulously filmed according to a Hollywood model, and
the results were jarring, if not unrealistic, in an urban context that Italian
spectators had been accustomed to perceiving as familiar. It is no coincidence that one of the first films of the detective-movie trend was titled

Roma come Chicago (1968, directed by Alberto de Martino). Rome was dismantled and reassembled exactly like the Tolfa Ravine in order to resemble a fictional Chicago, which in those years Hollywood had elected as the icon of metropolitan violence.

Spencer and Hill

The americanization of landscapes, the use of pseudonyms on the part of directors and stage names on the part of actors all worked on the same principle of complicity with the spectator.[5] An exemplary case is that of the pair Bud Spencer and Terence Hill, the comic duo of Carlo Pedersoli and Mario Girotti, who, until recently, were the protagonists of numerous slapstick comedies made for cinema and television. Both started out using pseudonyms in the years of the spaghetti Western, and they initially undertook separate careers. Before long, however, the director E. B. Clutcher, aka Enzo Barboni, had the idea of pairing the handsome, clever, blond gunslinger played by Hill/Girotti with a character like Spencer/Pedersoli, who was corpulent, slow-witted, and slow on the draw, but was nevertheless unbeatable when it came to dealing out justice with fisticuffs. The couple had already been tested on the set of *Dio perdona ... io no!* (*God Forgives, I Don't*, 1967), where Spencer had, however, a minor role. In the spaghetti Westerns directed by Barboni, of which *Lo chiamavano Trinità* (*They Call Me Trinity*, 1970) was only the first of a long series, the two characters were reconsidered, their roles were balanced, and Pedersoli and Girotti began an artistic association that continued through the 1980s. In *Anche gli angeli mangiano fagioli* (1973), *Altrimenti ci arrabbiamo* (1974), and *Due superpiedi quasi piatti* (1976) the formula is always the same: Spencer and Hill are two Americans who embark on incredible adventures that are destined to culminate in blows and insults, in homage to the purest slapstick hilarity. All of the pair's films were Italian productions, but the misadventures of Spencer and Hill were always set in Miami or Chicago or New York and were often filmed on the authentic locations.

Carlo Pedersoli and Mario Girotti conducted their entire cinematic careers under their pseudonyms. Even when the comic duo separated they continued to perform as Bud Spencer and Terence Hill without distancing themselves much from the roles the public associated with their American pseudonyms. In the course of thirty years the two actors did nothing to maintain the secret of their real identities. Both extremely famous, they were spoken of in newspapers, appeared on television, and released interviews in an Italian that was provincial and dialectal, leaving no doubt as to their true origins. It is thus difficult to imagine that even the most distracted viewer could still have mistaken them for Americans. Their destiny as actors was not only tied to the fortunes of their "personalities," but also to the fact that in their case the conventional pairing of actor and character was supplemented by a third element, which was the pseudonym. Bud Spencer and Terence Hill were recognizable and identifiable fictional characters, but situated *outside* of the filmic fiction, in a "role-playing game" that involved spectators as well. In the case of these popular comics, the spectator was put in the position of perceiving a sole figure with three different "faces" and three different names that corresponded to the same number of interpretive levels. For years the formula of Spencer and Hill remained substantially unaltered. In the tracks of their more illustrious predecessors, Laurel and Hardy, the two actors continued to perform the same roles and reenact the same clichés, film after film, collecting box office successes. But unlike Laurel and Hardy, the names of the characters in their films changed from time to time. Trinità, Piedone l'africano, and Banana Joe lived exclusively for the duration of the film, while Spencer and Hill, even though they, too, were "characters," were situated outside the film's story on a level that was intermediate with respect to the anagraphic identities of Girotti and Pedersoli.[6] The case of Spencer and Hill merits a deeper analysis, but we can affirm that it was more of a strategy for involving the public than a "compromise for the sake of authenticity" with the spectators.

The level of extrafilmic fiction in which Spencer and Hill can be situated is the dimension or space between the officially recorded identities of the actors and their characters. This distance exists even if we disregard the space, opened up by the pseudonyms, where an extremely important phase of the cooperative creative activity of the spectators is accomplished.[7] But in these particular circumstances, the pseudonyms Bud Spencer and Terence Hill do not allow this space to remain an unarticulated and private work of fiction. Instead, the pseudonyms confer upon this dimension a name and an identity that can be shared, thereby creating the conditions necessary for a less ambiguous reading of that dimension. It is in this space of extrafilmic fiction that we should seek several of the interpretive keys of the "fake American" phenomenon. Along with historical, sociological, and strategic reasons, the pact of cooperation between the directors of B-movies and their viewers was an indispensable element for the survival of the pseudonyms. When they did not serve to disguise a product (if they ever really served such a function), Bob Robertson, Robert Hampton, and Anthony Ascott remained "characters" who were indispensable to the spaghetti cinema. Regardless of its quality, spaghetti cinema was metacinematic by virtue of the simple fact that it was born of the cinematic imaginary of Italians and survived thanks to mechanisms of recognition and identification.

Even before it became a cult phenomenon, before being exhumed by historians and cinephiles, spaghetti cinema differed from genre cinema pure and simple. It was the cinematic representation of an imaginary. It was the image of Hollywood cinema and its profound influence on Italian popular culture, reconstructed by the cinema itself. Its poverty of resources, and at times of talent, did not deter the public's appreciation. Spaghetti cinema survived for a long time despite the competition of Hollywood. The association between B-movies and their spectators was held together by a shared cinematic imaginary and the more or less conscious interpretive cooperation practiced by directors and viewers vis-à-vis this subgenre, or better, metagenre. The "fake Americans," the pseudonyms used by directors and actors, and the transformation of landscapes were all fictions that sustained this metagenre. These characters and iconic symbols lived on the border of fiction and reality, carving out for themselves a dimension that would perhaps be worth taking into greater consideration, above all when thinking in terms of the relation between filmmaker and spectator. In the case of spaghetti cinema, pseudonyms bring to light the shadowy zone between fiction and reality, by identifying characters, or more exactly, by identifying some of the functions of cooperative interpretation, with names.

This intermediate space of extrafilmic fiction is a dimension that operates as a filter between the two extremes of the officially recorded identity of the director and the empirical viewer, a filter through which pass strategies of reading and writing in an operation that is reciprocal. Bob Robertson, Leone's alter ego, and the other pseudonyms of spaghetti cinema, more than mere marketing strategies, were also interpretive and creative strategies. If B-movies pretended to be made in the USA with the complicity of spectators, these latter also constructed for themselves a character/filmmaker (or a character/actor) with the complicity of directors. This type of interpretive cooperation is certainly not exclusive to spaghetti cinema, nor even to cinema in general. Perhaps the "fake Americans," without having either this intention or too much awareness of it, can only be credited with having made explicit certain of this relationship's ambiguous dynamics by forcing out of their anonymity some of the functions and strategies of the relation between filmmaker and spectator.

Notes

1. Gary Arnold, "The Death of a Gunfighter," review of *Death of a Gunfighter*, *Washington Post* 16 May 1969: B10.

2. *Translator's note*: *Peplum* films were a group of mythological films created in Italy in the late fifties and early sixties, including, most famously, *The Labors of Hercules* (1958). The term refers to the skirts worn in ancient Rome and by the body-builder protagonists of the films. *Peplum* films often reacted against the fascist use of mythological film, but their ideological suppositions remain questionable.

3. *Translator's note*: Maciste was a muscleman/superhero invented for the film *Cabiria* (1914), and originally played by Bartolomeo Pagano in a long series of Maciste films, including *Maciste* (1915), *Maciste the Alpinist* (1916), *Maciste the Athlete* (1918), *Maciste in Love* (1920), *Maciste against Death* (1920), *Maciste's Voyage* (1920), *Maciste's Testament* (1920), *Maciste on Holiday* (1921), *Maciste Emperor* (1924), and *Maciste in Hell* (1926). It has been suggested that the many-faceted career of Maciste provided a model for the newsreel coverage of Mussolini, who

appeared in the media as a hero with many guises. Maciste was then resurrected in the genre of *peplum* film. Ursus (from the Latin for "bear") was a similar pseudomythological personage. See *The Companion to Italian Cinema*, ed. Geoffrey Nowell-Smith with James Hay and Gianni Vopi (London: BFI, 1996).

4. Raimi himself assumed the Alan Smithee (Jr.) pseudonym for his work on the 1992 film *The Nutt House*.

5. Comparing the Smithee effect to Duchamp's aesthetic strategies, Jonathan Eburne describes this sort of complicity, in the essay that follows, as a film's appeal to the spectator to "nominate it as art."

6. *Translator's note*: In Italian, the *anagrafe* is the register that is used to record births, deaths, and changes in legal status of the citizens in a community. *Anagrafico* thus refers to the officially recorded identity of a person.

7. *Translator's note*: Parigi is here drawing upon the work of Umberto Eco in the eponymous introductory essay to *The Role of the Reader* (Bloomington: Indiana University Press, 1979). Eco sees "the model reader" as the device that accounts for the role of "foreseen interpretation as a part of [a text's] generative process" (3). Eco does explore the feedback loop that Parigi postulates, but (as she concludes) the space of "extra-filmic fiction" is not delineated by Eco, but is instead a foreseeable modification of his theory, as presented in "The Role of the Reader." However, in his discussion of the Western, Eco does posit the "great train robbery" as a topos of intertextual competence (22), and his ideas about ideology's role in the interpretation/generation of texts seem to include the possibility of Parigi's thesis whereby pseudonyms function as objective correlatives, acknowledging the role of American cinema in fabricating the West that they themselves evoke.

CHAPTER 10

The Cheerless Art of Industry: Marcel Duchamp and the Smithee Readymade

Jonathan P. Eburne

If it is shoes that you want, I'll give you shoes that you will admire to such an extent that you will lame yourselves trying to walk in them.

—Marcel Duchamp, 1936

It is indecent and pretentious to appropriate body and soul, blood and sweat, the work of another.

—Jean Suquet, on reading Duchamp's *Notes*, 1991

On the morning of the conference from which this volume arises, I was introduced to the man named Alan Smithee,[1] who was to make a brief speech and accept a token of appreciation later that day. Elegantly middle-aged, he was tanned and wore a light linen suit, a dark T-shirt, and sunglasses dangling from his neck. Rather than showing up at the last minute, he attended the entire conference, for he was determined to hear what people had to say about his work. He arrived with little fanfare, and listened politely and without comment to the discussions of his films and "pseudonymous" persona. Few people, therefore, were aware of his presence until he stood up to deliver his speech. Unsurprisingly, the general reaction to this appearance, this sudden emergence from anonymity, was mixed, ranging from mild surprise to annoyance and confusion. Several people refused to acknowledge him as anything other than a fake, the sham impersonation of an already "artificial *auteur*." Others expressed a kind of relief in finally encountering, in person, the subject of an academic conference with whom they had little familiarity. This emergence of a face from the crowd provided a way of making sense of things, a way of fleshing out the unfamiliar name to which so large a body of films had been ascribed. As the photograph published in the following Monday's university newspaper suggested, the man who may or may not have been "Allen Smithee" was certainly a worthy photo opportunity insofar as he proved that the conference was at least *about* somebody.[2] Regardless of their mixed feelings about his legitimacy, though, the realization that dawned on everyone was that the elusive figure of Alan Smithee, suddenly embodied and quite real, had been amongst us all along.

The fact that someone stepped in to complete, or at least to flesh out, an incomplete portrait of Smithee—incomplete insofar as Smithee is normally imagined as incomplete, without identity, indefinite—is particularly fitting to the nature of Smithee's own work. Although it is easy to think of Smithee as a pseudonym "standing in" for a missing film

Figure 10.1. Alan Smithee. Courtesy of the *Daily Pennsylvanian*; reprinted with permission. Photographer: Jennifer Arend.

auteur, that is, as a name that marks incompleteness, it seems more productive to consider him quite literally as the figure nominated by the film industry to *complete* a film. On the one hand, Smithee's intervention in a film is designed to complete it in both the legal and financial sense, steering it away from disaster, however marginally, by enabling its commercial release. "My life's work," Smithee explained during his brief speech, "is really about the turnaround of movies."[3] In accordance with the policies of the Directors Guild of America, Smithee steps in to complete a film only after its original director abandons ship, refusing to have his[4] name attached to the finished film. Since the Guild insists upon a director having "reasonable grounds" for doing so, such an abandonment signals more than an artistic failure; rather, it indicates deep contractual and financial crises, personnel problems, or breakdowns in management. The appearance of the name "Alan Smithee" in the credits is both the symptom of and the solution to such difficulties. Without necessarily making a film watchable, he spares a production company considerable financial losses by making a film *releasable,* allowing the company to cut its losses and to stave off further expenditures, losses, and potential lawsuits. By "hiring" Smithee, the corporation can salvage a product that would otherwise demand drastic rehiring and refilming, as well as extensive and potentially fruitless marketing.

On the other hand, Smithee could also be said to "complete" films aesthetically, by structuring the way audiences receive them in much the same way that Marcel Duchamp anticipated how the viewers of paintings "complete" their qualification as art. Writing that "the spectator completes the painting," Duchamp proposed the term "pictorial nominalism" to describe how a picture demands that its spectators "nominate" it as art.[5] Aesthetic value, in other words, is neither a quality essential to a work of art nor can it be definitively proclaimed by either an institution (a museum, exhibition, or panel of judges) or even its artist. Instead, as Thierry de Duve has explained, Duchamp locates aesthetic value as the product of an individual judgment "this is art," which only begins to function as a work's "proper name" if repeated enough times by enough people.[6] That is, the judgment "this is art" works like a name that, in order to be identified with a particular work, must be connected to it with enough determinacy to be recognized as its "name." This recognition, in turn, has the tautological effect of guaranteeing the existence of whatever qualities or concepts its viewers consider intrinsic to "art": if it is called art, it must *be* art.[7] Smithee, likewise, is the figure whose own proper (or improper) name represents the outcome of a particular judgment upon the value of a film. Of course, it is not primarily the *aesthetic* value of a film that Smithee determines, but its monetary value: Smithee's name almost certainly guarantees an astonishing degree of obscurity and a margin of commercial loss. Nevertheless, the fact that Smithee's films are often not only virtually unwatched, but virtually unwatchable, confirms the degree to which Smithee stands in the position of Duchamp's viewers, as the spectator of his own films. That is, he is nominated, not only by a corporation, but by his own films, to "finish" them—or to "finish them off"—in a way that assigns a readymade "proper name" to them immediately, both anticipating and determining how they will bear public scrutiny. However, such a solipsistic strategy for producing films that "consume themselves" represents more than a coy way of saying that the name "Smithee" signifies, or is the signature of, a bad film. Rather, this strategy embodies Smithee's true genius: in his "turnaround" of failed enterprises into films, Smithee transforms the film industry's cycle of production, artistic creation, public reception, and aesthetic judgment into the contingencies of a single name. In doing so, he demonstrates how the production of films can be understood not just as the assembly of moving pictures, but as a vast industry for producing meaning and opinion, which can be studied and manipulated independently of the actual commercial product. Alan Smithee, in other words, is an industry unto himself.

In what follows, I will discuss the implications of thinking about Alan Smithee in terms of "industry"—that is, as both a product and agent of the film industry, and as a productive industry unto himself. Marcel Duchamp is particularly useful to the study of Smithee because he developed a strategy for producing works of "art" that understood this production as a proliferation of aliases. With the readymade, Duchamp, like Smithee, did not "invent" or "create" so much as he devised ways of exhibiting or reproducing other objects, even other works of art, under aliases designed to complicate the all-too-automatic process of using art "as a proper name." Abandoning the "physical aspect of painting" soon after 1910, Duchamp's development of the readymade suddenly made it impossible—or at least extremely difficult—to understand a work's artistic value on the basis of its stylistic, allegorical, or physical properties. As he explained, "I wanted to get away from the physical aspect of painting ... I was interested in ideas—not merely in visual products. I wanted to put painting once again at the service of the mind."[8] By presenting a workaday, mass-produced snow shovel or urinal in the place of crafted, pictorial art, Duchamp's readymades wrought havoc upon the assumptions of so-called avant-garde art movements like cubism and futurism, whose names represented shifts in pictorial convention, but not in the broader convention that all such shifts remained *pictorial*. Adorning a snow shovel bought in 1915 with both a signature ("Marcel Duchamp") and a title ("In Advance of the Broken Arm"), Duchamp gave it two new names; with the urinal, called "Fountain" (1917), his more intricate methodology involved signing the object and entering it into an exhibition under the name "R. Mutt." In so doing, he provided aliases not only for the objects, but for the *artist* as well. Furthermore, in referring to these objects as "readymades," Duchamp placed them under yet another alias, appropriating a term used in New York City in the teens to describe mass-produced, ready-to-wear clothing.[9] Duchamp began using the term in 1915 to describe the objects that, likewise, no longer required the "tailoring" of painterly art, but required only the new names that would allow him to present the objects as "ready-to-wear" works of art.

As I have suggested, this proliferation of titles and names both parodies and repeats the process through which a work of art is presented before its public: it identifies a title, a genre, and an artist, thereby somehow accounting for the object's appearance within a gallery space. However, by attaching these supplementary names to an object whose name is already firmly fixed—"snow shovel" or "urinal"—Duchamp's aliases have the combined effect of alienating the art object itself from the names, words, and terminologies used to describe it, as well as inciting disagreement about which of these names can be considered "proper" ones. The field of discourse and disagreement that Duchamp hoped would "complete" his readymades would, in turn, constitute the industry these "machines," as he called them, could churn out—only it would be an industry of thoughts and ideas, and not an industry of actual "products." Indeed, as Jean Suquet writes about a work contemporary to the readymades, the *Large Glass*, or, *The Bride Stripped Bare by Her Bachelors, Even*, this intricate and complex work functions as a machine that "runs only on words."[10] The "words" Suquet mentions refer both to the copious boxes of notes Duchamp published about the *Large Glass*, as well as to the "words" of interpretation and critical judgment that both the work and its notes would provoke. Begun in 1915 and assembled in tandem with the majority of the readymades, this work was designed not to be "completed" by spectators but to remain indefinitely perplexing: in 1923 Duchamp called the work "definitively unfinished."

Smithee, on the other hand, is himself a symptom of corporate dissent and the "words" exchanged between the people implicated in the death-throes of a floundering film. By the time Smithee is hired, the cycles of perplexed arguments and serious negotiation have, to a large degree, already run their course; rather than risking the possibility that a film might remain "definitively unfinished," Smithee's job is to make sure it gets finished, definitively, if not gracefully. The possibility that Smithee is himself analogous to the discursive field of "words" that is both the product and the fuel of Duchamp's machines is further supported by the degree to which, as I have suggested above, he forecloses on the cycle of aesthetic judgment as the "spectator" of his own films. What is "readymade" for Smithee, therefore, is not only the virtually completed film his presence recasts as "an Alan Smithee film," but also much of the debate and judgment that, in Duchamp's case, the works were intended to inspire. Smithee himself becomes a kind of alias for the *effects* of his own "art."

At the same time, Smithee provides an additional alias, standing in for the "readymade" quality of his own function as an artist. Although, like Duchamp, Smithee distances himself from the actual labor of creating the objects he presents as his "work," he has no hand in the decision to perform the *secondary* labor of transforming these objects (whether urinals or reels of film) into "readymade" films. Rather, Smithee is nominated by the film corporation for this exact purpose, and thus his presence in the production of a film is, however crucial, not one of artistic intentionality—Smithee serves instead as the *corporate representative* of this intentionality: he is its figurehead, its overseer, its alias. For this role, too, Duchamp can offer insight, since he was similarly invested in distinguishing, to the best of his abilities, both the labor and the intentions involved in making art from an artist's *persona*.

The Alias Men

In his 1961 lecture "Apropos of 'Readymades,'" Duchamp explains the lack of aesthetic consideration behind his choice of objects to baptize as readymades, though he says this in a way that seems almost to divest the decision of consciousness altogether: "The point which I want very much to establish is that the choice of these 'readymades' was never dictated by aesthetic delectation. This choice was based on a reaction of visual indifference with at the same time a total absence of good or bad taste ... in fact a complete anesthesia."[11] Duchamp's "indifference" and "anesthesia" suggest the degree to which he was attempting to abstract himself entirely from the intentionality of his art. His "baptism" of anonymous objects was not the mandate of a supreme will, an official induction into the sacred realm of art; rather, this renaming was "a choice based on a reaction of visual indifference," that is, a chance encounter, or, as Duchamp has elsewhere described the "reaction" behind readymades, a *rendez-vous*. Duchamp's experimentation with chance—as well as with the *rendez-vous* of chance and strategy he called "canned chance"—at this moment further suggests the degree to which he was attempting to abstract the artist's creative work of "authorship" from the artist's persona, as well as from the work itself. Duchamp's subsequent development of a series of alter egos is a function of this abstraction that seems to have arisen itself in the wake of the readymades. In developing these alter egos and determining their consequences for the nominalism of his art, Duchamp anticipates Smithee's own role as an "alter ego" for the authorship of films in a way that can help us understand his consequences for the definitions of authorship and artistry in Hollywood.

One of Duchamp's most famous images is the work entitled *L.H.O.O.Q.* (1919), a readymade that uses an art-book reproduction of Leonardo da Vinci's *Gioconda*, the *Mona Lisa*, as its everyday object. Allegedly "defacing" the painting with a mustache and goatee, Duchamp adds a title that likewise assaults the painting's value for posterity by punning on its subject's posterior: pronounced in French, the letters spell out "elle a chaud au cul," meaning something like "she has hot pants," that is "she's turned on." However, the effect of this defacement is, ironically, that it actually attaches a face to Leonardo's notoriously anonymous (is this a woman or a man? is it Isabella d'Este, the wife of a patron, or a self-portrait?) portrait; as numerous scholars have suggested, Duchamp's graphic alteration transforms the painting with all the thoroughness of an alchemical change; as Duchamp himself writes, "The curious thing about that mustache and goatee is that when you look at it the *Mona Lisa* becomes a man. It is not a woman disguised as a man; it is a real man, and that was my discovery without realizing it at the time."[12] Duchamp's graffiti proposes that the painting has represented a man all along, a man whose name is, in a sense, both Leonardo da Vinci and Marcel Duchamp. This alteration thus performs a "turnaround" upon the painting, smilingly inverting its image to reveal a self-portrait of the artist who, in all but the goatee, is in drag.

From revising (or re-visaging) the *Mona Lisa* as an alter ego in 1919, it was a short step to inventing a similar persona, from scratch, in 1920. As Moira Roth has suggested in an influential article on Duchamp as a "Self Ready-Made," the fabrication of Rrose Sélavy, Duchamp's drag alter ego, is the hypostasis of R. Mutt and *L.H.O.O.Q.* alike.[13] Both a self-portrait and an alias, Rrose becomes the coauthor of many of Duchamp's works after 1920, beginning with *Fresh Widow* (1920), and including *Box in a Valise* (1941), a collection of meticulously reproduced miniatures

L.H.O.O.Q.

Figure 10.2. Marcel Duchamp, *L.H.O.O.Q. (Replica of, from Boite-En-Valise)*, 1919.
Courtesy of Philadelphia Museum of Art: The Louise and Walter Arensberg
Collection. Photograph by Lynn Rosenthal. Copyright 2000 Artists Rights Society
(ARS), New York/ADAGP, Paris/Estate of Marcel Duchamp; reprinted with permission.

of Duchamp's early works that is "copyrighted" by Rrose Sélavy. Like Alan Smithee, Rrose has even less of a hand in the actual production of "works" than Duchamp himself; yet the attribution of such works to Rrose Sélavy produces a significant effect on the work's status as a presentation. Since *Fresh Widow* is not a true readymade but an "assisted" readymade—a French Window with its panes covered in black patent leather and, in the title, with two "n's" removed from its name—Rrose steps in to account for the "assistance" that would otherwise implicate Duchamp's hand in crafting, rather than merely re-presenting as a readymade, an object.

To compare Rrose Sélavy with Alan Smithee produces a startling resemblance. Certainly, the photographs bear a degree of similarity: both are formal portraits of men in drag—Duchamp in fashionable female attire, Smithee in a somewhat dated corporate uniform. More significant, however, is how this effect draws attention to the phenomenon of Smithee's name. "Rrose Sélavy," indeed strange-looking for a name, pronounces itself as "eros, c'est la vie," or, "eros, that's life." This pun might be interpreted as a witticism based on Gertrude Stein's famous dictum "a rose is a rose is a rose," to which Duchamp adds an extra spin, an extra turn: in Duchamp's French accent, "a rose" would form the easy homonym to "eros," which its spelling as "Rrose" confirms. For Duchamp, a rose is *not* just a rose, evoking the ability of readymades to transform an object from itself into something else: a urinal is no longer a urinal but a fountain as well, a rose is no longer just a rose but *eros* as well, and Duchamp is no longer a male artist but a female alias as well.

Alan Smithee's name, too, seems a little strange, though it pronounces itself comfortably enough. Applying a degree of scrutiny made possible by the comparison to Duchamp's pun, however, reveals a possible source for this orthographic strangeness: spelled as "Alan Smithee," the name breaks down as an anagram for "the alias men." What does this signify? First, it further suggests that Smithee's appearance as a corporate businessman can be read as a kind of Duchampian drag performance. Like the *Mona Lisa*'s goatee, the anagram's "defacement" of Smithee's proper name reveals the truth of the portrait: he is not, to paraphrase

Figure 10.3. Man Ray, *Marcel Duchamp Dressed as Rrose Sélavy*, 1924. Photograph by Lynn Rosenthal, 1993. Courtesy of Philadelphia Museum of Art: The Samuel S. White, 3rd, and Vera White Collection. Copyright 2000 Man Ray Trust/Artists Rights Society (ARS), New York/ADAGP, Paris; reprinted with permission.

Figure 10.4. Studio portrait of Alan Smithee. Collection of the author.

Duchamp, a man dressed up to look "corporate"; he *is* a real corporation, insofar as his name incorporates the (to date, exclusively male) filmmakers whom he replaces contractually[14] The defacement, ironically,
attaches a face to Hollywood's notoriously indeterminate body of industrial laborers and executives; the photograph thus represents a kind of
"cross-dressing" in the sense that it depicts a corporation dressed up to
look like a man. As a result, Smithee is transformed from a mere signature into a carefully crafted artistic product himself—a reasonably slickly
dressed corporate representative of artistic intentionality. Smithee's sudden appearance "in drag" thus provides a *visual* example of the way his
name collapses the distinction between an author's signature ("an Alan
Smithee film"), a name for an artistic object ("an Alan Smithee film"),
and a critical judgment ("oh ... an Alan Smithee film"). That is, like his
name, his photograph provides an alter ego not only for the anonymous "alias men" themselves, but for the tautological closure his presence is designed to guarantee: *here* is a man who represents the making
of films, regardless of how good or bad those films might be. What makes
Smithee's drag performance particularly interesting, then, is how its
very closure, its exaggerated determinacy, opens up a whole series of
questions about what this ability to "represent" filmmaking says about
filmmaking—problematizing the tendency for its codes, its business
practices, its gender biases, and its political ideologies to remain invisible and anonymous.

At the same time, although its existence may be coincidental—and
indeed, certain (mis)spellings of his name as "Allen" frustrate it—the
notion that Smithee operates on a logic of anagrams, as opposed to Rrose
Sélavy's logic of puns, is itself significant to Smithee studies. If punning
evokes the multiplicity and simultaneity of meanings played upon by the
readymade, as Octavio Paz has argued,[15] then Smithee's anagram evokes
both his "turnaround" role in film production, as well as the solipsistic
and ephemeral logic of his existence as a film "author" or *auteur*.

Puns, as Duchamp explains, are "like rhymes" in the sense that their
sound alone "begins a chain reaction" of "considerations, connotations,
and investigations." For Duchamp,

words are not merely a means of communication. You know, puns have always been considered a low form of wit, but I find them a source of stimulation both because of their actual sound and because of unexpected meanings attached to the inter-relations of disparate words. For me, this is an infinite field of joy—and it's always right at hand. Sometimes four or five different levels of meaning come through.[16]

The simultaneity of associations offered "right at hand" by such rhyme-like strokes of wit are not, however, so readily produced by anagrams. Emphatically spatial rather than aural, anagrams, particularly complex ones, exist only in one particular configuration or another. Their multiplicity resides only in their use and reuse of the same material, the same letters, in different configurations. Considered an even lower form of wit, the anagram's source of stimulation lies in its cryptic near-invisibility and in the sheer difficulty of proving its significance as anything other than an interpreter's overestimation of coincidence. An anagram thus presents itself as a solipsistic, involuted linguistic trick whose intentionality is imposed upon the interpreter or spectator. Rather than offering a "field of joy" that is always "right at hand," the anagram implicates the "hand" of a spectator's involvement: the spectator completes the picture.[17] By transforming "Alan Smithee" into "the alias men," I can literally change what the "picture" of the filmmaker by that name looks like, summoning instead the multiplicity of writers, executives, actors, studio hands, editors, engineers, and camera operators for whom "Alan Smithee"—or the name of any director whose name "authors" a film—serves as the alias. On the other hand, though, just as Rrose Sélavy both assists and embodies the punning logic of the readymade, Smithee stands in for the nearly alchemical transformation that occurs somewhere between the mechanics of a film's creation—its writing, filming, and financing—and its completion as a finished "film" (as opposed to a mere collection of reels). Duchamp referred to this "alchemical" distinction as the "infra-thin" separation between non-art and art; for Smithee, then, it is the infra-thin separation between a non-film and a film that his name both exemplifies and bridges. As both a "turnaround" artist and a "big name" in the film industry, Alan Smithee, in other words, fully exploits the degree to which a "work" of filmmaking is no more—nor no less—than the alter ego of a failed endeavor that doesn't "work" at all. Both this alias and this difference are so slight, so subject to interpretation and disagreement, that they invite the same scorn as the anagram, the debased form of wit that governs them.

Of Industry and Idiocy

The understanding that qualifies Marcel Duchamp as a useful interpretive tool for thinking about Alan Smithee relies heavily upon an interpretation of Duchamp that does not merely depict him as a nihilistic "anti-artist," but rather as a serious—if witty and playful—artist and thinker who was more interested in how art "works" than in the "works of art" themselves. The resulting interpretation of the Duchampian readymade as a kind of machinist "idea-works" (much like a waterworks or steelworks), rather than as pictorial "works of art," was largely the product of Duchamp's reevaluation by young artists, art critics, and interviewers in the years following World War II. The critics who first encountered Duchamp's early works, on the other hand, were less understanding. Though he gained fame and notoriety for his quasi-cubist painting, *Nude Descending a Staircase, No. 2*, when it was exhibited at the 1913 Armory Show in New York, Duchamp's readymades were, like the other avant-gardiste experiments of New York's dada artists, almost universally panned. In a characteristic effort to explain such experiments, the *World Magazine* published an article in 1921 titled "Dada: The Cheerless Art of Idiocy."[18] Though it only marginally implicates Duchamp as one of the "idiots" of dada art—printing a wire portrait of the artist rather than quoting him directly—the article seriously questions whether dada's avant-garde practices have any ideas at all. Appropriating a line from Tristan Tzara, one of the Zurich dadaists, to incriminate dada activity as a whole, the article concludes with Tzara's "single intelligible sentence: 'What Dada-ism is working for is to make the people idiots!'" Nevertheless, the article's opening line, however snidely intended, describes Duchamp's own nominalist practices more accurately: "Dada offers the latest guess at Art's eternal enigma." In Duchamp's case, this "offer" represents less a provisional answer to this enigma than a solicitation, a demand for spectators (including the author of the article) to make their own "latest guess" at it. What such guesswork might entail is suggested by the future surrealist André Breton, who writes, later in the article, "All is Dada. Everyone has his Dadas. You worship your Dadas and make gods of them. The Dadaists know their Dadas and laugh at them. It shows their great superiority over you." Here, it seems that Breton transforms "Dada" from the name of an art movement into another name for the ideology, or the fetishism, that it calls into question. As a bilingual Frenchman in New York, Duchamp would understand "Dada" as baby-talk for both a hobby-horse (French) and a father (English). From this perspective, the "Dadas" known and laughed at by Breton might, for Duchamp, include an artistic paternity through whose legacy the radical artistic inventions of a previous generation become the second-hand conventions, the childish toy horses, of younger artists. Duchamp's abandonment of "the physical aspect of painting" for a mode of artistic production that produced, if not idiocy, then an industry of guesswork, represents an abandonment of this paternal legacy. It suggests that Duchamp's goal was to mass-produce a way not only to "laugh at" the fathers of art, but to approach, first hand, the "eternal enigmas" they were attempting to address.

The fact that Duchamp, toward the end of his life, was being resurrected as a father-figure for many conceptual artists, such as Joseph Kosuth, Robert Morris, Sherrie Levine, and Bruce Conner, suggests the deep, structuring influence of Duchamp upon the art scene at the historical moment—the middle to late 1960s—during which Alan Smithee himself was "born" as a filmmaker.[19] And, if we might offer that Duchamp was thus somehow the "father" not only of conceptual art but of Alan Smithee as well, this paternity was neither biological nor even directly genetic in its theoretical basis. Rather, Smithee was the offspring of another kind of "Duchamp industry": the dissemination of Duchamp's individual work as an artist into the discourse and artistic work of the conceptual artists who invoked him. Unlike many of the conceptual artists who fetishized Duchamp, however, Smithee does not understand his "Dada" as someone or something either to laugh at or worship, whether in statement or in habit, in name or in hobby. As an author, Smithee betrays no "anxiety of influence," in this sense. Unlike other film "*auteurs*," who maintain a kind of pact with their audiences that maintains each film's creation by a singular author, an "Alan Smithee film" imposes such a transitive, "infra-thin"—and merely contractual—singularity upon the composite labors of countless writers, actors, studio hands, editors, and subordinates that the onus of the question of which "Dadas" Smithee might be addressing is placed upon us: not as spectators of Smithee's *films*, but as spectators of Smithee himself.

If Smithee can be considered the prodigal sibling of 1960s conceptual art, it is not the works articulating a singular "concept" that he resembles, but the quieter, wiser ones that speak only about the concepts asked of them. One such latter work, installed in a room near the Duchamp collection at the Philadelphia Museum of Art, is Richard Long's *Limestone Circle* (1985), whose ring of stones demarcates a "sacred" space upon the otherwise ordinary museum floor. Once circumscribed, that part of the floor becomes something akin to "art"—not in the positive, aesthetic, or titular sense (since the work's title refers to the stones, not the museum), but in the *affective* sense of a restriction, a sudden alteration of the "everyday" quality of the floor it demarcates. What happens when you step into it? Will the guard come after you? Like Smithee's anagrammatic name, the *Circle* functions as a trap for a spectator's interpretive efforts, successfully diverting attention away from its own material appearance, toward an investigation of what you can make it do *to you*. Otherwise inert, the piece only "works" at all if you ask the right questions ("Can I step inside?" for example, or "Does the museum care about what's inside the circle?"), and it continues to work only as long as you continue questioning. Without this suspense, it falls back into quiescence and materiality, a cheerless piece of dumb art: most people pass it by altogether. The same is true for Smithee, whose anagrammatic persona can cause him to disappear entirely from existence. In order for him to be anything other than an inert, contractual presence in a film, in order, that is, for his existence to be anything other than a closed circle, Smithee has to be "inhabited" by ideas, used as a means of questioning what his presence achieves, what new ways of thinking he makes possible. As Smithee himself explained at the Specters of Legitimacy conference, "you all expect mediocrity—so I won't disappoint you." If Smithee's genius lies in his ability thus to live either up or down to expectations, it is because this way of responding to an audience—again, not a cinematic audience but an audience engaged in "Smithee studies"—is based on a Duchampian "reaction of visual indifference with at the same time a total absence of good or bad taste ... in fact a complete anesthesia." As the subject of "Smithee studies," Alan Smithee himself will answer only the questions we ask of him.

Notes

I wish to acknowledge the significant role that David Quintiliani has played in the development of this essay. A fellow member of the Allen Smithee Group at the University of Pennsylvania, David presented a paper on Smithee and Duchamp at the Specters of Legitimacy conference titled "The Smithee Readymade: Duchamp and the Anti-Art Object." David and I exchanged ideas about Duchamp and Smithee throughout a number of conversations before and since the conference, and the current essay is deeply indebted both to these conversations and to his paper. I wish also to thank Donald Pease, Hester Blum, and my father, Timothy Eburne, for their assistance.

1. As Jeremy Braddock and Stephen Hock discuss, the name's original spelling was "Allen Smithee." See chapter 1 in the present volume (n. 10).

2. Jennifer Arend, "Will the Real 'Allen Smithee' Please Rise?" *Daily Pennsylvanian* (29 Sept. 1997): 2.

3. Alan Smithee, acceptance speech, Specters of Legitimacy, University of Pennsylvania, Philadelphia, 27 Sept. 1997.

4. To date, it appears that all such directors have been male.

5. Duchamp writes, "All in all, the creative act is not performed by the artist alone; the spectator brings the work in contact with the external world by deciphering and interpreting its inner qualifications and thus adds his contribution to the creative act." Marcel Duchamp, "The Creative Act" (1957),

trans. Elmer Peterson, *The Writings of Marcel Duchamp*, ed. Michel Sanouillet and Elmer Peterson (New York: Da Capo, 1973) 140. For a provocative book-length study of Duchamp's pictorial nominalism, see Thierry de Duve, *Pictorial Nominalism: On Marcel Duchamp's Passage from Painting to the Readymade*, trans. Dana Polan with the author (Minneapolis: University of Minnesota Press, 1991).

6. As Thierry de Duve writes, "Art, you say, is everything we call art, but the *we* is not given." See de Duve, *Kant After Duchamp* (Cambridge: MIT Press, 1996) 19. De Duve continues, "The phrase 'this is art' is the expression of your judgment, arising case by case. And so is the phrase 'art is this.' In spite of the fact that it sounds like a definition, it is merely a quasi-definition, an empirical one if you like, since it is based on sense experience, but more precisely an aesthetic one, inasmuch as the word 'aesthetic' precisely means: that which has to do with a sentimental, not with a cognitive, experience. In baptizing the examples of your taste with the name *art*, you are thus making an aesthetic judgment. Most often of course, as in the case of established masterpieces, you are simply repeating a christening that has long since been performed. Your personal *habitus* confirms a more or less general consensus. But from time to time, you call art something unexpected, or you refuse to call art something too expected" (de Duve, *Kant After Duchamp* 32).

7. In an effort to describe how this works, Duchamp gives both an explanation and an example of his nominalism: "As a good nominalist, I propose the word patatautological, which, after frequent repetition, will create the concept of what I am trying to explain." Marcel Duchamp, unpublished letter to Jean Mayoux dated "8 mars 1956," cited in Carol P. James, "An Original Revolutionary *Messagerie* Rrose, or What Became of Readymades," *The Definitively Unfinished Marcel Duchamp*, ed. Thierry de Duve (Cambridge: MIT Press, 1991) 280.

8. James Johnson Sweeney, interview with Marcel Duchamp, *Museum of Modern Art Bulletin* 13.4-5 (1946): 20.

9. See, for instance, Eric Cameron, "Given," *The Definitively Unfinished Marcel Duchamp* 19.

10. Jean Suquet, "Possible," *The Definitively Unfinished Marcel Duchamp* 86.

11. Marcel Duchamp, "Apropos of 'Readymades,'" talk delivered at the Museum of Modern Art, New York, 19 Oct. 1961. Reprinted in *The Writings of Marcel Duchamp* 141.

12. Herbert Crehan, interview with Marcel Duchamp, "Dada," *Evidence* 3 (fall 1961): 36–38. See Dalia Judovitz's insightful commentary in *Unpacking Duchamp: Art in Transit* (Berkeley: University of California Press, 1995) 142–44.

13. Moira Roth, "Marcel Duchamp in America: A Self Ready-Made" *Arts Magazine* 51.9 (May 1977): 93–94.

14. See "Smithee's Incorporation," Jeremy Braddock's essay in the present volume.

15. Cf. Octavio Paz, *Marcel Duchamp*, trans. Rachel Phillips and Donald Gardner (New York: Seaver Books, 1978), especially page 21, where Paz makes the influential assertion that the readymade "is the plastic equivalent of the pun."

16. Katherine Kuh, interview with Marcel Duchamp, *The Artist's Voice: Talks with Seventeen Artists* (New York: Harper and Row, 1962) 89.

17. Laura Parigi argues elsewhere in this collection that the phenomenon of americanized pseudonyms in the Italian cinema operated by a similar kind of completion (or "cooperative interpretation") on the part of the audience, who knew all along that these figures of the cinema were pseudonymous personages.

18. Henry Tyrell, "Dada: The Cheerless Art of Idiocy," *World Magazine* 12 June 1921: 8, 13. Reprinted in Rudolph E. Kuenzli, ed., *New York Dada* (New York: Willis, Locker and Owens, 1986) 142–45.

19. For a helpful collection of studies of Duchamp's influence on the conceptual artists of the 1960s, see Martha Buskirk and Mignon Nixon, eds., *The Duchamp Effect: Essays, Interviews, Round Table* (Cambridge: MIT Press, 1996).

CHAPTER 11

A for *Auteur* and F for Fake:
A Case for Raoul Walsh

Tom Conley

The beginnings of *auteur* theory in France were summed up in a slogan François Truffaut borrowed from Jean Giraudoux, "Il n'y a plus d'oeuvres, il n'y a que des auteurs" [Works are finished, there are only authors]. We might say that the origin of the cinematic movement associated with the *auteur* takes the shape of a quotation attesting to its own borrowed nature. The work of the author is anything but original or originary. It is pocked with the names of others that have informed it, that have hollowed it out, that have evacuated it from the word go, its contribution to tradition not being any individual talent of its own, other, perhaps, than its will to build itself as a hieroglyph of citations. If a work there is, it is constructed through the presence of others, or "autres," who inhabit the world of creators, who determine their form, sensibilities, and their styles. Authors are worthy of their name when their works are so riddled and striated with allusions and references to *others*—to other films, other works of literature, other political events—that they begin to resemble crossword jumbles of proper names and places with their attendant signatures and toponyms. Without arching back to Andrew Sarris's groundbreaking article of 1962 on the politics of *auteur* theory or to *The American Cinema*,[1] his great catalog of film treating of the conscience of its myriad directors, and without rehearsing the rewriting of film history done by the authors and editors of *Cahiers du cinéma* under the spell of André Bazin in the postwar years, we can modestly assert that since then film theory and history have utterly changed. In each of the three decades since the 1960s we have said without any nostalgia that the *auteur* is not what it used to be.

The dilemma is clearly drawn in the current frame of *Cahiers du cinéma*. In recent discussions and writings, its editor, Antoine de Baecque, has noted that the journal has lived through three phases of its relation with the *auteur*. The first, at its inception, developed its politics along the lines of cinematic form insofar as the technical virtues of the medium were seen consubstantial with the vision of a consciousness, that of the director, who is no less a writer, who makes of thought itself a dialectics of filmic process. There resulted, as it were, a cockleshell politics in which the filmmaker and the cinéphile found themselves spiraling into bodies of work, often extensive collections of feature films, for the purpose of making of the seventh art what both Aristotle and Jean-François Lyotard called the mission of politics: the art of the possible. But the art of *auteurist* possibility seemed, in its affiliation with Hitchcock, Hawks, Welles, Rossellini, and Lang, to be one mixing the missions of commemoration, erudition, and, like it or not, a type of historical consumerism. Only in 1971, with the impact of close—and even psychoanalytical—readings of Marx did *Cahiers* change its stance by noting to what degree the "author" of a film tended to be a function of regimes of classification within a broader history of social contradiction. Younger cineastes and those of different cultural traditions could not be put under a rubric that seemed, by then, obsolescently historicist.

In the later 1980s, noted Antoine de Baecque, the journal turned full circle to espouse, again, the idea of the *auteur*, but with the difference that it had to be seen within a multinational matrix. Herein the point where the *auteur* meets Allen Smithee: how can a formerly effective interpretive model be adapted to corporate cinemas that indeed sell their commodities on the basis of the so-called art, now incredibly degraded, that would identify the pertinent traits of a directorial signature in films that are made with nauseatingly munificent budgets? How could a director such as Steven Spielberg ever be called an "*auteur*" in view of the corporate style of films marketed to push the affective buttons of a public at correctly political moments, whether in memory of the concentration camps (*Schindler's List* being tantamount to what has been coined as Shoah-business), social oppression in America (*Amistad*, a confusion of the history of slavery and Grecian bodies in black recalling Leni Riefenstahl), or the "liberation" of Europe (*Saving Private Ryan* commemorating D-Day in 1944 to launch an economic "star war" of cinema on Europe in 1998)? At *Cahiers*, however, aesthetic aura is still awarded to directors such as James Cameron for *Titanic* and other features, for which the art of the medium is celebrated while the echo of Freud's Marxian expression of doubt, "Je sais bien, mais quand même" [I know, but all the same ...] is heard through the praise. Within the "return" of the *auteur*, somewhat unlike that of the repressed, lurks the cinema of simulacrum, that of Allen Smithee, that perpetually calls into question the redemptive features of the *auteur*. The unsettling effect wrought by Smithee, I should like to argue in the paragraphs below, can bring a sharpened consciousness to the practice of the *auteur* in both history and theory.

Like it or not, we still categorize films by the name of the director. What we would like to believe to be the film's "vision of the world," in the fashion of the term that Lukács used to organize his readings of the nineteenth-century novel, applies to a style and mode of production that cannot be set outside of historical classification. It appears that practically all American cinema up to the 1970s can be categorized according to directors, but that since then the names of stars and corporate enterprises have become prevailing modes in a taxonomy that uses the past to camouflage other agendas. The director is a simulacrum and not an essence.[2] Yet the demise of the *auteur* in the world of the cineplex and in strategies of multinational distribution eternally promises its revival in forms *other* than the contours of the molds that shape it in film history. The *auteur*, like the Allen Smithee syndrome, is associated with surface tensions, with stylistic turns that bend or strain the codes of the classical styles they convey. If a directorial signature reiterates the "world-vision" of the *auteur*, his or her vision is forcibly out of place and, further, out of style when it is productively displaced or misused in what might be called the age of the production of mechanical *auteurism*. Hence, para-doxically, a curious affinity that ties Allen Smithee to the bedrock of classical cinema.

The basis for that affinity might be seen in what an unnamed author of sixteenth-century France states about a motley book of only his or her publisher's signature that includes a mix of philosophical observation, citations from problem-books, *varia* about Latin and vernacular usage, the relation of language to belief, and even the art of tuning guitars and lutes:

> J'ai recouvré les discours, dont est fait ce livre, & maints autres escrits, & labeurs divers de plusieurs ... aucunesfois des auteurs mesmes, aucunesfois d'autres que des auteurs, qui avoient cela retiré des auteurs, ou en quelque sorte leur estoit venus entre les mains sans savoir rien des auteurs.[3]

> [I have recovered the discourses of which this book is composed, and many other writings, and many various labors of different people, sometimes with the authors themselves, sometimes with others than the authors, who had drawn what they had from authors, or in some way material come into their hands without their knowing anything about those authors.]

The introduction, a piece of prefatory smokescreen in this work of 1556, indicates, first, that the Allen Smithee syndrome does not entirely belong to cinema, and second, that in the years of bloody reprisals against humanists in the reign of Francis I to be an author publishing anything in the public sphere meant risking one's life. Such was the dilemma for Bonaventure Des Périers, the libertine who might indeed have penned the beginning and the chapters of the *Discours non plus mélancholiques que divers* cited above. The humanist and rationalist reputedly plunged a sword into his belly after it had become known that he was responsible for an infamous series of anticlerical dialogues titled the *Cymbalum mundi*, which appeared in 1538. In this posthumous text the editor pro-tects himself from the risk of publishing a dangerous author by appeal-ing to some of the ground rules of *auteur* theory: the author of the book may well be dead and gone, for which cause the work can be necessarily of greater value; even if it has a single author, the origin of the book is collective; it may have individual attributes, but those attributes may indeed be those of others who wrote unbeknownst to those who collected the information included in the patchwork of *meslange*. The poetic gist of the locution stating that the material is taken, "aucunesfois des auteurs mesmes aucunesfois d'autres que des auteurs, qui avoient cela retiré des auteurs," tells us that the *auteur* celebrating the self is someone *other*.

If these words are pasted over what Arthur Rimbaud, in the celebrated "Lettre dite du voyant," stated about the condition of an author, an even broader historical (and citational) perspective is gained. "C'est faux de dire: Je pense: on devrait dire: On me pense.—Pardon du jeu de mots.—Je est un autre"[4] [It's wrong to say: I think: they ought to say: I am thought.—Pardon the play on words.—I is another]. The other who is I is an author. Whatever we use to identify ourselves in our writings has long before inhabited the traits of one's own signature. The overlay of Rimbaud and his sixteenth-century forebear proves what was evident both in etymology and in creative practice at the cusp of manuscript and print culture. The author survives as long as he or she is *l'acteur*, the performative agent whose creation is textualized only in the event of its expression. *L'acteur*, the designation coextensive with *l'auteur*, shows that the authority of the latter is tenuous because of the durational fragility of the former. The implied dialogism of the relation between the performer, the work performed, and the virtual—but not necessarily existential—audience is such that by a slight bend of a syllable or inflection the *acteur*, *l'auteur* echoes the reader, or *lecteur*, the *auctor* and *lector* sharing an intimate and cohering rapport.

If we consider *auteur* theory in the light of a coproduction of alterity, performance, and of the confusion of the sites of origin and reception of an act of communication, it is impossible not to return to the celebrated title of and conclusion to the essay ending *Marges de la philosophie* (published in 1972, a decade after Andrew Sarris scripted his polemical "Notes"). Therein, in "signature événement contexte" [Signature Event

Context] Jacques Derrida argues that an event amounts to the performance of the name of its origin as a reiteration.[5] The element of spacing at the basis of the title (the original in lower case, without commas punctuating the areas between *signature* and *événement* and *événement* and *contexte*) offers dimensions immediately lost upon monolingual anglophone readers. Each of the terms has an equipollent value in the string. No term is grammatically or parenthetically in a subordinate relation to the others.

Each is a "keyword" in a self-translating formula that cues on its own acronym, as Derrida insists time and again in the French version of the text, in what he calls a "dry" (or *sec*) summation of the principle that absences or gappings (even misunderstandings) are required for the process of communication. By insisting at length that he must offer an aridly stenographic conclusion of his discussion he also draws his reader's eyes to the visual agglutination of the title, *s* ignature *é* vénement *c* ontexte. It plays on the reminder of what he calls the "Securities Exchange Commission" of "limited responsibility" for communication in his essay, "Limited Inc a b c . . . ," all the while playing on the relation of an *event* to the construction of the author as a figment of translation.[6] *Sec* transliterates into "est-ce (s) i (e) ci (c)," or "is it here?" Is it—communication—right here and now? Or is it based on a delay, no matter how infinitesimal it might be? On looping and translating in the gaps that assure the authority of the author who reiterates a signature in order to keep its integrity possible? In every event the title of the essay plays on the presence of the old French verb *texter*, held within the difference of its spoken and graphic articulation, that emerges in the difference of "signature événement contexte" and "signature, événement, contexte." With the assurance of an equivalence that we would habitually locate between a signature and an event comes the equivocation of *contexte* and *qu'on texte*. *Texter* meant to "write," with the inflection that the reader sees in the expression the echo of the principle of the act of inscribing. "Signature, an event that one writes": thus implied is that the "author" becomes a reiterated event of writing, the latter being understood in at once manuscriptural, printed, photographic, and electronic technologies. A signature is not merely what confers authority upon its author. Its reiteration is needed in the field of its own resemblance and difference in respect to other signatures. Only in its perpetual rewriting or repetition of a common look does it obtain an appearance of singularity.

These seemingly archaic principles of deconstruction, mapped out in Derrida's critical account of speech-act theory of 1972, also heralded the demise of *auteur* theory at the time of their enunciation. What had been understood as the relation of a signature-style to an artist's consciousness in the industry of cinema was suddenly projected into the pragmatic world of reiteration in a world of printed rhetoric. The essay was delivered and written at the same moment that *Cahiers du cinéma* rejected the tenets of the *auteur*. Nonetheless, Derrida's work did not— nor has it since—eradicated the broader historical and political implications of the theory associated with Bazin and Andrew Sarris. Somewhat to the contrary, it has served to refine them. By way of "Signature Event Context" it can be argued that if we *fold* the longer history of the author—and not that merely of the history of Hollywood or of the tradition of modernism that reaches back to the nineteenth century, but to at least the last five centuries—over the debates concerning the directorial signatures in the film industry, some pertinent traits emerge. One is that of the author functioning as an agent of *reiteration*, but also as a difference obtained through the process of repetition. The author is glimpsed as a minimal but decisive shift perceived in each signatory instance that upholds the ambient codes it at once repeats and on which it varies.

It might be said, too, that in each event a transgression upholds the codes in the very act of renaming and recalling what comes with the signature. In cinema the transgression can be sensed in various ways, many of which can be at once thematic and cinematic. In the work of critics following Bazin, attention was brought to a director's general depiction of a way of rewriting a convention, or of distorting expectations.[7] The idea of the *auteur* as a reiterative element brings issues concerning the effect of the medium to any number of topics by virtue of a discernible articulation of a cinematic process and whatever it conveys.

The *auteur* somehow makes his or her form a function of what is being put forward. The reiterated signature both calls into question the thematic illusion of the narrative and points to the cinematic effects that make it possible. Thus in the thirty years that have been gained since the heyday of *auteur* theory we can say that its insistence on the director's unvarnished authenticity and on an "absence of clichés" actually carried a critical dimension of utopian (hence political) vision: it asked the viewer to use the stylistic trait associated with a personal name not just to celebrate a consciousness that could move across different themes, genres, or situations but, especially, to bring a critical view to the mechanism of reiteration in cinema that exploits feeling and illusion.

As a prelude to a study of the ways the grounding themes of the *auteur* can "return," somewhat in the manner of a nagging memory, to displace or to make us reconsider the economy of current film practices, I should like to look at some of the signature-effects of the work of Raoul Walsh. Walsh is the Hollywood *auteur* par excellence, but his work also, insofar as the criterion of "excellence" can be ascribed to the work, bears a power of performativity, falsehood, and, above all (without being essentialized), in its entirety, that of continual transformation. Its own tendency to turn itself into its own simulacrum; to reiterate the context and the event of its own signature; to counterfeit the ostensive truth of its representations, be they of war, of love, or whatever aligns it with the issues raised by Allen Smithee. The affinity is the topic of the conclusion of this essay.

The quantity and variety of films Walsh produced can be taken as a standard for the possibility of his classification as an author. A director who was born into, grew with, and died in the midst of the medium, Walsh has been awarded the dubious epithet "the director's director" for a no-nonsense approach to film. He was the man of action who created features that are more about movement than psychology.[8] Andrew Sarris was the first American viewer to note that an extraordinary relation of tenderness in relation to environment gave to Walsh's heroes and heroines an uncommon mix of strength, fragility, and sensitivity to the world at large.[9] In the classical phase of *auteur* politics such as they have been categorized by Antoine de Baecque, Walsh was a shoo-in by the 1950s by dint of having produced enough films to merit transverse analysis. Like Hawks or Hitchcock, the wealth of themes and genres, along with the reiterated styles of given actors and actresses or screenplays by favored writers, allowed for a then new historical treatment. Yet, inasmuch as the films could never claim to offer much extensive psychology in the labor of their production—120 features over fifty years being unparalleled— the signature was discerned with greater difficulty. It could be wagered at the same time that many of the overtly cheapened decors or dime- store scenarios gave to many of the films—say, *Salty O'Rourke* (Para- mount, 1945) or *Background to Danger* (Warner, 1943, a film that James Agee called a "good" fake of Hitchcock)—a countervirtue that can now be taken as belonging to the overall force of the director's oeuvre.

Jean-Louis Comolli, perhaps the first of the classic *Cahiers* critics to write on the purity of movement of the camera in *Objective, Burma!* (1945), furnished an initial view of the classic *auteur*. He noted how Walsh brings the spectator's eye to the surface-effects of the film and not the abstraction of its psychology. Since then, over a telling gap of twenty years, a striking difference in the reception of the work emerges. In the last monograph on the director, Pierre Giuliani has emphasized how much we see in the film "l'aveugle nécessité du processus onirique au travail dans le processus cinématographique pour conclure que le cinéma privilégie toujours, au bout du compte, l'objet de pulsion à l'ob- jet marchand" [the blind necessity of the oneiric process at work in cin- ematography in order to conclude that the cinema has always favored, ultimately, the object of basic drives over the market impulse]. The priv- ilege awarded to elemental drives are summed up in the director's desire to "aller vite, être violent ou n'être rien" [go quickly, be violent, or be nothing].[10] Giuliani's remark recalls a tendency ("nonetheless," as Freud's ghost would whisper) to revise the stronger sense of *auteur* aesthetics in its identification of an "object of a basic drive" that replaces the "mar- ket impulse." Drive is discussed in a relation to a market impulse, as if a purer drive, seen in the all-or-nothing, in the unchecked speed of Walsh's cinema, will eventually supersede a grounding condition of commodity exchange. Giuliani suggests that the latter is almost immutable. "Basic drives" are tantamount to what market strategists, often weaned on their readings of Freud and Durkheim, circulate in the name of *needs*. A marketing agency such as cinema will use as the alibi for its sales its commitment "to meet the needs" of consumers, even if those are located in the intermediate realm of fantasy. Giuliani's appreciation of Walsh therefore bespeaks the history of the economic and political relation of the *auteur* to the industry of cinema.

Between the French and American reception of the director we might say that for the latter an existential relation with the world is shared by personages standing with affective grace and humility beneath overriding forces of nature and fate. If a single Walshian hero would be chosen from that world, it would be Robert Mitchum, the Freudian character par excellence in search of a key to his troubled past, on the American mesa of *Pursued* (1947), a film that Martin Scorsese has disinterred and claimed to be formative for his own oeuvre. For the former, *action*, a grounding component of Aristotelian poetics, shows that psychology of human beings is less consequential than the sight of force and effect deployed on a greater landscape. It defines the movement of horses in front of the massive cliffs thresholding the desert of *Colorado Territory* (1947). A cinema of depthless surface becomes vital for narratives that otherwise seem deprived of even an iota of redemptive content or emotion.

Seen in another light, the performative traits of the signature, what assures the reiteration of the paradox of their industrial look invested with some distorting features that bring attention to the mechanism of cinematic illusion in general, include several aspects. The first, apparent from a film as precocious as *The Regeneration* (1915), is the presence of optical elements that play on the coexistent depth of field of the long shot and the flat surface of the frame. Elements that are in extreme depth of field are also in utter depthlessness, leaving the effect of a mix of binocular and monocular perspective. Walsh uses an extreme depth of field in the outdoor photography in the silent years and transposes that style to films, especially in the work done in the Warner studios from 1939 to

1949, to promote optical paradoxes. This aspect of the style gives rise to the existential quality of the surroundings that frame their narratives: a hero marked by fate is seen "isolated" in the space of the world that contains his or her person, but in turn he or she moves about its surface in ways that give it an uncommon character. A space of fear is conveyed through the machinations of illusion, whereas its creative practice is seen by the character's traversal over its contours. In this fashion an almost cartographic style marks the deep-focus photography that runs from the takes of the tenement neighborhood of the Lower East Side in *The Regeneration* (1915) to the shot that records a tiny car crossing the desert in the beginning of *High Sierra* (1941).

Insofar as film often calls attention to its own workings by setting extreme close-ups next to deeply focused establishing shots, its own predilection for movement is underscored when the near and far are set in counterpoint.[11] Walsh clearly exploits this element in films of different genres, even in costume epics such as *The Thief of Baghdad* (1924). But it acquires a special valence in the work filmed after 1928. Walsh's autobiography, *Each Man in His Time*, is a work of mythomania, to be sure, but it also seems to be a performative autobiography ("as told to" his editor) that loosens the grip that a traumatic event, enucleation, might have held on the director. Much of the book turns around the moment when a jackrabbit jumped in front of the windshield of a car he and a friend were driving from the set of *In Old Arizona* (1929) on location in Utah.[12] The animal was dazzled by the lights before it sprang up and shattered the glass that splintered into the director's right eye. The bloody event becomes a parable for the mythic virility of the Walshian stereotype, the hypermasculine male vulnerable to the imminent event of one more instance of castration, and it also demonstrates the shift between illusion and flatness, between a depthless take of the world and a penchant to look into and about three-dimensional space.

After 1928 Walsh continually inserts into his cinema various references to that event. Sometimes they become a topic of narrative, as in *High Sierra*, when a jackrabbit sprints across a highway and almost precipitates a crash.[13] Sometimes the moment is inferred, as in the title and the many ocular shapes that inhabit *The Cock-Eyed World* (1929), a film that was finished on the heels of the accident when it happened. At others it folds curiously into the films as a strange object of perspective that mirrors the way we look at film: in *They Drive by Night* (1940) a monocular electric eye installed in the garage of Ed Carlson (a comic entrepreneur played by Alan Hale) becomes the apparatus of fear, loathing, and murder. In *Colorado Territory* (1947) the gaping holes in the cliffside behind the desert appear to be gigantic pupils mirroring the spectator's gaze upon the landscape. It recurs in *The Strawberry Blonde* (1941) and in *Gentleman Jim* (1942) with the shenanigans and fisticuffs that blacken the protagonists' eyes. In each instance the allusion arrests the narrative, bringing into the montage a momentary and often dizzying speculation about the *auteur* and the question that concerns how one looks at a film through a trauma about the origins of vision itself. The reiteration of enucleation exceeds the life and world of Walsh by pertaining to the limits of sight itself.

Another, correlative feature of the signature is displayed in the erotic dimension of the cinema that coextends viewing with an anal drive by which regression leads to tenderness brought forward by the refusal of sexual difference. This dimension would seem to be entirely psychogenetic were it not for the fact that emergence into visibility constitutes the adventure of spectatorship. The viewer is continually rehearsing his or her entry into the world—such are the stakes of perception that entail the continuous invention of the visible—in visual ways, in which sexual difference is not yet (or ever) a problem before one's eyes.[14] The perception of visibility in the action of viewing a film is coded in Walsh's work as a productive regression to a stage in which the five senses are in dialogic play. Concomitant confusions of erotic roles enhance this sensibility. Men and women become children who bear polymorphic qualities as objects of a desire that does not discriminate on the basis of sexual difference. In this way Walsh is a quintessentially "woman's" director in the garb of misogynistic narratives (e.g., *A King and Four Queens* [1956], *What Price Glory* [1926], *The Naked and the Dead* [1958], and so on).[15] When men are in congress they mime prevailing heterosexual codes, but in general all of the players are forces of a desire that is not given a privileged valence that would be either male or female. There exist no phallic females or males, no phallambules of the horror movie genre but, rather, Melvillian types who find erotic pleasure in any bodily or geographical zone. The camera tends to use the military comedy to foster the regression. Films such as *What Price Glory* (1926), *The Cock-Eyed World* (1929), *Manpower* (1941), *Objective, Burma!* (1945), and *White Heat* (1949) exploit sexual isolation in order to create worlds of homoerotic tenderness. The privilege gained by exclusion spills onto the register of visibility by making the entire field of the image an object of desire.

In this way the image in much of Walsh's work carries the bonus of being both something seen as a detail, a partial object detached from a maternal world that is sought by the central figure, who is more often than not a wanderer or a searcher, and a totalizing space, an expanse that the film or the frame cannot contain in its view. A film bearing a title as innocuous as *The World in His Arms* (1952) in fact crystalizes the relation of parts and wholes in the overall oeuvre. *The Horn Blows at Midnight* (1946), derided by many (Jack Benny stated that it was the worst film in which he ever played), uses the motif of heaven and the world below to imply a baroque volume of intimate closure that is countered by an uncertain and dubious, postconcentrationary immensity. It confirms what Andrew Sarris noted about the existential plight of the Walshian protagonist, but the staging links the surface of the image to the curvilinear reflection of a world on the pupil of an eye. Even *Distant Drums* (1951), a remake of *Objective, Burma!*, suggests that the great expanse invented by the relation of spaces far and near—tom-toms heard from afar by figures lost in the Everglades, their feverish and sweaty faces seen in abruptly proximitive close-up—is the real subject of the film. In much of the film the cinematic geography is constructed to imply that something erotically other and more is within the scopic grasp of the camera.

In every aspect of the defining traits of the signature we discover over and again attention directed away from the illusion of the narrative—a central theme, a plight, or a problem that serves as a cinematic pretext or even an alibi—to the apparatus that produces the illusion. In

the categories reviewed above—the tension of the monocular and binocular field and a traumatic event given to be informing that vision;
action theorized as a play of relations of figures and grounds; a regressive eros, as it might be seen in a Freudian scheme of sexual development,
that alloys tenderness and empathy with sexual isolation in an expanded
visual field; finally, no less, a geography of a simultaneous linkage and
breakage of partial and expansive worlds—the power of an "effect" that
might cause the viewer to lose a critical hold on the film is broken or
sundered.

Here the association of the *auteur* with a neo-Brechtian process
of viewing becomes more than an implication. It may be at the basis of
the history and what might have inspired monographs and analyses that,
written when they were in new beginnings of the globalization of American cinema, appealed to the cult of the individual, the center of consciousness, and the aura of the "work." No matter how much the style
of interpretation may seem anachronistic thirty years later, even a cursory review of the *auteur* shows that a politics of viewing is present. One
cue to the politics is that of reiteration, the continuous reenactment or
rearticulation of a trait bearing a sign of identity, understood not as
unity but as seriality, such as we see in the rapport that Derrida's work on
the signature shares with *auteur* practice as a production of simulacra
that casts originality into a problematic sphere. The originality of the
auteur, given the proximity of Derrida's work on recurrence, thus shifts
onto a plane of repetition and difference by which attention is drawn to
the speed, pace, and economy of what goes by the name of the director's
individual talent in the industry of cinematic tradition. The "event" of
the authorial signature is thus based on something else or other that
emerges from its reproduction, which is tied to mechanisms of greater
strategic order.

Nothing makes the partisan of the *auteur* so apprised of the pre-
dicament than the Monday tallies of film-viewings and monies gained
after a feature is shown nationwide over the duration of a weekend. Reiteration becomes a dizzying thought when the number of tickets taken
at cineplexes, malls, and first-run theaters is tallied to chart the future

course of a fresh release. Compared with the mass-marketing of *auteur-ism* and corporatization of cinema today, the foundations of the theory can now, nonetheless, and I would daresay thanks, too, to the Allen Smithee syndrome, be deployed for more politicized ends now than they were in the 1960s.

Andrew Sarris wrote of his taste for directors in the cast of "confessions of a cultist,"[16] cultism being in his eyes a productively tactical way of extracting oneself from surrounding economic strategies in order to inaugurate *other* practices. These other practices, indeed author-practices, happened to be ways of inventing sensibilities that at the time resisted cooptation. If a Certellian figure used at the beginning of this essay can be invoked again, they were ways of practicing "culture in the plural," or of inventing critical speech among discerning people who would otherwise be as a *public* spoken for, its "needs" met, and thus consumed in the economic strategies of a rapacious industry.[17] We might say that *auteur* theory was the "capture" of a different analytical speech at the moment of its birth and its extraordinary growth, but that it has been coopted by institutions—cinematic, academic, journalistic—that redirect its implicit (but often unstated) politics for unavowed purposes.

A repoliticization is required. One way is to return to the work of *auteur* theory in its early expression and to see how its quasi-Brechtian elements were unconsciously soldered to its well-known taste for purely aesthetic issues. As even a cursory review of the take on Walsh's oeuvre seeks to demonstrate, the fact of the "return" to the era and style of the *auteur* brings forward a new difference in relation to the marketing and the definition of the *auteur* in the current time. Brought forward is not a way out of a dilemma, as what the editors of *Cahiers du cinéma* might have seen as a passage out of the labyrinth of the *auteurist* cockleshell in the early 1970s, but the need to use the dilemma in an ethics of viewing that copes, without any easy solutions, with the relation of film to consumerism.

One important point that follows the rewriting of the principles of directorial consciousness in the wake of performance, reiteration, and difference that meld the "author" with the "other" and the "sender" with the "receiver," along with an increased emphasis on the psychoanalytical roots of that consciousness, concerns the return to history. If *auteur* theory comprises one of many chapters in the expanding volumes of film histories rivaling each other for their archival mastery and comprehensiveness of documentation, it also has force enough to summon the veracity of those histories and to bring fresh agency to film-work in general. Histories are by nature economic products and betray "centers of consciousness" of discursive formations that reiterate them. The *auteur*, insofar as it is also a figure that plays and moves about the works in which and by which it is identified, is a demonic agent who erotizes and destabilizes the controls that are used to define it. It appears that the stakes of *auteur* theory in the light of the "Allen Smithee" phenomenon become greater, and the need to reconsider it in its past and present forms even more urgent. Orson Welles, the *auteur* written in upper case by André Bazin, ended his career with *F for Fake*. Through the "powers of the false" that are implied in his work, and in the context of the counterpractices we associate with Allen Smithee, we can now propose a gay science with A for *auteur*.

It can be affiliated with the broader stakes of form if we consider now, as perhaps the adepts of *auteur* politics had earlier intuited, that cinematic "form" is a function of its "truth." In the work of Gilles Deleuze, a philosopher of cinema who never abandoned the concept of the *auteur*, directorial consciousness is taken through what he calls "les puissances du faux" [the powers of the false].[18] At stake is how cinema, especially in light of Welles, can be raised to quanta of power that are finally free of the inflections of either veracity or mendacity. "By raising the false to an exponential power, life would be liberated from appearances as much as from truth: neither true nor false, an undecidable alternative, but a power of the false, a decisive will. Welles is the director who, as of *The Lady from Shanghai*, imposes a single and unique personage, the falsifier."[19]

These same falsifiers are obsessed with matters of form. It is only the creative artist, adds Deleuze,

> who bears the power of the false to a degree that is brought no longer into form but into transformation. There exists no more either truth or

appearance. There exists no longer either an invariable form or a variable point of view on form. There is a point of view that is so intimately of the thing that the thing endlessly is transformed into a becoming identical to point of view. A metamorphosis of the veracious. The artist is a creator of truth, for truth cannot be attained, found, nor reproduced, but created.[20]

In the world of market-driven cinema, in which the creation of truth is as difficult as that of the work of an *auteur*, it would seem that the political dimension of Allen Smithee's work is vital for showing the contours of a different relation to film form in difficult times. Smithee grants a shift whereby power and agency, by dint of falsehood, move to those who do not meet the needs generated by the film industry. The failure of illusion offered by work of his signature is a sign, in a more pervasive critical relation to cinema, of implicit success.

Notes

1. Andrew Sarris, "Notes on the *Auteur* Theory in 1962," *Film Theory and Criticism: Introductory Readings*, ed. Gerald Mast and Marshall Cohen, 2d ed. (New York: Oxford University Press, 1979) 650–65; Andrew Sarris, *The American Cinema: Directors and Directions 1929–1968* (New York: E. P. Dutton, 1968).

2. A comparison is noteworthy. Richard Roud's *Cinema: A Critical Dictionary*, 2 vols. (New York: Nationwide Book Services, 1980) is almost entirely classified according to directors. The massive five-volume second edition of the Saint James *International Dictionary of Films and Filmmakers* (London: St. James, 1990), completed a decade later, delineates entries according to its volumes on films, directors, writers and production artists, and actors and actresses. Craig Saper has astutely remarked that Tarantino, Lynch, Lee, and Scorsese have become "market-*auteurs*" identified as directors in the place where commanding strategies of organization use proper names to confuse art and sales. He notes, too, that "artificial *auteurism*" has replaced the vision born of the labors of the *Cahiers* authors. In a strong sense the appeal to a tactics of bogus *auteurism* in the name of Allen Smithee constitutes the beginning of a counterpractice, of an *art of doing* cinema that the religious historian Michel de Certeau had called the "art de perruque" in matters of hidden or secret ways of living in the midst of societies of both discipline and control. When, as shall be argued above (and noted

below), a return to *auteur* cinema is engaged, it must of needs be conceived as a type of counterpractice that veers away from the consumerism that film studies can often sustain. The trick is, of course, that of combining what Saper notes about defamiliarization at the basis of *auteurism* with the design of creating—before they are coopted—productive vacuities in the present world of film studies that are not merely "lacunae" to be filled in an overarching history of cinema. The *auteur*, then, is disinterred in order to be used differently—and not merely in a history of forms—in a time other than that of his or her own work. See Craig Saper's essay and the editors' chapter 1 in the present volume.

3. [Bonaventure des Périers], *Discours non plus mélancholiques que divers, de choses mesmement qui appartiennent a notre France: & a la fin la maniere de bien & justement entoucher les Lucs & Guiternes*. A Poitiers, De l'imprimerie d'Enguilbert de Marnef, 1557.

4. Arthur Rimbaud, *Poésies complètes*, ed. Daniel Leuwers (Paris: Librairie Générale Française, 1984) 199.

5. Jacques Derrida, "signature événement contexte," *Marges de la philosophie* (Paris: Minuit, 1972) 365–93. The date of publication is identical to the completion of Jean-Luc Godard and Jean-Pierre Gorin's *Tout va bien*, a film whose credits perform many of Derrida's hypotheses. The spectator witnesses a close-up of a pen signing checks that disburse sums of money to each of the agencies responsible for the production of the film that follows.

6. Jacques Derrida, "Limited Inc a b c ...," *Limited Inc*, trans. Samuel Weber (Baltimore: The Johns Hopkins University Press, 1977), 29–110.

7. We can recall in *Howard Hawks* (New York: Gardner and Doubleday, 1968), Robin Wood's benchmark work on the director, *Rio Bravo* is analyzed in view of Hawks's own avowal that the film was written *against* the clichés with which Fred Zinneman constructed *High Noon* (32–35). Wood's essay is built from differences it detects in the way cinema has a vital feeling for what it portrays. Hawks transgresses where Zinneman does not, even though "judgements of this kind are notoriously difficult to enforce when dealing with the cinema" (34). Hence (and here the reader of today smiles with approbation at what Wood stated in 1968) "there are no clichés in *Rio Bravo*" (36).

8. "Movie fans," notes Douglas Gomery, "have long appreciated the work of this director's director. But only when auteurists began to closely examine his films was Walsh 'discovered,' first by the French (in the 1960s), and then by American and British critics (in the 1970s). To these critics Walsh's action

films come to represent a unified view, put forward by means of a simple, straight-forward technique. Raoul Walsh is now accepted as an example of a master Hol-lywood craftsman who worked with a naive skill, and an animal energy, both frustrated and buoyed by the studio system. Unfortunately, this view neglects Walsh's important place in the silent cinema." *International Dictionary of Films and Filmmakers*, vol. 2, 886.

9. Sarris makes his observation in the entry on Walsh in *The American Cinema* 119–21.

10. Comolli's essay, "L'esprit d'aventure," appeared in *Cahiers du cinéma* 24 (Apr. 1964): 11–14. Giuliani hinges his remarks on desire, illusion, and signa-ture in *Raoul Walsh* (Paris: Edilig, 1984) 28, 17.

11. In his redefinition of the principal styles of "image" in film, Gilles Deleuze notes that classical film, based on the identity of the image qua move-ment (hence the recourse to the hyphen in *Cinéma 1: L'image-mouvement* [Paris: Minuit, 1983]), draws attention to its own virtuality in montage. Deleuze also set his discussion of the "perception-image" (or deep-focus shot) adjacent to the "affect-image" (or close-up) to imply that classical cinema can make the one the identity and the obverse of the other (99–135).

12. Raoul Walsh, *Each Man in His Time* (New York: Farrar, Straus and Giroux, 1972) 224.

13. I have studied the insertion of the episode into John Huston's screen-play of W. R. Burnett's eponymous novel in more detail in *Film Hieroglyphs* (Min-neapolis: University of Minnesota Press, 1991) 168, and in "L'auteur énucléé," *Hors cadre* 8 (1990): 77–95.

14. See Deleuze, *Cinéma 1* 101.

15. In a celebrated treatment Pam Cook and Claire Johnston argue for "The Place of Woman in the Cinema of Raoul Walsh" along Lacanian lines, in *Raoul Walsh*, ed. Phil Hardy (Edinburgh: Edinburgh Film Festival, 1974): 93–110, showing that the woman questions the macho look of the male in the sound films, especially *The Revolt of Mamie Stover* (1956).

16. Andrew Sarris, *Confessions of a Cultist: On the Cinema, 1955–1969* (New York: Simon and Schuster, 1970).

17. Michel de Certeau, *The Capture of Speech and Other Political Writings*, and *Culture in the Plural*, trans. Tom Conley (Minneapolis: University of Min-nesota Press, 1997). In an essay on the will on the part of the media to turn May 1968 into oblivion in the weeks following its happening, he noted, "[i]n order to

be seen, innovations are disguised, and often stifled under borrowed old clothing. The fragile moment is no less that of human decision, which will select among possible destinies. To this instant that allows for the glimpse of a mutation corresponds the memory of a few words that, when a whole system is ajar, announce the color of another culture, with a different kind of taking of speech" (*Culture in the Plural* 31). Set against the backdrop of the fact that May 1968 *performed* what it could not say in the language of its time, *auteur* theory might be seen *saying all too well* what it cannot state about the economy of its process, even if it is critical of it. To transpose this double bind into the aftermath of the *auteur* is one way of inaugurating a different deployment of its principles.

18. "Les puissances du faux" is the title of the sixth chapter of *Cinéma 2: L'image-temps* (Paris: Minuit, 1985) 165–202. Translations from the French, quoted from the pages of the French edition indicated above, are mine. It suffices to recall that at the beginning of *Cinéma 1: L'image-mouvement* (Paris: Minuit, 1983), Deleuze remarked, "[t]he great *auteurs* of cinema have appeared to us comparable not only to painters, architects, and musicians, but also to thinkers. Instead of concepts they think with movement-images, with time-images. The enormous production of stupidity [*nullité*] in the film industry is no cause for objection: it is neither here nor there, although the economic and industrial consequences are beyond comparison. The great *auteurs* of cinema are thus only the most vulnerable, given that it is infinitely easy to keep them from making their works. The history of cinema is a long scroll of martyrs" (7–8).

19. Deleuze, *Cinéma 2* 189.

20. Deleuze, *Cinéma 2* 191.

Bastard *Auteurism* and Academic *Auteurs*: A Reflexive Reading of Smithee Studies

James F. English

What should we make of the fact that, in addressing ourselves as cultural theorists to the figure of Allen Smithee—which is to say, to the problem of authorship and authority in a cultural arena (Hollywood) dominated by the fetish of the name, the economics of the brand, and the logics of celebrity and stardom—we turn, automatically it seems, to the names, the stars or celebrities, of our own cultural arena: to, as one of the participants at the Specters of Legitimacy conference expressed it, "the Jeans, the Jacques, the Jean-Jacques" of contemporary theory?[1] What, to quote another contributor, is the significance of the particular "path dependence"[2] that leads us so consistently to invoke, even and especially when we fashion ourselves "illegitimate" or maverick intellectuals, the same handful of proper academic names? What is the nature of our own name-dependency, how is it manifest in a cultural-studies anthology such as this one, and what does that tell us about the implication of our own practices of cultural production in the Smithee phenomenon?

As the contributors to this collection all recognize, Allen Smithee exists not just because the Directors Guild of America needed to assert the legal and economic interests of its members, and therefore to foster the extension of Hollywood's "star system" onto the category of the director. Smithee exists because a first generation of film theorists, of artists and intellectuals bent on producing and institutionalizing a theoretical discourse about film, had its own more specifically cultural interests to pursue. Film studies needed a canon of Great Authors or star *auteurs* in order to ground and organize its textual materials, and Smithee appeared as the strange but inevitable symptom of this practical and professional desire. One aim of the present anthology is to appropriate this symptom of authorial star-lust, Smithee, in such a way as to disturb our habitual thinking about, our habitual investment in, authors. The pieces collected here undertake in various ways to deploy a kind of bastard *auteurism* whose effect is not merely a further stellification of author-stars, a further consecration of Names, but a new opening onto more obscure and less nameable dimensions of authorship.[3]

This bastard *auteurism* plainly has implications for the production of academic articles as well as for the production of films. The author who writes on the problem of authorship is perforce engaged in a double discourse, a double critique. Smithee critics address themselves in potentially disruptive ways to the conceptual ground on which rests not only the ideology of the Great Director but also that of the Great Critic. It is, of course, a commonplace that the academy supports its own version of the Hollywood star system, that the academic field is largely defined by the names of the stars who occupy its positions of greatest visibility and influence. There has been much discussion of this feature of academe lately, both inside and outside the academy—most of it "critical" in facile and misapprehending ways. Often conducted in tones of personal resentment, the discussion has tended to represent the academic superstars, and especially those working in literary theory, cultural studies, or other fields of perceived social resistance and subversion, as opportunistic hypocrites, lackeys of capitalism, betrayers of their presumed collectivist roots, even co-conspiring agents of the job-market crisis in higher education. The stars, that is to say, have been looked upon as a "them," as outsiders or interlopers or traitors of the scholarly and intellectual worlds, "individuals who are not part of the community."[4]

This stance of simple opposition can yield only half-truths, and rather self-serving ones at that. The undeniable convergence of the symbolic and material economies of culture, such that one's stature as a scholar or intellectual among scholars and intellectuals is more and more directly correlated with one's extra-academic visibility and economic success, may indeed be a development against which we need to focus our collective energies, as Pierre Bourdieu and others have argued.[5] But, as Bourdieu has also insisted most strenuously, this collective act of resistance can achieve no efficacy unless it is genuinely *reflexive*, that is, unless it addresses, and incorporates rigorously into its analysis, the rules of academic practice and the particular positions and dispositions of the academic players themselves. The productive desire for great authors, celebrity authors, stars of the intellectual and artistic realms, the need to overvalue and overcompensate a very few individual writers, to circulate their names with maximum redundancy: these are not simply imposed upon us. We need to recognize them as *our* desires and needs, part of our academic habitus, intrinsic to the very practices we rely on even as we seek to rethink and perhaps to unsettle the author function itself. Allen Smithee, the name that names the fetish of the Name, holds a place in and among us, whose professional inclination and whose monopolistic right it is to produce cultural theory about Allen Smithee. Let us therefore attempt, in concluding this volume devoted to such theory, to perform a brief Bourdieuian act of sociological self-scrutiny, addressing ourselves to the very fact of this anthology and to the scholarly practices and arrangements through which the Name is produced, and the credit of authorship secured, within cultural study itself.

Theory-Stars and the Work of Intellectual Production

Stars have emerged in many if not all academic disciplines, and no doubt there are important differences between the way stars are produced and circulated in, say, music departments and in departments of astronomy. Some of the most aggressive bidding wars and highly publicized compensation packages occur in economics and the natural sciences, partly because those are the academic discipines in which superstardom can be most concretely and indisputably certified, in the form of the Nobel Prize.[6] Indeed, someone who is tipped to win the Nobel in the near future can be even more attractive to a university than an actual laureate, since the moment of consecration itself is often the moment of greatest visibility and renown. In 1998 Columbia University offered Harvard economist Robert Barro a $300,000 base salary plus control over six additional hires, a job for his wife, a spot in one of Manhattan's elite private schools for his son, a newly renovated 2,200-square-foot apartment on Riverside Drive at about half the market rental rate, and other perks.[7] (According to some writers at the *Harvard Lampoon*, "the deal also included a tenure-track position in the comparative literature department for his dog, Dizzy, use of the university helicopter and a cameo in the acclaimed Broadway musical 'Bring In da Noise, Bring In da Funk.'")[8] This was partly a bid for Barro's services as a teacher and research colleague—as a "builder" who could gather good people around him. But the university was also counting on a certain "surplus," as one economist put it, a surplus of which the Nobel Prize was potentially the biggest piece.[9] Columbia had finally added a Nobel economist to its ranks the year before, when the department's *eminence grise*, William Vickrey, was named a co-laureate. But Vickrey, already well into the emeritus phase of his career, passed away a few weeks before the prize ceremony, putting Columbia back at the starting gate in the medal chase.

What David Shumway has called the "star system in literary studies" may seem small-time in comparison with this kind of deal-making; no literary or cultural critic makes $300,000 a year.[10] But it is the stars of our discipline who have attracted the most attention from the media, and who are seen, not without reason, as being most perfectly representative of the academic star system as a whole. As Shumway makes clear, these stars are not simply the outstanding critics and historians of English literature but the outstanding practitioners of what has come to serve as the unstable center of our increasingly marginal and centrifugal field, cultural studies, and especially of the more theoretically oriented forms of cultural studies.[11] There are highly respected, well-compensated, and relatively visible scholars of Restoration drama or of nineteenth-century American poetry, but these are not the individuals whose names are ordinarily invoked in analyses of the star system. The "stars" are

overwhelmingly theorists (and theorists of culture, addressing themselves to the broadest problematics of the discipline—language and
sexuality, race and power, late capitalism and postmodern art—rather
than to more narrowly "literary" questions such as the rise of the novel).
They are inventors of new terms and concepts, leaders of schools or
movements with which scholars in many different fields of specialization
might align themselves. Shumway's examples include "Judith Butler,
Jacques Derrida, Stanley Fish, Henry Louis Gates Jr., Fredric Jameson,
[and] Gayatri Chakravorty Spivak."[12]

Our deference toward, and dependency on, these stars seems first
of all to be bound up with our anxieties about social consequence. The
stars are not just those perceived to be the most vivid or the deepest
thinkers among us, but those perceived to be, at least potentially, the
most consequential agents of social transformation. When we invoke
them, we enlarge our sense of our own relevance and efficacy, and when
we engage in intellectual practices whose legitimacy is yoked to this
sense of relevance and efficacy (as cultural studies and theory manifestly
are), we engage also in the production of stars. This is so regardless of
the particular content of our analyses and speculations. We may, for
example, be quite expressly concerned to critique the ideology of liber-
alism, with its voluntarist baggage and its deep confusions about the
nature of individual freedom; we may be explicitly emphasizing social
structures or systemic effects over deliberate acts and initiatives. Our
practice as cultural theorists will nevertheless be guided by a certain
faith in the power of the individual cultural theorist (our own power here
mirroring that of the authors we name) to shape theory, to shape culture,
ultimately to shape society itself, in accordance with a more or less radical political agenda that has been taken up freely and may therefore be
worn as a badge of collective and individual courage. As John Guillory
has remarked, the "national intellectual field" of contemporary America
is characterized by an unacknowledged "ethos of voluntarism" to such
an extent that the conscious political agenda, and the possibility of its
realization, have become the necessary and sufficient justifications for
academic cultural study.[13] The scholar's personal political intentions, and

personal political credentials, are determining factors in establishing the legitimacy and value of his or her work.

What is interesting about this situation is that it arises at the moment when the "national intellectual field" appears to most observers to be irrevocably atrophied and impotent, when the very notion of an "intellectual" in the classic sense—as one whose substantial accumulation of cultural knowledge and competence and of "specific" symbolic capital, or prestige among other highly cultured people, opens for him or her a specially advantaged position on the larger field of power—seems an anachronism.[14] As Bill Readings has described, the last quarter century has seen the "virtual elimination" of this historically important "speaking position": "The intellectual no longer appears authoritative when speaking either from the university or outside of it."[15] The academic stars are not regarded as contributors of special consequence to debates of national importance. Their knowledge and accomplishments in the domain of culture are in no way qualifications to speak and be listened to on questions of broad social urgency. Rather, their cultural and symbolic capital are put into circulation as exchange value pure and simple. Stars are worth something outside of their limited fields of production only inasmuch as they help academic institutions to differentiate structurally similar products according to quality—or, to use the term of whose current predominance Readings has offered a very astute reading, "excellence."[16] Following the circular logic of the contemporary economy of academic prestige, a "star-studded" faculty is the most reliable index of a university's "excellence." It assures high placement on the journalistically produced, and increasingly dominant, hierarchy of value whose key artifact is *U.S. News & World Report*'s ranked list of "America's Best Colleges." It thereby helps, perhaps more than any other single differentiating factor, to justify the kind of high-end tuition that runs two to three times that which an institution lacking in Names and hence in "excellence" can hope to charge.

Shumway and other commentators have questioned whether cultural theorists should allow themselves to be put into play in this special market—put into play, in effect, as instruments of intraconversion, whereby the symbolic and cultural capital of specific academic achieve-ments and competencies are converted by means of journalistic capital (visibility, celebrity) into economic capital. Shumway points out, first of all, that in an era of academic downsizing and retrenchment, the fact that universities are devoting an "ever larger share of shrinking resources" to the "care and feeding of stars" assures a steeper decline in real wages for other faculty. Indeed, he remarks, the star system may be an important factor in the universities' increasing reliance on part-time, temporary, and nonfaculty instructors.[17]

More pointedly, Shumway sees the cultural theorist's metamor-phosis into a star as a betrayal of the collective or communitarian orien-tation of cultural studies and of the new social movements with which cultural studies has been aligned: "Marxism, feminism, queer theory, and the various ethnic-studies projects have all attempted to build knowl-edge collectively. The star system has been and will continue to be an obstacle to such collectivity."[18] There is a certain truth in this, but these various projects seem to me less clearly oriented toward collectivity, and more actively and unavoidably productive of academic stars, than Shum-way suggests. Certainly, they all entail, or claim to entail, broad social agendas. But we are speaking here of highly specialized academic work—work that, star system aside, enjoys an elite status even within academe, where only a privileged minority engage in research and writing, as opposed to teaching and administrative labor, at all. The actual collec-tivities in question consist of at the very most a few thousand professors and graduate students, their relationship to academics as a whole, much less to the larger populations whose circumstances they hope radically to alter, being by no means a simple one of representation or leadership. In general, that relationship is closer to the kind of homology that Bour-dieu warns us not to overextend: the "homology of position" between the "dominated fraction of the dominant class" (i.e., among the holders of significant capital, those whose capital is mostly cultural in form) and the "dominated as such" (those who have little capital of any kind).[19] In attacking the star system as anticollectivist, Shumway and others seem not only to be (justifiably) emphasizing the class division within the dominated fraction of the dominant class, the split between the have-everything stars and the ordinary rank-and-file cadres of cultural studies and theory, but also, and less justifiably, to be deemphasizing the even more fundamental and pronounced division between that whole culturally privileged fraction (the fraction that comprises the producers and consumers of this anthology) and the dominated as such.[20] The star system, in Shumway's view, "obstructs" the collective enterprise in part by placing the stars between committed academic cultural workers and the masses with whose interests the committed academics' interests are assumed in large measure to coincide.

Because those interests, and the systems of dispositions through which they are expressed, in fact do not substantially coincide, the project of, say, postcolonial or queer cultural studies is only a collective project in a sharply limited sense, the collectivity of co-investing participants extending scarcely at all beyond the doors of the elite universities and colleges. Moreover, the group of academics primarily involved here is not an ideally unified and cooperative team, each member altruistically serving some collectively recognized and collectively pursued set of objectives. To be sure, these players are profoundly involved with one another and must attend closely to each other's moves. They do share certain objectives, hold certain interests in common. But only a very impoverished sociology of the academy would neglect the competitive or antagonistic dimension of academic practices, or imagine that the practice of cultural theory is somehow exceptional in this regard. Like the job shortage at the entry level of the professoriat, the star system in its upper echelons has simply brought more starkly into view the fact that academics are always pitted against one another in a struggle for recognition and resources—for authorial *credit*. This does not mean that we are all just in it for lofty titles, light teaching duties, frequent research sabbaticals, and comparatively high pay (though the extent to which our practice is guided by the system of professional incentives, our dispositional preferences geared to performing just the sort of work that the profession materially and symbolically rewards—which is to say, anything but teaching—should not be underestimated). It is enough to say that we must struggle to be read, struggle to take and hold a place among the very few academic writers who are at all widely read even by academic readers; each of us must struggle, on a field of effectively anonymous authors, for the name credit of authorship.[21] And this struggle is all the more obligatory for those of us who work in cultural studies and theory or other subfields whose existence is routinely justified (not just by others, but by us, in our own published work) on grounds of social utility, in terms of its functioning as part of what Foucault famously called "a tool kit" for the use of "new political subjects."[22] A work of cultural theory that is read and admired in manuscript by a few friends, positively evaluated by two readers and an editor for a prestigious university press and then by a handful of departmental colleagues and a few outside evaluators for a promotional case, and that is ultimately consulted by another dozen specialists who cite it in their own work, has enjoyed a reasonably successful trajectory in professional terms. But in terms of its social effectivity, its impact on a politically articulated collectivity, it has never gotten off the ground. One need not be seeking journalistic visibility or "cross-over" book sales to desire a more substantial form of author credit for one's work than this.

In comparison with other disciplines, literature, cultural studies, film and media studies are actually among the least collaborative or "collective" in their relationship to research and publication, and these disciplines' especially personalized conception of authorship has not changed with the rise of Theory. We readily acknowledge the collaborative dimension of much that we do, in our departmental and other administrative work, in our teaching (our classes being a kind of collective enterprise in the production of knowledge), in our on- and off-campus cultural and political work. With regard to these practices, we are prepared to disregard authorship. And of course we know that our research and writing make sense only within a social network of cultural production, that we are none of us isolate producers. But a glance at the authorship credits in other disciplines discloses the extent of our investment in the single byline, the sole author, the charismatic individual producer. In economics, engineering, health and medicine, the natural sciences, law, education,

sociology, anthropology, architecture, and other fields, multiple authorship is common, and elaborate protocols have had to be negotiated concerning the hierarchical ordering of names, primary versus secondary
researcher status, and so forth.[23] In our discipline, apart from a handful of
collaborative pairs—Laclau and Mouffe, Stallybrass and White, Deleuze
and Guattari, Bersani and Dutoit—publications are presented and circulated almost exclusively as the products of individuals.[24] A few collectives
have appeared over the years, most of them connected with cultural
studies and theory: the *Tabloid* Collective, the Miami Theory Collective,
and so on. But the members of these groups almost always published, or
went on to publish, much more work under their own individual bylines
than under the auspices of the collectives. And even the publications of
these collectives conform very rigorously, in their deployment of names,
to the scholarly protocols that support the star system. Partly because
they are *theory* collectives, carrying forward a continental-philosophical
project that has been mostly abandoned by American philosophy departments, they reinforce what Jürgen Habermas has characterized as the
"uninterruptedly personalized form of appearance taken by philosophical thought." "It is no accident," says Habermas,

> that the philosophical constellations can be characterized without great
> difficulty in terms of names. Up to our own day philosophic thought has
> moved in a dimension in which the form of presentation does not remain
> extrinsic to the idea. The factual unity of theoretical and practical reason
> that till now has been expressed in this sort of individualized thinking
> requires communication not just on the level of propositional content
> but also on the metacommunicative level of interpersonal relations. In
> this respect philosophy has never been a science; it remained constantly
> bound to the person of the philosophical teacher or author.[25]

If anything, Habermas understates the case: the philosophical con-
stellations, the "isms" of "Theory," cannot without great difficulty be
characterized *except* in terms of names. It is only by means of names, by
constant reference to the names of the great authors, that we are capable

of "doing" theory or any of the theoretically inflected forms of cultural study. And in order to keep cultural theory moving forward, in order not to be merely practicing the refinement of the history of philosophy, we must constantly produce new names, new "teacher[s] or author[s]," new stars: not many, but a few. Without the proper names, the credited authors, there can be no contemporary theory, no cultural studies—or none that we are remotely equipped to practice. Which is to say that, far from being an external "obstacle" to cultural studies as currently practiced, the star system is a condition of its possibility.

The Conference-Anthology and the Star System

The rising importance of the anthology in scholarly publishing today, and in particular of the anthology as theory-primer or cultural-studies sampler, with its promise to acquaint the uninitiated with the most lately emergent discourses and fields, might seem a notable deviation from the discipline's longstanding attachment to "the person of the ... author." The anthology, after all, has multiple authors; it also generally has multiple editors, cowritten prefatory material, and other seeming indicators of collective enterprise. To some extent, moreover, the cultural-studies or theory anthology seems to be functioning as a sort of one-off avant-garde journal, assembled by a radical (albeit temporary) editorial collective, at a time when the print journal itself may be proving an unsustainable form—when, indeed, the print journal appears to be trying, through ever more frequent recourse to thematically unified "special" issues, to market itself as a series of cutting-edge anthologies.

But the shift in our discipline away from individually authored books toward anthologies, like that from scholarly monographs treating individual writers to studies of more disparate (and less "literary") cultural phenomena, does not in fact interfere with the production of superstars and the circulation of Names. As a reader's ostensible shortcut to the newest, the latest, the most excitingly radical contributions to a theoretical conversation the full history and sweep of which no one any longer feels capable of mastering, the anthology holds great attraction for cultural workers under intensive pressure to professionalize, to

appear fully up to date in their professional practice, to position themselves on whatever cutting edges the discipline can still offer. This means
that its primary readership is probably graduate students, who have been
pressed by the conditions of the job market into what Guillory characterizes as "a new professional domain," a zone of "preprofessionalism"
in which the only availing strategy is that of cultivating an impossibly
premature and necessarily distorted professionalism (the professionalism of those who are not yet allowed to be professionals).[26]

The cultural-studies or theory anthology is tailored to the needs
and desires at work in this domain, just as the scholarly conference has
come to be; and, as is plainly the case with the conference, its orientation
toward the preprofessional does not at all prevent it from serving as a
major support to the star system. Indeed, the conference, the essay collection, and the star system are mutually supportive formations. Many
anthologies, the present volume included, have their apparent origins
in conferences, the essays collected being mostly revised versions of the
papers delivered. And yet the conference was as likely as not conceived as
a means of generating essays for just such a collection, with in some cases
an acquisitions editor actively taking part in the decisions about what
speakers/writers to invite. Whichever way one understands the vector
of production here, it is evident that the very structure of such undertakings secures certain empty slots or positions for "Names" ultimately
to occupy (the position, for example, of keynote speaker). The more
marginal or ostensibly illegitimate a conference/anthology's topic—the
more likely its being taken (as the Smithee conference frequently was)
for a kind of graduate-student hoax—the more imperative that some
quite legitimate or proper names, some stars or near-stars, appear on the
bill (Andrew Sarris, Robert Ray).[27]

A prominent case in point here is *Cultural Studies*, a collection of
essays that emerged from the Cultural Studies Now and in the Future
conference at the University of Illinois in 1990, was edited by Larry
Grossberg, Cary Nelson, and Paula Treichler, and was published by Routledge in 1992. This is an exemplary anthology, assembled by a knowl-
edgeable group of scholar-editors, and making available under the covers

of a single 700-page book a substantial range of up-to-date work by many of the most influential thinkers in the then-emergent field. To be sure, as Laurie Langbauer pointed out in an intemperate diatribe in 1993, the book is also an exemplary artifact of the star system, an academic *star vehicle* that lends itself very nicely to the purposes of Routledge's marketing department and to what she calls the "celebrity economy of cultural studies," an economy whose ultimate function is to expedite the marketing of cultural goods through the production and manipulation of celebrity personae.[28] Langbauer denounces cultural studies, in familiar terms, for operating too complacently within this economy, and especially for allowing its "celebrities, the *big* names who can draw an audience to a conference or readers to a book" to claim any sort of emancipatory or anticapitalist social agenda.[29]

This is not the position I am adopting in relation to the present anthology. As I have been trying to indicate, the sort of outcry we hear from Langbauer misconstrues the problem that "*big* names" represent because it insists on locating the agency of the star system wholly among the stars and/or their capitalist handlers. Our discipline, like many others, concerts its production around relatively few, and hence "big," authors and their works; for reasons that are neither simple nor new, we find it impossible to proceed as responsible practitioners (and even as responsible *provocateurs*) without a *canon of authors* (formerly a canon of poets, novelists, and film directors; today, for many of us, a rather smaller canon of theorists).[30] This profoundly internalized, *practical* orientation toward proper names and individuated theory—which secures preexisting slots or positions for "stars" not just on the empty conference program but in the citational framework of the as-yet unwritten conference paper itself—does more than anything else to assure the very high concentration of our profession's symbolic and material rewards in a few hands. The publishers whose marketing strategies lead them to prefer an all-star anthology, or an anthology with a few stars whose names can be prominently highlighted on the cover, over an anthology of worthy unknowns and preprofessionals ("new voices," in the language of academic marketing), are reflecting and probably amplifying this situation, but they are no more directly responsible for it than are the stars themselves. Those of us who produce the academic discourse of and about culture are the real supporting actors of the star system, and we lend our support every time we address ourselves to the tasks of research and publication. Langbauer herself, in her polemic against *Cultural Studies*, proceeds quite in accordance with the citational protocols of star-production, even borrowing a quote from Homi Bhabha as her closing rhetorical gambit. Indeed, her piece, with its special focus on the collection's best-known editors and authors, makes a definite contribution to their status as emergent stars.

My point is not that the academic star system, this contemporary manifestation of academe's name-dependency, is benign, nor that those who denounce this system are fools. My point is that even the most commendably illegitimate *auteurists*, such as we find contributing to this volume, theorists who aim, reasonably and without hubris, to trouble the regime of author, signature, and name, are unlikely to reflect very hard on the fact that their own trafficking in symbolic capital conforms more or less perfectly to the protocols of the authorial credit and the laws of the legitimate economy of authorial prestige. What is at stake in the matter of the author-as-star is not just the way we think and write about "the author"—as romantic individual, as structural function, as the genius of the system, or what have you—but the way we and the institutions we are a part of distribute the symbolic capital we and they produce. It is hard even to imagine our discipline distributing its symbolic capital in an ideally equitable and, as it were, nonpersonal or *name-independent* way. Certainly we cannot hope to pursue this objective simply by refusing to adopt a fan mentality or reaffirming our commitment to a collectivity or fighting for equal teaching loads and an end to honoraria at conferences, however admirable those stances might be. Nor is it simply a question of occupying tactically, like cultural insurgents, the spaces that have opened up between authors and texts. As is clear not only from our extraordinary reliance on credentials, honors, titles, prizes, awards—our fetish of the curriculum vita (see, e.g., the vita-blurbs in this volume)—but, even more fundamentally, from the evidence of the citation indexes, our practice as scholars and intellectuals simply will not support a socialism of the symbolic economy, an infinite extension of the author-credit line, let alone a withdrawal of all value from the author position as such. As I said at the outset, Allen Smithee stands as a symptom not just of somebody else's desires and dispositions, but of the desires and dispositions that form us as academics. To rid ourselves of this symptom would require a transformation of the academic field more radical than anything that most of us are prepared to contemplate, a dismantlement of the research-university paradigm itself, and, concomitant with that, a drastic devaluation of our own labor as writers. In the meantime, even the most impertinent and challenging engagements with *auteurism* will have to assist, more or less unproblematically, in the further production of academic *auteurs*.

Notes

1. Tom Paulus, "Let's Get Harry Fixed: Putting a Tail on the Elusive Mr. S. in at Least Three Critical Modes," Specters of Legitimacy, University of Pennsylvania, Philadelphia, 27 Sept. 1997.

2. See Robert Ray, "The Automatic *Auteur*; or, A Certain Tendency in Film Criticism," chapter 3 of the present volume.

3. Leo Braudy traces the verb "to stellify" to Chaucer's *House of Fame* and says it is probably Chaucer's own coinage. Braudy, *The Frenzy of Renown: Fame and Its History* (New York: Oxford University Press, 1987) 246, 246n.

4. David R. Shumway, "The Star System in Literary Studies," *PMLA* 112 (Jan. 1997): 98.

5. Much of Bourdieu's work over the last fifteen years has been devoted to the analysis of this "penetration," by the logic of commerce, into such formerly "autonomous" zones of artistic and intellectual production as the academy and avant-garde literary coteries. For a directly relevant discussion, see the third appendix in *Homo Academicus*, "The Hit Parade of French Intellectuals, or Who Is to Judge the Legitimacy of the Judges?" (Stanford: Stanford University Press, 1988) 256–70.

6. The fact that there is also a Nobel Prize in literature does not really matter, since those who win the literature award are almost never academics. One would suppose, however, that Toni Morrison's compensation from Princeton was adjusted after she won the Nobel in 1993.

7. Sylvia Nasar, "New Breed of College All-Star; Columbia Pays Top Dollar for Economics Heavy Hitter," *New York Times* 8 Apr. 1998: D1, 3.

8. Erik J. Kenward and Matthew J. T. Murray, "Tenure is Not Enough," *New York Times* 10 Apr. 1998: A19.

9. Nasar D3.

10. In 1998 Stanley Fish signed a contract with the University of Illinois for $230,000 a year, suggesting that he has realized the stated ambition of Morris Zapp, the character in David Lodge's campus trilogy, supposedly modeled on Fish, whose aim is to be the highest-paid English professor in the world. But while Fish remains a professor of English, he has taken the position of Dean of Humanities at Illinois, stepping across onto the administrative track, where compensation packages routinely eclipse those of superstar humanities faculty. See Ron Grossman and Patrice Jones, "Universities Pay Big Bucks to Get 'Star' Professors," *Chicago Tribune* 20 July 1998: A1.

11. I am bracketing here the tendency among some commentators to view cultural studies and theory as antagonistic strains within the profession, usually by positioning the latter as a Eurocentric, poststructuralist, and essentially apolitical foil for the former. This way of conceiving the divisions within the discipline never seemed to me very satisfactory; today it seems merely a vestige of the disciplinary struggles of the 1980s.

12. Shumway 85.

13. John Guillory, "Bourdieu's Refusal," *Modern Language Quarterly* 58 (Dec. 1997): 369.

14. Influential accounts of this attenuation of the role and function of intellectuals include Russell Jacoby, *The Last Intellectuals: American Culture in the Age of Academe* (New York: Basic, 1987); Samuel Weber, *Institution and Interpretation* (Minneapolis: University of Minnesota Press, 1987); John Guillory, *Cultural Capital* (Chicago: University of Chicago Press, 1993), especially chapter 4; Bill Readings, *The University in Ruins* (Cambridge: Harvard University Press, 1996), especially chapters 9 and 12; and the essays collected in Bruce Robbins, ed., *The Phantom Public Sphere* (Minneapolis: University of Minnesota Press, 1993).

15. Readings, "The University without Culture" *New Literary History* 26.3 (1995): 466; see also *University in Ruins* 139–40, 192–93.

16. Readings, "The Idea of Excellence," *University in Ruins* 21–43. The University of Pennsylvania, which hosted the conference out of which the

present volume of essays emerged, is currently operating under the slogan "Agenda for Excellence."

17. Shumway 94.

18. Shumway 98.

19. In his interview-essay "The Intellectual Field: A World Apart," for example, Bourdieu characteristically observes that "alliances founded on the homology of position (dominant-dominated = dominated) are always more uncertain, more fragile, than solidarities based on an identity of position and, thereby, of condition and habitus." As Guillory argues in "Bourdieu's Refusal," this habit of reminding academics of their determined and determining positions in an essentially reproductive system of social relations contrasts vividly with the voluntarism and self-declared altruism of the practitioners of cultural studies, and probably accounts for the hostility with which Bourdieu's work has been received in that quarter. It is worth noting, therefore, that Bourdieu goes on here to say, "The fact remains that the specific interests of cultural producers, in so far as they are linked to fields that, by the very logic of their functioning, encourage, favour or impose the transcending of personal interest in the ordinary sense, can lead them to political or intellectual actions that can be called universal." Bourdieu, *In Other Words: Essays Towards a Reflexive Sociology*, trans. Matthew Adamson (Stanford: Stanford University Press, 1990) 145, 146.

20. The others to whom I refer here include the participants at the 1990 Cultural Studies Now and in the Future conference in Illinois. Graduate students at that conference famously called attention to the hierarchical division of labor informing virtually every particular of the event, from the distribution of travel reimbursements and honoraria, to the positioning of bodies in the auditoriums and the granting of access to microphones (which amounted in effect to "the right to speak" for cultural studies). In this way, the stars of the conference were forced to address institutional questions about the star system and structures of domination more forthrightly than they might otherwise have done. But this discussion of the local distribution of power, however valuable, seems to have prevented the dominated majority fraction from considering the problems raised by their own advantaged position on the field of power.

21. In *The Employment of English: Theory, Jobs, and the Future of Literary Studies* (New York: New York University Press, 1998), Michael Bérubé makes the point that cultural-studies and theory writers, MFA-program poetry and fiction writers, and nontrade avant-garde poetry and fiction writers are to a large extent

pitching to the very same readership: "they're all fighting for the same small subculture of active, intellectually engaged readers," the ".00001 of the American public that buys the work of those jargon-addled theoreticians and talented small press poets and fiction writers no one's ever heard of" (117–18). This suggests that when one of "those jargon-addled theoreticians" manages to break out to the larger audience of buyers of "important" books, he or she does so as an author very much on the model of the suddenly "discovered" novelist, that is, as an *author*, not as a participant in a collective philosophical or political project.

22. Michel Foucault, "Intellectuals and Power," *Language, Counter-Memory, Practice: Selected Essays and Interviews*, ed. Donald F. Bouchard, trans. Donald F. Bouchard and Sherry Simon (Ithaca: Cornell University Press, 1977) 205–17.

23. To some extent, the practice of working in teams, coauthoring books and articles, and so forth, interferes with the production of individual stars, leading instead to clusters of stars, as when two or three scholars share equally a prize or honor for their collaborative research. But even in disciplines where collaboration is common there can be a strong orientation toward the individual star or "genius." For an example of the by no means socially innocent process whereby the fact of collaboration can be set aside in the interest of promoting one particular collaborator to the level of stardom, see Denise Scott Brown's discussion of her working partnership with her husband Robert Venturi, in "Room at the Top? Sexism and the Star System in Architecture," *Architecture: A Place for Women*, ed. Ellen Perry Berkeley (Washington: Smithsonian Institute Press, 1989) 237–46.

24. It may be worth noting that even most of these collaborative pairs in our discipline are understood, however unjustifiably, to consist of a dominant and a subordinate partner, an author of "genius" and a more or less ordinary helpmate.

25. Jürgen Habermas, *Philosophical-Political Profiles*, trans. Frederick G. Lawrence (Cambridge: MIT Press, 1985) 5.

26. John Guillory, "Preprofessionalism: What Graduate Students Want," *Profession* (1996): 92.

27. In academe as elsewhere, the star legitimates the project and not the other way around; one way to demonstrate your star status is to publish something apparently nonacademic and even frivolous: a study of dogs and dog-owners, say, or a baseball-obsessed memoir, or a science-fiction novel. There is

a rule of the academic game, perhaps a vestige of the era of the true public intellectual, which holds that the greater your status, the further your publications are expected to stray from your presumed area of scholarly expertise.

28. Laurie Langbauer, "The Celebrity Economy of Cultural Studies," *Victorian Studies* 36 (1993): 466–72.

29. Langbauer 470.

30. Guillory notes in *Cultural Capital* that "the names that circulate as 'theory' in this canonical sense are actually very few in number, much more restricted a list than that which constitutes 'canonical' literary work" (203).

Allen Smithee Filmography

1955 *The Indiscreet Mrs. Jarvis* (TV, released 1992)[1]

1968 *Iron Cowboy*, aka *Fade-In* (TV)
     The Omega Imperative[2]

1969 *Death of a Gunfighter*

1970 *The Challenge* (TV)

1971 *Goose Filburn*

1972 *A Cup of Sugar*

1973 *Kid Mann*

1978 *The Barking Dog*
     Campaign

1979 *Tell 'Em Suzy Knows*

1980 *City in Fear* (TV)
     Fun and Games (TV)
     Gypsy Angels (released 1993)

1981 *Student Bodies* (producer)

1982 *The Horrible Terror*
     Moonlight (TV)
     Shock Treatment

1983 *Twilight Zone: The Movie* (second assistant director on John
     Landis's segment)

1985 *MacGyver* (TV) (both the pilot and the first season episode,
     "The Heist")

Stitches

The Twilight Zone (TV) (episode "Paladin of the Lost Hour")

1986 *Dalton: Code of Vengeance II* (TV)

Let's Get Harry, aka *The Rescue*

1987 *Appointment with Fear*

Ghost Fever

Karen's Song (TV)

Morgan Stewart's Coming Home, aka *Homefront*

Riviera (TV)

1988 *Dune* (TV edit)

I Love N.Y.

Juarez (TV)

1989 *Backtrack*, aka *Catch Fire*, aka *Do It the Hard Way*

Ganheddo aka *GUNHED* (U.S. version)

House III, aka *The Horror Show*

1990 *Shrimp on the Barbie*, aka *The Boyfriend from Hell*

Solar Crisis, aka *Starfire*, aka *Crisis 2050*, aka *Kuraishisu Niju-Goju Nen*

Tiny Toon Adventures (segments "Duck in the Muck" and "Pit Bullied")

1991 *Bloodsucking Pharaohs in Pittsburgh*, aka *Picking Up the Pieces*

The Owl (TV)

1992 *Bay City Story*, aka *Deadline* (TV)

Fatal Charm (TV)

"I Will Always Love You" (music video)

The Nutt House (writer)

The Red Shoe Diaries: Auto Erotica (segment "Accidents Happen")

Scent of a Woman (airline and TV edits)

Thunderheart (TV)

1993 *Call of the Wild* (TV)

Notes from the Attic (production designer)

Rudy (TV edit)

1994 *Heat* (TV edit)

The Birds II: Land's End (TV)
While Justice Sleeps (TV)
1995 *The O.J. Simpson Story* (TV)
Raging Angels
1996 *Hellraiser: Bloodline*
1997 *Firehouse*
Sub Down
Le Zombi de Cap-Rouge
1998 *Burn Hollywood Burn: An Alan Smithee Film*
Illusion Infinity
The Disciples (TV)
1999 *Meet Joe Black* (airline edit)
To Light the Darkness
2000 *The Frozen Inferno* (TV) (writer)
Starforce

Notes

1. *The Indiscreet Mrs. Jarvis* is a half-hour television drama that was retroactively attributed to Smithee, as is evident from the director's first name being spelled "Alan." Tellingly, Rhino's 1992 video rerelease does not bear the program's original credits.

2. Production on both *The Omega Imperative* and *Iron Cowboy* began in 1968, before *Death of a Gunfighter*, Smithee's first credited film, was released. It was the appearance of that Western that enabled the two earlier productions to be released anachronistically as Smithee films.

Contributors

Jeremy Braddock is former editor of *Verbivore* magazine. His writing has also appeared in *Andere Sinema*. He currently teaches and is a Ph.D. candidate in English at the University of Pennsylvania; his dissertation is titled *The Modernist Collection and African-American Modernism, 1914–1934*.

Tom Conley is professor of Romance languages and literatures at Harvard University. He is the author of *Film Hieroglyphs: Ruptures in Classical Cinema* (Minnesota, 1991), *The Graphic Unconscious in Early Modern French Writing*, and *The Self-Made Map: Cartographic Writing in Early Modern France* (Minnesota, 1996). He has also translated several books, including works by Michel de Certeau and Marc Augé.

Jonathan P. Eburne is a Ph.D. candidate in the comparative literature and literary theory program at the University of Pennsylvania. He is the author of articles on William Burroughs, Raymond Chandler, and surrealism, and is currently working on a dissertation titled *Surrealism and the Art of Crime*.

James F. English is associate professor of English and acting director of film studies at the University of Pennsylvania. He is coeditor of *Postmodern Culture* and the author of *Comic Transactions: Literature, Humor,* *and the Politics of Community in Twentieth-Century Britain.* He is currently completing a book titled *Winning at Art: Prizes, Awards, and the Economy of Cultural Prestige.*

Stephen Hock is a Ph.D. candidate studying twentieth-century culture in the comparative literature and literary theory program at the University of Pennsylvania, where he has taught in the English, German, and comparative literature departments.

Christian Keathley is assistant professor of English at Clemson University.

Jessie Labov is studying in the comparative literature department at New York University, where she is working on an intellectual history of the dissident movements of Central Europe. She has written on film and censorship during the Cold War, and on Krzysztof Kieslowski in the forthcoming collection *Screening the City.*

Laura Parigi is a freelance journalist and reviewer for the Italian magazine *Primissima.* She has a degree in Italian literature from the Università degli Studi di Firenze. Her dissertation is titled *Alan Smithee: The Notion of Author in the Contemporary American Cinema.*

Donald E. Pease is Avalon Foundation Chair of the Humanities at Dartmouth College and the founding director of the Futures of American Studies Institute at Dartmouth. He is author of *Visionary Compacts: American Renaissance Writings in Cultural Context*; the senior editor of *New Americanists*; and the editor of seven books on American studies.

Robert B. Ray is director of film and media studies and professor of English at the University of Florida. He is author of *A Certain Tendency of the Hollywood Cinema, 1930–1980* and *The Avant-Garde Finds Andy Hardy.* He is a member of The Vulgar Boatmen, whose recordings include *You and Your Sister, Please Panic,* and *Opposite Sex.*

Craig Saper is author of *Artificial Mythologies: A Guide to Cultural Invention* (Minnesota, 1997) and *Networked Art* (Minnesota, 2001). He was guest editor of a special issue of *Style*, "Interactive Style."

Andrew Sarris is professor of film at the School of the Arts, Columbia University. He is film critic of the *New York Observer*, and author, most recently, of *"You Ain't Heard Nothin' Yet": The American Talking Film, History and Memory, 1927–1949*.

Index